A LATE DINNER

A LATE DINNER

Discovering the Food of Spain

Paul Richardson

BLOOMSBURY

First published in Great Britain 2007

Copyright © 2007 by Paul Richardson

The moral right of the author has been asserted

Bloomsbury Publishing Plc, 36 Soho Square, London W1D 3QY

Photographs courtesy of the author

Map by Jonny Hannah

A CIP catalogue record for this book is available from the British Library

ISBN 9780747588030 (hardback)
10 9 8 7 6 5 4 3 2 1

ISBN 9780747594550 (trade paperback)
10 9 8 7 6 5 4 3 2 1

Typeset by Hewer Text UK Ltd, Edinburgh
Printed in Great Britain by Clays Limited, St Ives plc

Bloomsbury Publishing, London, New York and Berlin

The paper this book is printed on is certified by the © Forest Stewardship
Council 1996 A.C. (FSC). It is ancient-forest friendly. The printer holds FSC
chain of custody SGS-COC-2061

www.bloomsbury.com/paulrichardson

ACKNOWLEDGEMENTS

To thank individually everyone who has contributed to the existence of this book would take up more space than is reasonable or practical. However, there are certain debts that need declaring. I am permanently grateful to my mother – who was, after all, the first person to put food on my table – and to my father, brother, sister, and sister-in-law. On the Spanish side, my thanks go out the extended Trives family, whose loyalty and love have been a constant in my chaotic expatriate life.

A heartfelt *gracias* to all the chefs and cooks, farmers and fishermen, who gave freely of their time and expertise – especially to those whose names appear in the text, but also to Javier Oyarbide, Serxio Ces, Sergi Arola, Francis Paniego, Carme Ruscalleda, Angel León, Dani García, Abraham García – and to all those Spanish friends, contacts, and acquaintances, who have added in small or large measure to my vision of the country and its way of eating. Just a few of these people are: Piluca Molina, Vicente, and all my friends in Valencia; Ana Valls in Madrid; the Arribas family in Plasencia and Bilbao; Wulf and Edwina Taeger in Riudarenes; Maria Fernández in Granada; Shelagh Vanderpool in Barcelona; Caridad Hernández, Claudio and Cesárea, Antonio, and little Jara; Eva Rincón; Jesús Ladero and Petri García; Antonio Navarro and Luigina diMeo; Mikel and Miren; Miguel Muriel and Nazaret Téllez; Pepa Miranda and her parents; Paloma Rozalen; Caco and Torro; Loli and Siro, María Vázquez, José and Mencía, and all our good neighbours in the Sierra. Special love and thanks – though she is sadly not around to receive them – to the late Sally Stein. Not forgetting those friends in the UK who are still on my virtual Christmas card list, despite the distances in time and space, including Katie Owen, Katy Emck, Neil Crombie and David Brooke, Sacha Schoenfeld, Alex Willcock and Charlie, Adam and Emma Barker, Carol Downie, Catherine Heard and Carla Pinto, Marlena Spieler, John and Antonia Price, Jason Lowe and Lori de Mori, Colin Spencer and Claire Clifton.

On a professional note, I would like to register my gratitude to María José Sevilla, who unwittingly kick-started my adventures in Spanish food, and Sarah Spankie and Sarah Miller at *Condé Nast Traveller*, whose commissions for the magazine have formed the basis of my knowledge of modern Spanish restaurant cooking. Thanks, too, to my agent Julian Alexander for his many years of loyal support, and to editors Alexandra Pringle and Mike Jones for their enthusiasm, encouragement, and efficiency.

'Cuisine may be generally regarded as a part of a people's culture. The quality of the fare, the manner in which it is prepared, the time devoted to its ingestion, the conventions of the dinner table: these are intimately related to, and frequently reflect, a people's aesthetic development.'

Angelo Pellegrini, *The Unprejudiced Palate* (1948)

CONTENTS

INTRODUCTION

Travel broadens the mind, that's true enough. But a whistle-stop on the Grand Tour, or a weekend break via a low-budget airline, won't widen it very much. Real understanding of a country and its culture takes longer: years and years must go by, practically a lifetime.

The surfaces are what impress us first: they are palatable, curious, striking, or at least inoffensive; they either confirm our prejudices, or ask a bigger question, leading us in. So we nibble away at the edges of the place, telling ourselves with every mouthful that the centre will have the same flavour – anything to insure ourselves against the thousand natural shocks of foreignness. But, little by little, perhaps, we begin to acquire the taste. The phrase is precise and oddly profound; it implies that the experience of food is more than a spectacle, something external to ourselves, but can eventually be interiorised and possessed, coming to form part of who we are. Manuel Vicent, the Spanish novelist, says that eating is a mystical act – it converts what you consume into yourself.

When, as a teenager, I crossed the border at Port Bou on the night train from Paris, I had never been to Spain before. As a middle-class family from a well-to-do county of southern England, we generally took our holidays in Italy or France. Spain was not much favoured by those from our social group. Whereas Italy and France had bourgeois social stability and a solid infrastructure, Spain seemed somehow rickety, the cheap package hotels lining the coast, the interior as scary as Africa. In short, it had a dubious reputation. Perhaps that was what attracted me to it.

My formative experience of Spain, my earliest gingerly taste of the way it lived and ate, was a two-month stint one summer on the Interrail – that great early experiment in European relations. Interrail was travel on the cheap at a time when there were no budget airlines, no mobile phones, and no email for keeping in touch with home. You carried your life in a belt around your midriff, and, if you ran out of money, you were in trouble, because the cash machine was not yet a feature of life in southern Europe, and, as a callow nineteen-year-old, I was not yet of an age to be trusted with credit cards. Mostly I survived on cheapo bar food: *tortilla de patatas*; meatballs from tins; *patatas bravas* laced with spicy sauce (the student standby); and what I call public-transport *bocadillos* – wodges of bread with a something laid inside them, such as cheese, ham, or chorizo, but never any olive oil, no tomato, nothing to mitigate their ascetic dryness.

What I knew about Spanish food as a teenager were the standard tourist clichés: paella and gazpacho, gazpacho and paella. My knowledge of Spanish ingredients could be scribbled on the writing side of a postcard, one of those kitsch tourist postcards with the flamenco dancer's dress standing out from the photo. Olives, oranges, saffron, garlic . . . what else? I was unfamiliar with the excellence of Spanish ham – unsurprisingly, I now know, since, after an outbreak of swine fever in the early 1980s, none reached the outside world for almost a decade. I must have heard of manchego cheese, but could hardly imagine there were any others. Spanish wine was Rioja or sherry, sherry or Rioja.

My introduction to Spanish cuisine was largely conditioned by my limited vocabulary: there were only certain words I knew, and I was too embarrassed to order unfamiliar dishes. My backpacker's budget was dreadfully meagre, but I still liked to mark the close of day with a glass of sherry and a plate of almonds. I must have imagined this was a profoundly Spanish thing to do, though, given my age and status, and the aperitif's inelegant backdrop of station bars and hotel cafeterias, a beer and a packet of crisps might have been more appropriate.

None the less, there were meals I have never quite forgotten. At a little *pensión* in the Mallorcan town of Deyà, on a terrace in late-summer smelling of pinewood and sea air, I was served a fragrant rice dish – my first true Spanish rice, made in the paella with chicken and peppers, golden and glowing and pungent with saffron – drank a bottle of iced rosado all by myself, and gazed down at the dark sea in a euphoric, alcoholic blur.

It was August, and Spain was in its usual summer limbo land, the cities like ghost towns, the beaches pullulating, the signs in the windows of shops and restaurants bidding their clients farewell until September. Armed with a motley list of contacts, I roamed the country on the cheapest, slowest trains. Spain was in the throes of a democratic revolution, did I but know it; even in 1982, it felt under-developed, and pungently exotic.

The trains were stinky old slam-door carriages with compart-ments, windows you could pull down and lean out of, and soap in the toilets that you ground into your hand in a powder, like pepper from a pepper mill. It was entirely normal, at that innocent time, for rail travellers to offer their food to those sitting around them. One time, on the night train from Paris, a Spanish family took me under its wing and invited me to share their midnight feast: cold breaded lamb chops, tortilla sandwiches, thin-sliced jamón serra-no wrapped in aluminium foil, and gazpacho poured into plastic cups from a thermos flask. The next morning, with an hour to go for Barcelona, out came the picnic box again, and there was café con leche and sweet María biscuits. I was struck by the way the family all dunked their biscuits in the coffee with gusto, raising the cup the better to convey each coffee-soaked biscuit to the mouth. It was my first contact with the sensible Spanish tendency to use solids as a vehicle for liquids: sauce is automatically mopped up with bread, sponge cakes made 'drunken' with sweet wine, and hot chocolate used as a dip for piping hot lengths of crisp, oily churros.

I was keen to avoid the expense of staying in hotels, so my route was determined by the dates I knew my acquaintances would be at home. After Mallorca, I headed inland to Madrid, where I had the address of a school friend. There was no answer at his family's apartment in the posh Salamanca district; the concierge told me they'd gone for the summer to their seaside home in Santander. It was a big house with a big garden, right on the seafront at Sardinero Beach, I couldn't miss it. So I caught the train north and found the house, and spent a week with the *jeunesse dorée* of Santander, roaring around town at night with the rich kids in their flashy cars.

On my last night, we all went out for a late dinner. I had never before eaten supper at midnight, and found the idea madly decadent. We ate at the fishing dock, where canteen-like restaurants dished up plates of seafood for the crowds that came in ravenous from their day on the beach. Tin platters of prawns *a la plancha*, squid in its own ink, crisp fried battered rings of calamares, juicy steamed mussels, clams *a la marinera* with parsley and white wine, huge boiled crabs, and heaps of little black winkles, seemed to emerge from nowhere to land chaotically on a white paper tablecloth that quickly became a stained and crumpled mess. A heady atmosphere flooded the room as a hundred happy eaters shouted their heads off between mouthfuls. There was a squeezing of lemons, a sucking of shells and a cracking of claws, a dunking of bread in the slopping juices, and a swigging of jugsful of sticky sangría packed with ice. This was nothing less than a full-on Spanish feast, loudly vocal, apparently anarchic, but actually quite under control. The platters kept on coming and we kept on eating, late into the night. It was all a revelation to me, in my cloistered, cut-and-dried Englishness. I had no idea that it was possible to have so much fun.

The years went by, there was university, then a life in London. After spells as a waiter and wine-merchant's apprentice, I landed an editor's job on a publication with the brave, but, in retrospect, embarrassing, name of *Taste*, run on a shoestring in a former garage near the old docks at Fulham.

The truly pivotal moments in life are those that happen, as John

Lennon once said, when you are busy doing other things. I was clearing my desk on a Friday night when the phone rang: it was a woman from the food export department at the Spanish Embassy in London. Breathlessly, she gave me the lowdown: there was a food fair in Madrid this weekend at which all of the important Spanish chefs of the moment would be present. Someone from the press had dropped out at the last minute: could I go in their place? It would mean taking the first flight on Saturday morning. Everything was paid for: I would be the honoured guest of the Spanish government.

For a few seconds, I hesitated. I had nothing very important planned for the weekend. And the proposal did sound intriguing. In the late 1980s in London, the very idea of a Spanish chef sounded, at the very least, unusual, if not actually oxymoronic. In the wake of the nouvelle cuisine, creativity in restaurant cooking was still essentially the domain of the French, while the rustic cooking most valued at the time was undoubtedly Italian, and the gastronomic avant-garde was most active in California. Spain simply didn't figure.

That May weekend proved to be a watershed in at least two major ways. On the Saturday, I went to a birthday party on a lake and met the person with whom I was to share my life. Nacho was an agronomist with the Ministry of Agriculture who specialised in the genetics of seeds and knew more about the growing of vegetables, grains, and fruits than anyone I have met before or since. It was with Nacho that I first set up house in Spain, on the island of Ibiza, and with him that I still live, on a farm in Extremadura, where the two of us produce most of our own food, drawing on Nacho's expertise and my own decade and a half of agricultural experiment.

Nacho had grown up in a family of seven children in which life was lived in a vortex of noise and emotion. In charge of the family kitchen was Nacho's mother, María Teresa, a remarkable cook and woman who, over the years, has become one of my guiding lights in the simple yet variegated art of Spanish home cooking. For almost half a century, she has cooked two meals a day of two

and sometimes three dishes each, catering to a public that fluc-
tuates wildly, depending on which of her children and their
spouses, offspring, and friends happens to be passing through
their small flat in Alicante.

Maria Teresa cannot be persuaded to think there is anything
especially remarkable about the food she prepares. But, for me, the
remarkable fact about her cooking is precisely that which she thinks
unworthy of mention – her innate understanding that the food you
make to please and nourish a family is less about fireworks or fancy
produce, and more about the quiet rhythm of balanced eating, meal
after meal. Her cooking is careful, economical, and flavoursome.
She is not given to extravagance, except on a few particular occasions, notably Christmas. The type of cuisine she practises, if one
could characterise it in a few words, is a Spanish domestic cookery
that cuts across regional differences – though her rice dishes, her skill
with vegetables like artichokes and cardoons, and her Levantine
specialities, like *pelotas de pava* (meatballs made from turkey, with
pine nuts and lemon), reflect her roots in the communities of the
south-east coast, Alicante and Murcia. Her family, though originally from Asturias in the north, came down in 1910 to run the salt
flats at Santa Pola, and never went back.

If that Saturday in Madrid was a red-letter day in my senti-
mental education, the following day at the food fair was when I
realised for the first time that something remarkable was going on
in the world of Spanish cuisine. Cooks had come from all over the
country to represent their regions in a contest of high-flown
culinary ambition. They were mostly men and women of my
own age, working away with enormous seriousness at field kitchens set up around the fair, producing sophisticated dishes that used
Spanish ingredients in radical new ways. The language may have
been beyond me, but there was no doubting the sensory impact of
beetroot gazpacho with saffron foam; rice with goat's cheese,
octopus, asparagus, and paprika; or essence of fresh peas with
jellied barnacles and salted butter toffee. On this late spring day
flooded with sunshine, there was warmth and colour in everything

I saw, everything I tasted. There was a stall where fine jamón serrano was being sliced and served – the deepest-flavoured ham I had ever tasted, making Parma seem sweetly innocuous. There was a multiplicity of cheeses, wines, sausages, and preserves. All of it seemed to suggest what I had never considered before – that, in the matter of ingredients, and in the richness of its regional culinary tradition, Spanish food was worthy to be compared with the famous cuisines of Italy and France. I remember that weekend as a blaze of newness, marking out paths in my life which I am still travelling, a decade and a half after the event.

In 1991 I left London in a brown Mini, as economic recession turned my homeland a shade of ashen grey, and a year's sabbatical turned into a new life.

Over the years, cooking in the Spanish manner became second nature to me; its techniques and rhythms became part of my life. When I wasn't travelling around the country, meeting fishermen and farmers, cheesemakers and chefs, I was cooking for friends, talking about Spanish food, or eating it. My larder filled up with Spanish ingredients, my library with Spanish cookbooks.

In the early years of the twenty-first century, Spain was at a crossroads. It maintained a fusion of old and new, of solidly traditional and madly futuristic, in a balance so delicate it seemed almost schizoid. On one level, the country seemed uninterested in its own past: the peseta had been discarded, the new euro currency embraced without a whimper of nostalgia. Yet history was clearly still embedded in the culture, in individual lives, in families and communities, in the form of tradition. The observance of time-honoured modes of behaviour, ethical, linguistic, celebratory, religious, agricultural, architectural, or culinary, was still central to the Spanish modus vivendi. But for how long could the balance last?

Little by little, I conjured up a grand design: a year-long voyage that would take me to the heart of the Spanish culinary universe. I would work from the outside in, as I had got to know the country in the first place, drawing on formative experiences of Spanish food and life, seeking out the people and landscapes that had shaped the eating habits of the nation. In the course of the year, I would spend time hunting down the traditions of the rural interior, and the creative cooking of the modern Spanish city. But, for one summer at least, I would stick to the Costas. I would start with the tourist heartland of Alicante, then move northwards to Valencia, the place which indirectly defines the outside world's perception of Spanish food, providing it with its defining symbol, its 'signature dish', the paella. Up north on the Costa Brava, beside the French border, there would be tourist food in its most shameless form, but also *alta cocina* at the most exalted level. In the coastal communities of the far South, richly traditional, but deeply colonised by tourism, I might find that providing for visitors and catering for locals are not such very different things. But the Spanish coast is not only the Med. There is also the Atlantic, and a very different culinary culture which, none the less, has certain crucial elements in common. There was a famous seafood festival I had been wanting to get to for years, up on the far western coast of Galicia. If I wasn't fed up with fish by the time autumn came around, this would be where you'd find me.

It was mid-June, a time of year that, in northern climes, would be hot enough for high summer, but, in Spain, is merely the first agreeable stage of summer's four-month journey into Hades. I loaded up the car with maps and restaurant guides, books on history and geography and the traditional food of the regions, and notebooks full of every contact I had ever made, every new friend whose number I had ever scribbled down in a drunken haze in some late-night bar. I got myself a mobile phone, an iPod full of music, and a box of heartburn pills for when the going got tough. And I did what thousands of European holidaymakers were doing at this very moment: I slapped on the sun cream and headed for Benidorm.

COAST

CHAPTER ONE

LEVANTE

The Spanish have a phrase, *leyenda negra*, to indicate a bad reputation so obstinately perdurable that it takes on the quality of myth. And there have been few legends blacker, if you discount the Inquisition, the expulsion of the Jews by the Catholic kings, and the atrocities of the Spanish Empire in the New World, than the abominable food supposedly served in the *fondas* and *posadas* of Spain. What was attractive about this country to foreign writers and artists were the exotic archaisms of a place out of step with the rest of Europe – its wild and little-visited landscapes; its immense wealth of architectural and artistic treasures – but never, or almost never, the quality of its food.

Generally speaking, when writers on Spain have turned their attention to the national cuisine, it has been to cast aspersions on it. Literary travellers of all eras turn up the same catalogue of shocking hygiene, primitive installations, and general ignorance of the culinary arts. Spanish food was thought to be monotonous, poorly prepared in foul conditions, swimming in rancid oil, and stinking of garlic.

The French, while thrilling to the passionate wildness of their southern neighbour, have traditionally turned their noses up at Spanish cuisine. A saying popular in nineteenth-century France declared of Spain: *des milliers de prêtres, et pas un cuisinier* (thousands of priests, and not a single cook). One of the earliest literary incursions by a Frenchman in the field of Spanish gastronomy is the account by Jean Muret, priest and diplomat, of dinner at a *posada* in Tolosa in 1666. The meal is presented as tragicomical: it begins with a bowl of thin soup, which is not intended to be drunk, but to have bread dunked in it. On so doing, the priest burns his mouth. The second course is a salad of 'grasses' with oil and vinegar, followed by a piece of goat which needs to be chewed for half an hour in order to be swallowed.

The account of a visit to Spain, a few years later, by the Comtesse d'Aulnoy, a lady of mode, exercised a powerful influence on subsequent writers on the subject, contributing in large measure to the popularity of Spain and Spanishness among several generations of French Romantics. The comtesse found *la cuisine espagnole* so repulsive, so excessively flavoured with saffron, garlic, and spices, that she would have died of hunger, were it not for the French cook she brought along with her. She did approve of the fruit, especially the figs, she adored the Muscat wine, and she thought Spanish lettuces sweet and refreshing. The favourite meal of her trip was a collation offered by an upper-class household in Madrid, at which she happily nibbled at fruit conserves served on gold paper, and drank hot chocolate with milk and egg yolks. With almost everything else, however, the comtesse found fault. In Spain, she pronounced, the roast partridge is 'usually' burned to a cinder. The lamb is tender enough (the quality of local lamb is often mentioned by early travel writers), but ruined by frying in filthy oil. Spanish table manners, or the lack of them, horrified the comtesse:

in some establishments she found no cutlery or napkins, her fellow diners burped openly at the table, and their custom of picking teeth with a stick seemed, to her, beneath contempt.

Taken as a whole, the image of Spanish food over the centuries is rather like that of the country itself: primitive, crude, and so strongly flavoured as to be shocking to delicate palates. Richard Ford, whose *Handbook for Spain* (1845) is possibly the best-researched (as well as the most opinionated) travellers' guide to the country ever written, describes the national cuisine as 'by no means despicable'. The major stumbling block, for Ford, as for most of the early travellers in Spain, is a somewhat too liberal infusion of garlic. 'From the quantity eaten in all southern countries, where it is considered to be fragrant, palatable, stomachic, and invigorating,' he writes, 'we must assume that it is suited to local tastes and constitutions. Wherever any particular herb grows, there lives the ass who is to eat it.'

It is true that, as author and gastronome Rafael Núñez remarks in his curious study of foreign attitudes to Spanish cooking, *Con La Salsa de su Hambre* (literally 'with the sauce of their hunger'), for much of its history Spain presented serious natural disadvantages to the visitor from northern Europe, unused to the country's extremes of heat and cold, its forbidding terrain, and its unfathomable bureaucracy. To cover the large distances between cities where there was, from the point of view of the nineteenth-century cultural tourist, something to see, required a dose of fortitude in the traveller, as well of plenty of money. (The trip from Madrid to Cádiz by stagecoach cost an astronomic 3,000 reales in 1844, three times a schoolmaster's annual salary.) The awfulness of Spanish hotels became one of the great clichés of travel literature – a much-repeated joke divided them into categories of bad, worse, and worst – and writers fell over each other to regale readers with bug-infested beds, towels the size of handkerchiefs, and sanitary arrangements that were an affront to civilisation. Travellers were often advised to bring their own sustenance, because the food provided was supposed to be inedible.

All the same, can the food these travellers were served really have been quite so extravagantly bad? As Rafael Núñez wistfully enquires, how much of what they found in Spain was simply what they expected to find? Spanish food was so routinely disparaged, just as the dreadfulness of its roads and accommodation were so ghoulishly dwelt upon, that one wonders whether readers didn't come to expect the thrill of horror these accounts so faithfully provided. It may be that, for early writer/travellers in the peninsula, Spanish culinary habits were another fine example of that savage exoticism, that primitive brutishness, which formed the basis of the romantic image of Spain.

The summer before I went to university, we broke with the habits of a lifetime and took a holiday flat in Jávea, on the Costa Blanca. As a family, we had little money to spend on what we were used to thinking of as luxuries, like groaning platters of fresh seafood. Our meals were taken at the apartment, with its perfectly awful view of a building site, keeping to the English timetable and mostly to the English culinary repertoire.

During the day, we lay on the beach, but, when the weather turned cloudy, we got in the car and drove along the traffic-clogged roads to take a look at the other resorts strung out along the Costa.

So, I had been to Benidorm before. To the snobbish middle-class juvenile that I was, Benidorm seemed the epitome of all that was vulgar and plebeian about holidays abroad. I remember the day we went there to laugh in the red, booze-shiny face of mass tourism. In the event, the soaring towers of this Manhattan-on-Sea amazed and rather shocked us; the sheer scale of the operation silenced our snickerings. There is something about the sight and sound of 20,000 people having fun in the sun that renders meaningless such elitist concepts as taste and authenticity.

At the beginning of the twenty-first century, Benidorm was still in rude good health. In early June, the place was full to the gunwales, and the Playa de Levante, Benidorm's spectacular arc of sand, was a panorama of pink flesh with a flotsam of sunshades floating above.

Environment, life, and food: all are interconnected. Driving into Benidorm, what you see of the countryside is almost all entirely new; the purpose-built *urbanizaciones* have been magicked out of a landscape as dusty and unforgiving as the moon. Olive trees that once provided oil for food and light now serve as decoration, islands in a bright green sea of irrigated grass. Carob trees whose long brown pods were once used as animal feed, and even kept human beings alive in times of scarcity, have long since been retired from a life of utility.

I parked behind the beach and walked along the Playa de Levante, dodging a succession of pale-skinned families in various states of undress. A background babble of European languages: French, Dutch, German, English, and what sounded like Finnish. A bar on the prom offered a complete list of the elements likely to appeal to the Anglo-Saxon male on his holiday abroad:

SKY SPORTS

BAR SNACKS

LIVE FOOTBALL

ENGLISH BEERS

LIVE RACING

HOT MEALS

There was a surreal, postmodern quality about Benidorm food, like something out of the twisted, out-of-kilter, sci-fi worlds of J. G. Ballard. There were pizzerias and pasta joints, English pubs and French bistros, Chinese and Indians and Moroccans and Thais. The menu at one bar zigzagged from spaghetti Bolognese and prawn cocktail, to French omelette, Hungarian goulash, and *arroz a la cubana* – the homespun Spanish dish of plain rice, fried egg and banana, and tomato sauce, supposedly invented in the 1920s by a Cuban exile in Madrid. Only in a place like this might you find a hybrid of Norwegian tavern and Spanish bar, the El Quijote

Nordiska Krogen, serving, on the day I put my head around the door, a choice of 'beef cordon blue and chips' or 'stroggenoff'.

In a documentary I once saw on the BBC about British expatriates in Spain, there was one unforgettable image – that of a corpulent English lady in the tiny kitchen of her restaurant on the Costa Blanca, serving up English roast dinners with gravy, three veg and Yorkshire puddings, the poor woman pink and sweating in the 100° heat of a Spanish summer. It is not that there is anything wrong with good old-fashioned British nosh, especially on a good old-fashioned British winter day, with a cold drizzle falling from a grey sky, but here, under a blistering sun that cracks pavements and strips paint off walls, it is as incongruous as a bullfight in the snow.

Everywhere you looked in the restaurants of Benidorm were photographs of food: colour snaps provided to indicate what would arrive on your plate, should you decide to order it. This entirely functional form of food photography is very much a part of Spanish life, and not just in tourist establishments. You see these photos in the kind of restaurant that serves up *platos combinados*, the 'combined plates' numbered one, two, three, in their various permutations of fried egg, bacon, pork chop, fried green pepper, tortilla, tomato, and chips. A sub-genre is formed by photographs of the *bocadillo*, the bread roll always pictured at the same angle with the filling poking out, though, if the truth be told, it is never very easy to tell the difference between ham, chorizo, jamón York, pork loin, or whatever. These images have canonised a certain type of proletarian cuisine, now going out of fashion as fast as the faintly kitsch images themselves. I find them strangely poignant, and often wonder about the anonymous photographer who must have taken them, probably back in the 1970s. At the café by the church, where a balustrade looks out over Benidorm's two magnificent beaches, one on each side of the peninsula, the photographs of ice-cream sundaes and banana splits were now almost completely undistinguishable, their once lurid colours bleached white by a decade of Costa Blanca summers.

The gastronomic history of Benidorm is not widely documented, but you can get some idea of it from the general history of the place and its sudden transformation from rustic village to tourist megapolis. Despite the soil of this barren coast, which is poor, chalky, and lacking in minerals, the village of Beni-Dorm (son of Dahrim) had always found a way of producing decent harvests of wheat, barley, maize, figs, and carob beans.

In 1926, when the population of the village was 2,160 souls, its main occupations were agriculture and fishing. Benidorm had no proper harbour, but the boats were drawn up on the beach. In 1944, at the height of its importance as a fishing port, no less than 500 tons of fish came in on Benidorm's fleet. By the start of the 1950s, however, it began to be clear that there were easier ways of making money, and the fishing industry foundered.

At the dawn of the tourist era, Benidorm tried hard to sell itself, if not quite as a gastronomic paradise, then at least as a place where the diet was healthful and affordable. A press advertisement for the 'Grand Sea Bathing Establishment of the Virgin of Suffrage in the Village of Benidorm, property of Don Francisco Ronda y Galindo', assured those readers tempted by the idea of a summer residence by the seaside that 'nowhere else will they find a more benign climate, more delicious beaches, healthier or cheaper food, or a bathing establishment with better conditions for the bather than that which Don Francisco Ronda has the pleasure of offering to the public.' A note at the foot of the advertisement draws our attention to the price of a kilo of lamb (one peseta), of a pound of beef (one peseta seventy-five), of chickens (one-fifty each) and boiling fowls (interestingly, hen was twice the price of chicken, at three pesetas each). Grapes, melons, pears, apples, peaches, and figs, were ten centimes a kilo. Vegetables were simply *'baratisimas'*: 'very cheap'. Most of this produce would have come straight from the gardens that stood behind the Playa de Levante, where forests of towerblocks now crowd the shoreline.

Leaving Nacho at home to look after the farm, I drove across the country to stay with his mother and father at their place in

Alicante. The morning after my arrival, we sat on the veranda with its distant view of the Mediterranean, drinking coffee in the early sunshine. When I told Nacho's father, Manuel, that I was off to Benidorm, he cast his mind back to the days of his youth, when the resort was just a scruffy village surrounded by almond orchards and dry-stone walls.

'I knew Benidorm when there was nothing. Nada. Just the village and the beach. What was it like then? It was *precioso*. Well, the whole coast was lovely,' he said mournfully. 'It was just a white village. There were fishing boats, pulled up on the sand . . . We used to go there on excursions, myself and a few friends. I used to know the man who went round the village on a horse and cart, selling vegetables. The beach had fields behind it, with fig trees. There was never anyone on it. At one end was a *chiringuito*, a beach shack built of bamboo, where you could have something to eat. It was very simple. I went there once with María Teresa, when we were courting. I think we ate tortilla. María Teresa, do you remember that day?' he called to his wife, who was busy in the kitchen. 'Didn't we have tortilla?'

'How should I remember what we ate?' she replied laughingly, bringing in more coffee. 'Honestly, Manolo, it was nearly sixty years ago!'

Nothing remains of that time, and few people now remember it. The dizzying changes Benidorm has undergone during the last half-century have given it an entirely new identity. The town's population has grown tenfold in forty years, from 6,202 in 1961 to 67,573 in 2004. Twenty-eight per cent of its inhabitants are English, French, Dutch, German, Moroccan, Ecuatorian, Swedish, or Norwegian. Of the town's 330 restaurants, according to official bulletins, around fifty are 'foreign'.

James Michener, in his post-Hemingway odyssey, *Iberia*, writes memorably, if fancifully, that the traveller arriving in Spain by boat could smell the orange groves even before he made landfall, as the perfume of their blossom was carried out to sea on the ocean breezes. Half a century later, the distant fragrance of orange flowers has its modern equivalent in the reek of frying oil, bubbling in a thousand deep-fat fryers in restaurants along the Spanish Mediterranean coast.

By midday, I had walked the whole length of the Playa de Levante, and the tourists were already sitting down to their steak pies and 'strogenoffs'. Caught between a French *pâtisserie* and a Spanish pizzeria was an unassuming bar specialising in the cuisine of the neighbouring region of Murcia. Laid out on the bar top were baskets of green peppers, artichokes, tomatoes, and broad beans. The *huerta*, the fertile well-watered region that cradles the city of Murcia, has inculcated a profound respect for vegetables that amounts almost to dependency. Some of the great dishes in the Murcian repertoire are entirely vegetarian. The murcianos' love of broad beans is proverbial, and it's not uncommon to see them munching their way through piles of raw beans, either as a bar snack or along with the main meal, a heap of them beside the plate. They remove the pods with a stroke of the thumb to devour the tender beans within.

'There used to be a walk along the river, when we visited Murcia,' Manuel had reminisced that morning, 'where we would all go to walk in the afternoon. In the summer, there used to be a stall selling lettuces, and people would buy one and walk along the river. It was funny to see all these young folk like us strolling along the river, munching these lettuces as if they were ice creams. But, actually, they were delicious, and a very refreshing food for a summer afternoon.'

Only in Murcia could lettuce be conceived of as a fast food.

I sat down gratefully at a table on the terrace and ordered a plate of snails, a handful of fried almonds, and a large Estrella Levante, the excellent local beer of Murcia. The snails – another great Levantine love, cooked in a sauce with a slight kick of chilli heat – arrived with a glassful of toothpicks for wiggling the creatures out of their shells. They tasted so good, and the beer was slipping down so nicely, that I decided to stay put and forget about a proper lunch. The barman brought me a plate of *michirones*, the classic

murciano stew made with dried broad beans, and another of
zorongollo, a variation on scrambled eggs with onion and courgettes, another large beer, and a couple of juicy salted anchovies
with toast and olive oil, and, before long, I was beginning to feel
the relief and satisfaction that come when you realise you have
made the right choice about a place to eat. It may have been the
purest fluke, but I had managed it. And, in a place like Benidorm,
the odds were not exactly stacked in my favour.

That afternoon I set out on foot from Manuel and María Teresa's
house along the beach, the towers of Benidorm gleaming in the
distance like a futuristic vision of some high-rise city on the water:
Manhattan *sur mer*. Between Alicante and Benidorm are a string
of minor towns that never quite made it to Benidorm's fame and
fortune, but were happy to chug along gently in its wake, often
preserving something of their original character in the process.
Where the Playa de San Juan, just to the south, is a magnificent,
wide swathe of sand, El Campello has an ugly, stony beach,
making it imperative for the town to possess some industry other
than tourism. Which is why it has clung with such tenacity to its
little fishing fleet, and still has a proper fish market, where the
general public can go most days and buy the fish straight off the
boats, without any of the intermediaries that cut the fishermen's
profits and push up prices at the larger Mediterranean ports.

   In the early evening sun, after a long hot day, commerce and
society spring back to life. Down on the beach at El Campello, a
game of pétanque was in progress, and a group of old men in
shorts and sandals looked on, calling encouragements in Catalan
and Spanish. Up on the harbourside stood the *lonja*, a newish
brick-built construction with the kind of all-purpose municipal
modern look that could just as well have been a primary school or
a library as a fish market.

   When I got there, the market was about to start. Two boats, tied
up in the harbour outside, had just got in from the day's work,
their nets lay in a heap on deck, and the blue plastic boxes of fish

were being unloaded from the deck to the harbourside, and from there to the backdoor of the *lonja*. From production to consumption in the shortest possible time, in the shortest possible distance. A crowd was gathering in the interior of the market, watching the fish come in from the boats in lots of a kilo or sometimes more, each lot on its own white tray.

The slab was filling up: I saw conger eels and flatfish and red mullet and *escórpora*, the ugly spiny orange scorpion fish that (as *rascasse*) is a main ingredient of the French bouillabaisse and bourride. I wandered away from the action to look at the photographs around the walls, which showed El Campello as it used to be in the 1950s: a line of dark little boats along the beach, with a row of low houses behind them; women and girls in rough black dresses, their hair pinned back, each sitting on a nest of nets like a giant spider on her web; the fleet's various boats with their picturesque names: *Marufina, Lolica, Fina Tendero de Terol*; the *Toñi Carmen*, tragically shipwrecked in 1954.

A man in a white coat with a head-mike, the auctioneer, was strutting about, explaining the process to his attentive audience, housewife/cooks of a certain age in flowery summer dresses with robust arms protruding from their short sleeves. One woman wore the *bata de casa*, the blue pinafore that is practically the uniform of the Spanish housewife. The big-bellied man who schmoozed with the auctioneer was clearly a restaurateur. As at any kind of auction, the public fell into two types: buyers and non-buyers. The latter looked on in curiosity, with the quick superficial gaze of the tourist; the former focused intensely on particular items, their eyes as beady as the specimens they examined so expertly.

The merchandise slapped and flapped in its white trays. First up was a flying fish: a novelty item. The auctioneer held it up for all to see, a box-like creature, like one of the Wright Brothers' early machines, pushing open tiny concertina wings. The bids went down and down, but the fish failed to take wing in a commercial sense and it was shunted away sadly, unsold and unloved. The unglamorous lots, the ugly and unfashionable fish, went for so little money one wondered whether it was worth anyone's while. An ashen-grey conger eel went for one euro and fifty cents. A kilo of dogfish could be yours for a euro.

One lady made off with a large *lampuga* (the common dolphin fish), then came back for three kilos of red mullet: 'Do that on the *plancha*, flip flip, bit of olive oil, bit of lemon, and you've got yourself a nice lunch,' spieled the auctioneer. And now we came to the rockfish, the bony little fish which are essential for a good fish stock, such as that needed for the fish-and-rice *caldero* typically eaten for Sunday lunch in El Campello. And, of course, it was a Friday evening, and the whole town was thinking about the weekend. Now, suddenly, there was a flurry of interest. Hands were going up all over the place. Each tray held three or four of these diminutive monsters – the man called them '*morralla*'. Caught up in the bidding fever, I bid three euros for a kilo, proudly taking them to the counter to be weighed up and paid for. I would take them back for María Teresa, and beg her to make me a proper *caldero* for lunch the next day.

A moray eel in an elegant mottled yellow and tan design. 'That's also a good one for stock,' confided the lady in the blue pinafore, who was now standing next to me. Then there was a tray of small *pargos*, with a huge tiger prawn that had somehow got in among the fish. And a greasy-looking dogfish, looking more like a catfish. The auctioneer held out the tray so the fish's toothy muzzle faced the audience, and frightened a little boy in the front row.

And now, *señoras y señores*, for the stars of the show. The *dorada*, or gilt-head bream, has long been one of Spain's absolutely favourite fish. But the *dorada* has has been so ruthlessly overfished in the Mediterranean that it is rarely seen in public these days, and depends on an army of farmed *doradas*, at half the price and half the flavour, to keep alive its reputation. The single, real, wild gilt-head bream at today's auction went for twenty-one euros to the big-bellied restaurateur. When the price was announced, the lady in the pinafore poked me sharply in the ribs.

*   *   *

In the summer of 1991, with Britain in the throes of economic recession and Peter Mayle's *A Year in Provence* reminding its millions of readers that life was easier in the south, I quit my job at the magazine and moved to the island of Ibiza. For the next ten years, I lived with Nacho in a house within sight of the Mediterranean Sea, on a stretch of coastline which had somehow escaped the rampant development that has pulverised the rest.

The island was a microcosm of Spanish food in the sense that it divided up into the coastal zone, where the cooking was mainly *marinera*, and the inland uplands, where a different kind of cuisine had developed, based more on meats, the products of the *matanza*, and vegetables from the *huerta*. The remarkable thing was the way that, on a scrap of land just forty kilometres by twenty kilometres, there could be such a world of difference between the two. But there was. In the centre of the island, where elderly peasants lived who had seldom been to the seaside, you might be served up a *sofrit pagès*, a popular dish of mixed meats first simmered, then sautéed with garlic and vegetables. On the coast, there were fish soup-stews, like *bullit de peix* and skate wings with potatoes.

Misery and starvation were just around the corner, historically speaking, for an island society that, thanks to mass tourism, had become extremely rich in a very short time. For centuries they had been paupers; now they were millionaires. But one understood, partly by intuition, that they had, by no means, always had it so good. Hair-raising tales were told of the war years, when the Republican militia commandeered any food they could lay their hands on, to the extent of robbing grain from underground stores, and the rural populace subsisted on carob pods. The tourist boom had been a blessing (though it may ultimately prove to be a deadly curse). Now the islanders could shop at hypermarkets like everyone else. They could buy smoked salmon, if they could afford it, and greenhouse tomatoes and Roquefort cheese.

Our village had been a fishing community, and still bore the marks of its centuries of dependence on the sea. The sandy bay where a couple of hotels now cater to tourism was still known as *es port*. On weekends, teenage boys from the village went out in dinghies from *es port* to fish for lobster and grouper, which they sold to the handful of restaurants along the seafront. The menu at these simple places was the epitome of *cocina marinera* as practised all along the Spanish Mediterranean coast, a nearly unvarying repertoire of rice dishes with fish and shellfish, whole bream or bass baked *a la sal*, *calamares a la romana*, cuttlefish *a la plancha* with parsley and garlic, as well as a few local specialities.

But that was restaurant cooking. In the daily lives of the locals, the 'cooking of the sea' was a simpler, saltier affair, based on whatever could be gleaned from the ocean in the immediate vicinity of the village. Every few days a man with a white van would appear in the village square selling *gerrets*, a small fish caught locally on an amateur and probably illegal basis. They were dirt cheap: a kilo of *gerrets* could be had for the price of a *bocadillo*. But it was their versatility that made them popular. You could do what you liked with them – fried, grilled over coals, or cooked up with rice, they always tasted good, their white flesh flavoursome in a straightforward sort of way, like sardines without the oiliness and pungent smell.

In his history of food, Felipe Fernández-Armesto claims that the appeal of fish as food is explained, not so much by contemporary ideals of healthy eating, as by its romantic status as the last important foodstuff obtained by something that resembles hunting. Certainly, the seafood the villagers enjoyed was not the kind of thing you would find in the fishmongers. One old man went fishing for moray eels down at a deserted cove, bringing them back slimy and squirming in a bucket, for his wife to cook in a saffron-scented stew for their supper. One moonlit night in high summer, we went out fishing for squid in a little wooden boat with a square sail. The boat belonged to Juan Antonio, a friend whose grandfather had built the *llaut* with his own hands at a time when it was thought entirely right and proper for a young man in a Spanish fishing village to build his own boat. We rowed out from the miniature harbour at the end of the beach, stopping within sight of the

shoreline where the water was calm and deep. Shreds of laughter
and guitar music drifted from the beach bar, a whitewashed shack
that had once been a fisherman's hovel. Juan Antonio showed us
how to drop the thick nylon line with sardine bits attached to big
hooks. From the rim of the boat hung two old flashlights upside
down, for attracting the squid to the surface. When we pulled in
the lines, they loomed up like ghosts through the blackness.

Nights on the water, days on the rocks. On summer afternoons,
we hiked down to the string of little bays along the coastline where
no one else went, since the access was only on foot down a long
mountain path. We collected sea snails and urchins – I learned that
the purple and brown ones were finer flavoured, though harder to
find, than the black.

The fun was in the hunting and gathering, and in the big
flavours that came as a reward for your efforts. One day I walked
down to the *cala* alone and lay by a rock pool, watching the tiny
shrimps, translucent wisps of nothingness, that paddled placidly at
the edge of the sun-warmed pool. I spent the afternoon painstak-
ingly catching them one by one with a butterfly net. When I had
myself a handful and the sun was going down, I walked back up to
the house, poured myself a beer, and stir-fried the whiskery, still-
twitching shrimps for a a second in a spoonful of oil with half a
clove of garlic. The shrimps went from glassy to deep orange in an
instant, leaching out some of their colour into the sizzling olive oil.

Just as well there was no one else around to share that meal, for
half of very little is hardly worth bothering with. On the other
hand, I sometimes curse the fact that no one was there to feel the
mild crunch of their shells giving way to a burst of flavour, rich
with minerals. It was one of the most delicious mouthfuls I can ever
remember taking.

Spanish gastronome Julio Camba once wrote that just one
sardine is the whole ocean. Well, those shrimps were the whole
Mediterranean sea.

CHAPTER TWO

VALENCIA

The season was kicking into top gear as I drove north along the motorway that hugs the coastline all the way from the deep Spanish south to the French border. Barcelona was 500 kilometres away, Perpignan, 750. On a weekend in late June, the big road was a six-lane roller coaster thick with tourist traffic; its broad chicanes swinging between sprawling orange groves and giant estates of back-to-back houses built as second homes for northern Europeans. To the left was a wall of blank, bare mountains; to the right, now and again, a flash of blue sea.

Turning off at the sign for Valencia, I fought my way into the *centro histórico*, disregarding the signs that advised me not to try, and parked in the cathedral square. The city was flooded with high-summer light. Fountains splashed in the squares; flowers blazed in the balconies. Browsing the souvenir shops around the Plaza de la Reina, I bought a few postcards and sat down to write them with a cold *horchata*, the pale, refreshing local drink of earth nut milk, sugar, and water.

At the table next to me, a time-honoured scene was being played out: the Arrival of the Paella. It steamed in its pan from the oven – or, which was more likely, the microwave oven – while the French couple who had ordered it bubbled over in their excitement. I leaned as close to the table as I dared, pretending to pick up a fallen paper napkin, and inspected the dish out of the corner of my eye. It had a garish yellow colour, more of a turmeric or tartrazine yellow than the luscious orange of saffron, and the strips of red and green pepper made for an alarming contrast. Lumps of something firm and white, possibly boneless chicken meat, could be seen buried in the rice. The paella gave off a damp, mucky smell, like clothes that have been left too long in the washing machine in hot weather.

Never was a dish so misunderstood, so misrepresented, so abused as paella. The crimes committed in the name of the Spanish national dish – mostly by Spaniards themselves – are horrible to relate. Even the name is a mystery to most of us. One (English) writer traces the etymology of paella to the Arabic word for 'leftovers', which could hardly be further from the truth. In fact, it derives from the Latin *patella* – the English word pail shares a common root – meaning a cooking utensil made of metal, and, more particularly, iron. It follows that, like 'casserole', 'terrine', and so on, paella refers originally not to the food, but to the utensil, a wide, flat, shallow iron pan with handles on the sides.

Of the three picture postcards propped up against the salt cellar on my breakfast table, the first showed a *paella de mariscos*, the standard beachside paella with fat pink langoustines and prawns and mussels on the half shell artfully arranged across its surface, the pan settled among pine branches surrounded with oranges and lemons. The second was of the original *paella valenciana* – made with rabbit, chicken, snails and beans, and cooked on a fire of orange wood (you could see the trunks poking out from under-neath, with a few glossy leaves still attached). And the third captured the making of a particular paella on a gigantic scale. This one was twenty yards or more in diameter; so wide, that a special rotating bridge had had to be constructed for the battalion of cooks to reach the centre of the pan with their long metal stirrers. This monumental paella, made to feed 100,000 people, was created in 1992, when Valencia's rival city of Barcelona was celebrating the Olympics and Seville the Expo. It has gone down in history and the Guinness Book of Records as the grandest paella ever made.

As any Spaniard will tell you, the people of Valencia are lovers of exaggeration, and especially fond of the categories of loudest, brightest, gaudiest and most spectacular. The baroque, with all its curlicues and furbelows, is undoubtedly the city's favourite archi-tectural style. The famous fiesta, known as *Fallas*, in which giant painted figures are set fire to amid an apotheosis of fireworks and supercharged bangers as loud as anti-tank missiles, is one of the noisiest and most ebullient in a country where noisily ebullient fiestas are the rule rather than the exception.

When it comes to the city's central market, said to be the food market with the largest surface area in the whole of Spain – 'a record it disputes with Barcelona's Boqueria' – it is not just size that's important; here are scale and substance, wonderfully com-bined. Grand and gorgeous, the airy spaces under its domes and halls echoing with the comings and goings of its floating con-gregation, the Mercat Central is a kind of cathedral.

It had been more than a decade since I'd last set foot in this, one of Spain's major temples of good food. Gratifyingly, nothing much seemed to have changed in the interim, except that the building's intricate ironwork and stained-glass panels had recently been given a handsome overhaul. Prices had risen hugely, of course, though the change to euros from pesetas made it difficult to tell exactly by how much. Everywhere in the western world, the out-of-town hypermarket poses an ever-present threat to traditional markets such as this. But the Mercat Central showed no sign of buckling under the strain. The market now had a home delivery service: details were available on its website.

Nothing that was good about the old place, however (apart from those low, low prices), had been sacrificed on the altar of modernity. At Caracoles Selectos – Select Snails – I stood for a minute or two to admire the stall with its pots of plastic flowers and fat snails hanging in string bags. Opposite, at the Lettuce Boutique, a greengrocers', an image in painted tiles depicted an idyllic rural scene in the Valencian countryside: a farmer with a square-ended Spanish hoe, up to his ankles in a paddy field, with a field of cabbages in rows stretching behind him. At the herboristería, bunches of dried herbs were tied up with lengths of esparto grass.

The Mercat is an anthology of local ingredients in all their variegated glory. There were four or five varieties of orange on one stall, six types of green bean on another; aubergines delicately striped in purple and white, taut-skinned and shiny as if polished with furniture wax; cardoons and artichokes at a euro the kilo, and radishes as big as turnips. A box of hard, wrinkly, coffee-brown pellets in a wooden fruit box beside the almonds and hazelnuts and walnuts turned out to be *chufas*, or earth nuts, produced in the village of Alboraia and mostly used for *horchata*. I crunched one: it was mildly bitter and astringent, with a subtle nuttiness reminiscent of almonds. At Vicent Peris, founded in 1870, the variety of cured and salted fish products, a great speciality of Valencia, ran from salt cod and tuna in oil and the classic *mojama*, to rare and exquisite delicacies, like sun-dried octopus and *bull de tonyina* – the salt-cured stomach of the tuna, looking like a relic from some medieval saint.

'Try one of these, they're lovely and sweet,' said a voice by my ear as I passed a busy fruit stall. The buxom market lady held out in her hand a orange the size of a grapefruit. I sank my thumbnail into the zest and rubbed the glossy skin on the back of my hand, sniffing the cologne-like fragrance of the citrus oil. I bit into the skin, Spanish style, and ripped off the white pith and peel to get at the cool flesh inside. I gulped down the segments: they were packed with juice, and a freshness that was palpable and tastable. It was a perfect Valencia orange, reminding me forcefully just how much we take this delicious fruit for granted.

After a swift beer in the market bar, I took the new tramway from the city centre to the sea, getting off at Doctor Lluch and walking briskly through some of Valencia's meanest streets. When the old harbour moved away to the grand new container port a mile or two further down the coast, the Grao neighbourhood fell into decrepitude. Indians, Moroccans, and South Americans had made the place their own, playing their lives out against a tawdry backdrop of convenience stores, video libraries, and neighbourhood bars with faded, tattered awnings. Children played in the gutters.

The neighbourhoods of Cabanyal, Grao, and Malva-Rosa were old-fashioned maritime *barrios*, existing between the poles of the harbour and city beach. If Cabanyal and Grao were rough, harbour-side districts, home to a shifting population of dock workers, sailors, and fishermen, the Malva-Rosa was a tatty Brighton of the South, a seaside pleasure zone where Valencia's poorer citizens once came to spend their Sunday afternoons.

But, down at the seaside, change, like the invigorating scent of salt and ozone, was in the air. New buildings were going up as fast as the old buildings crumbled. From the top floor of a brand-new block, where they were just putting in the windows, I heard Russian voices, bellowing at each other for more cement. The air was full of dust, the smell of decay and regeneration.

It being almost lunchtime, I directed my steps towards the

restaurant that is routinely spoken of as Valencia's best and one of the top ten or twenty in the country. Ca' Sento had always intrigued me as much for its history as for its fundamentalist obsession with the quality of its raw materials.

The Aleixandre family were natives of El Grao, the hard-living fishermen's district just behind the harbour front. In the early 1960s, Vicente Aleixandre and his wife, María Muria, emigrated to Switzerland, where they worked for fourteen years, returning in 1977 to open a bar in the modest Calle Méndez Núñez.

Their place was a sailor's bar with a TV blaring in the corner, beer on tap, Coca-Cola and plain table wines, and a bottle of rough brandy kept on hand for when the local gypsy baron came in to pay the couple a visit. What kept the business bubbling were the plates of food Sento (short for Vicente) and María served up at the bar.

'What have you got?' was the customers' cry as they came in the door.

'I've got prawns, langoustine, squid, cuttlefish, crab, red mullet, some nice mussels . . . I've got grouper, sole, monkfish, hake . . .' sang the reply from behind the bar. In the 1970s, Valencia was still an important fishing port, so that this fishy cornucopia was easily available and, what's more, affordable. It was normal, for example, for a working man to come in at midday and sink a few beers and a plate of gambas.

'How do you want it done? Fried, grilled, *a la plancha*, with garlic and parsley . . . ?'

Over time, the humble harbour bar became a proper restaurant. Sento's natural charm and acumen, María's inborn understanding of the subtle arts of fish and rice cookery, and their shared determination to make something of themselves, quickly turned the place into a success. And, in the course of things, their son Raúl, born in 1971, became an integral part of what went on in the kitchen. As a child, he worked in the bar while his schoolmates played football in the street. Seasons spent in important restaurant kitchens have taught him about the currents of modernity swirling about the world of Spanish food. But, in his heart, Raúl is the archetype of the Spanish chef, solidly rooted to tradition and family.

Ca' Sento is still to be found in its original location, on the corner of the down-at-heel Calle Méndez Núñez. The place has not grown or expanded, and can only serve a maximum of sixteen customers at one sitting. But, even so, the dining room now gleams with marble, the kitchen with stainless steel. The walls are lined with abstract art; a series of shelves accommodates a magnificent collection of single malts, aged rums, tequilas, Armagnacs, and grappas. On this weekday lunchtime, the majority of the diners were business people and politicians – it is only they, or their expense accounts, who can afford the prices at Ca' Sento.

Certainly, the cooking here is exquisite. The salad of clams (*vieiras*) and Dublin Bay prawns with baby chard and rocket leaves, turnip tops and violet petals, with a dressing of orange and lobster coral, was memorable as well as beautiful. The rice *a la plancha*, a dish of Raúl's creation, each spoonful given a golden crust by a few seconds of sizzle on the griddle, came with four enormous, juicy, deep red Palamós prawns. I thought of the workman and his four prawns, and wondered what he'd make of the price-tag attached to this dish, now that Palamós prawns are a scarce and expensive luxury.

Raúl came out into the dining room and sat at my table to smoke a cigarette. He was a roly-poly, friendly man with a well-suppressed stutter which hinted at shyness.

There are three main types of rice dishes to be found in the region of Valencia, Raúl explained, the classification depending on the amount of liquid left unabsorbed by the rice. *Arroz seco* is 'dry': paella is a dry rice. But then there is *meloso* and *caldoso*: 'creamy' and 'soupy' respectively. The menu at Ca' Sento included all three styles, but tended to concentrate on the lesser-known *melosos* and *caldosos*, in part as a reaction to the predominance of the paella.

It is the curse of being a Valencian that, wherever you go in the

world, people want to talk about paella. In the popular imagination, the paella has come to symbolise not just Spanish cooking,
but Spain itself. In its bright colours and hectic, but somehow
harmonious organisation, this dish seems to encapsulate what
non-Spaniards believe to be true about Spanish life and culture
in a wider sense.

'I always get asked the same question,' complained Raúl, tap-
ping his ash on the edge of a saucer. 'Where should we go for a
good paella? And, I have to tell them, the places you can find a
good paella could be counted on the fingers of one hand. There is
just so much rubbish about. And the worst rubbish is the paella
served to tourists, frozen and defrosted in the oven, with a jug of
sangría. It's a shame, because that paella is the impression they
take away with them. It's also a shame because there are so many
good rice dishes they will never try. Rice baked in the oven; rice
with beans and turnips; rice with pears and raisins, a dish you
don't see nowadays, but my grandmother used to make for us; the
arroz meloso that my mother still makes in the kitchen back here,
with the same pot she's been using for forty years. It's amazing, the
variety of the world of rice. It's a universe,' he said.

Rice is not just a primary ingredient of the region's favourite
dish. The grain Oryza sativa has an importance here that is
dietary, gastronomic, cultural, and economic. As the mayor of
Valencia, a lady of traditional build who obviously enjoys her
carbohydrates, is fond of saying, rice has contributed to the
promotion and diffusion of the image of Valencia all over the
world. Once could go further and say, as the Spanish do, that, for
valencianos, rice is nothing less than una manera de entender la
vida – a way of understanding life.

Spain is currently one of Europe's hungrier consumers of rice –
indeed, national production cannot keep up with consumption,
which runs at an average of six kilos per head per year (much of
the shortfall comes from Egypt). But it was not always so. The
thirteenth-century Llibre de Sent Sovi, the earliest surviving cookbook in any Spanish language, includes just one rice recipe, and

this is for a sweet pudding with almond milk and cinnamon. For many centuries thereafter, rice cultivation was closely associated with disease, since the standing water it required was an ideal breeding ground for the malarial mosquito, and rice as an ingredient, by association, was frowned upon.

For most of the history of its cultivation in Valencia, rice was a poor man's food. It took centuries to rise through society; even in the early 1900s, as Lorenzo Millo describes in his monograph, *Arroz*, the most typical and popular lunch dish among the Valencian middle and upper classes was not paella, but *olla* – a mixed stew of pulses, mixed meats, and vegetables, closely related to the *cocido* of Madrid, the *puchero* of Andalucía, and the rest of the family of Spanish one-pot stews.

The evolution of rice cookery in the region closely follows its economic development. The earliest paellas were probably made by farming folk in the rural flatlands around the city, cradle of Valencia's important fruit and vegetable production. For the ingredients for these primitive paellas, made over an open fire of orange or lemon wood, cooks would logically have used whatever was closest to hand. Vegetables like Swiss chard, artichokes, and beans, both 'broad' (*fabes*) and 'French' (*tavella*). Depending on the time of year, there might be snails. For protein, a nice fat rabbit or perhaps a chicken might be chopped and added, since everyone kept a few hens in the backyard. A rice dish was made (and still is) with wild ducks, or with eel and frog, both plentiful, and even, it is whispered, with the fat rats that gorged on the tender rice shoots in early summer. Another of these ur-paellas, dating back at least to the eighteenth century, was *arroz con bacalao y col* – a potent mixture of rice, salt cod and cabbage, especially popular during Lent, when meat was off the menu.

From the farmyards of Valencia's rural outskirts, the paella gradually took its place in public life. By the mid-nineteenth century, it had been adopted as a regional *plato típico*, with the name *paella valenciana*. It became a dish for Sundays in the country, the centrepiece of multitudinous fiestas in the open air, and part of the romantic upwelling of nationalist sentiment in the form of folklore and the picturesque. The paella, as it is known outside Valencia, a marriage of rice and seafood, came into being in the early twentieth century, in the *merenderos* (open-air eating places) down by the beach. Compared to the traditional inland paellas, which were relatively dull to look at, the *paella de mariscos*, the shellfish paella of prawns, crab, and mussels, must have been a revelation, the deep red of the fish standing out against the saffron gold of the rice like the red and gold of the national flag.

Valencia sits on the edge of what was once a marshy flood-plain criss-crossed with rivers and canals. As the city has grown, its consumption of water has grown enormously, the water table has plummeted, and, as a consequence, the plain has largely been drained of surface water.

But the Albufera remains – a freshwater lagoon closed off by a build-up of silt from the Turia and Júcar rivers, and by a slender sandbank on the seaward side. As described by Roman historians in the fourth century AD, it covered an area equivalent to 30,000 hectares; it was the Arabs, however, who christened it Al-Buhera – the lake. It was the Arabs, too, during the reign of Abderrahman III in the tenth century, at a time when agriculture in Muslim Spain was making dramatic technical advances, who began growing rice in the rich alluvial plains around 'the lake'.

Driving southwards on the A7, the city seemed endless, a dense tissue of motorways gradually strangling the remains of what were once prosperous farms, mills, store-houses, stables. Off the main highway on the old coast road, north of the Albufera, you are in rice country. The rocket-like silos of a factory proclaim their contents as 'Arroz SOS': a rice brand as familiar to Spanish consumers as Uncle Ben's is to Americans. During the winter, the flat fields are featureless, brown, and dry. Then, in the early spring, the ground is ploughed, the channels (known as *acequias* or *ullals*) are opened, the fields are flooded, the rice shoots sown, and the Valencian countryside begins to resemble the paddy fields of China. Now, at the height of summer, with two months to go before the harvest, the lush greenness of the plantations was shocking to the eye.

The restaurant Casa Salvador stands on a modest estuary at the point where the river Júcar meets the sea, on a marshy outcrop, a little uncanny in its humid silence, poised at the confluence of three waters, brackish, fresh, and salt. The Estany, as it is known, was where Salvador Gascón and his sister, Concha, pitched up with their parents in the year 1950 from the inland village of Tavernes de la Valldigna. Despite the certain disadvantages of the abandoned duck farm in which they installed themselves, such as the lack of electric light or running water, the Gascóns planned to start a bar serving drinks and snacks to the hunters and fishermen who visited the Estany at weekends. In the intervening years (during which the family boasts that it hasn't closed a single day), the bar has smoothly transmogrified into a fine restaurant, and, half a century later, Casa Salvador is famous above all for its rice dishes, over which it has attained a supreme mastery.

The restaurant is formed of two *barracas*, the original farm buildings, joined into a wide, airy space hung with eel nets, painted ceramics and other knick-knacks typical of the region. The menu at Casa Salvador reads like a treatise on the rice cookery of the Pais Valenciano, with curiosities that you'd be hard pushed to find anywhere else, such as a paella of duck, snails, and eels, another of salt cod and cauliflower, and a fine sounding *arroz del senyoret* – 'rich kid's rice' – so-called because the prawns and langoustines and fish chunks come ready peeled, shelled, and boned. I sat at a table on the terrace overlooking the estuary, where a salty breeze was coming in over the sandbar. Thirty minutes later, I was happily eating my way through a magnificent *arroz caldoso de cigalas, rape y setas* – a soupy rice, cooked not in the paella, but in a high-sided casserole dish, magisterially combining langoustines, monkfish, and wild mushrooms in a powerfully flavoured saffron-infused broth. I preceded this with a plate of clams, followed it with an ice cream, and then sat in a stupor looking at the view as the afternoon settled into siesta mode. A double café solo would, I calculated, provide me with just the boost I needed to drive back to Valencia, find a parking space, and fall through the door of the apartment before collapsing into an armchair.

There is no gold-standard paella, just as there is no absolutely archetypal quiche Lorraine, no Platonic pizza. But, if the tourist industry has messed around with Valencia's most characteristic dish, it seemed like a good idea to look for it in its original version, or at least as close to this ideal as possible. To this end, I would have to travel a little distance from the coast, for the classic *paella valenciana* has only been saved from extinction, like some shy wild animal, by careful protection away from built-up areas. In the forested uplands behind the Mediterranean seaboard, rabbits run wild and there is firewood in abundance.

I made a few phone calls and, next morning, took a train from Valencia's art nouveau jewel of a railway station, the Estación del Norte, to the mountain town of Buñol. The train clattered at a gentle pace through the agricultural zone upon which rests Valencia's fame as an important producer of vegetables and citrus fruit. As we climbed uphill, there were groves of oranges and olives, and almond trees, and pomegranates spattered with their scarlet flowers.

These days, Buñol is best known for a mad fiesta called the Tomatina, billed as Spain's greatest food fight, in which thirty tons of tomatoes are hurled in the streets and the world's media turns up to watch. Before the invention of the fiesta in the 1960s, Buñol was an important stop on the seven-day carriage route from Madrid to the coast, and the Venta Pilar was a kind of caravanserai where drivers, muleteers, and their charges could stop for the night. The house is a whitewashed, cuboid warren of a place, more than 300 years old, with a heavy wooden double door where the traffic came in and sepia photographs hanging in the hall.

'In the old days, one hundred people might sleep here of a night.

It was a tremendous business. But, of course, when the mechanical traction engine came in, the carriage business died,' mused Enrique Galindo Estévez, elderly owner of the Venta along with his son – also called Enrique.

Nowadays, the place functions mainly as a restaurant, its *especialidad de la casa* being a paella made in the old-fashioned way, over a wood fire.

'In the old days, everyone used wood. Then the gas came in. Now almost nobody does,' reflected Enrique. It could be any kind of wood: pine, olive, or almond. But today it was orange, loved by valencianos for the intense, continuous heat it gives out, as well as its fragrance. In a covered section of the backyard was a long stone platform where paellas were cooked on trivets, each on its own fire. The walls and ceiling were coated with a thick layer of shiny tar, the residue of years of paella making at the Venta.

Hauling a two-handled pan, almost a metre wide, from a blackened stack in the corner, Enrique laid it on the trivet and poured in a generous slug of olive oil. 'I do it all by eye,' he said.

First, he fried the chunks of chicken and rabbit, tumbling them in the sizzling oil. The flames licked greedily around the lip of the pan. Then came the beans: a large pale butter bean called the *garrofó*, found only in the region, and a flat green bean not unlike our own dear runner. A sloosh of tomato purée (leftover from the Tomatina, perhaps, I thought about saying, then thought better of it), then the rice and chicken stock, the fine threads of saffron, toasted and ground in a mortar, and a generous sprinkling of salt.

And that, said Enrique, was that. From then on, it was a matter of watching the fire, poking in more sticks as the fire burned low. The ideal is a constant level of heat that will cook the rice, not so fiercely as to burn it, but just strong enough to leave a crust on the bottom of the pan – this is known as the *socarrat*, and it's a delicacy that valencianos fight over.

We stood in the courtyard in the spring sunshine admiring the paella as it bubbled appetisingly, waves of aroma billowing out of the pan along with the clouds of steam and smoke. Enrique mopped his brow: it was hot work. A minute or two's rest and he was back on the job, busying himself with a second paella while the first was already on the home straight. It was a Sunday, and the Venta would soon be full of hungry families.

Before long, the day's first paella was a great glowing circle of Buddhist orange-yellow. The rice had sucked up all the stock and there were puffs of steam escaping from little blowholes that had formed in its surface. I tried a forkful. The rice was perfectly cooked, and had absorbed all the savouriness of the rabbit, chicken, beans and saffron. This may not have been the most elaborate paella of all time; it certainly wasn't the cleverest or the most inventive. It was, simply, authentic. Or authentically simple. Which, as with most of Spain's best traditional foods, pretty much comes to the same thing.

CHAPTER THREE

COSTA BRAVA

There have always been visitors to Spain, but, until the twentieth century, they were few, a handful of intrepid souls who were able to overlook the discomforts of travel in one of Europe's most backward countries for the sake of its magnificent artistic heritage. Spain never really featured on the Grand Tour: it was far too difficult a destination for those young aristocrats of the nineteenth century who flitted effetely from Switzerland and Tuscany to the English lakes, sketchbook in hand.

Tourism had its official birth a hundred years ago, with the creation of the National Tourism Commission by the Count of Romanones in 1905, but scarcely took off in a commercial sense until the mid-century, by which time the stage was set for the extraordinary tourist boom of the 1960s.

In 1950, there were 290,000 foreign visitors. In 1959, the Francoist policy of autarchy, or closed economy, was officially discarded. After that, foreigners, and foreign investment, flooded into the country. From 1960 to 1973, Spain had the second highest growth rate in the world after Japan. In 1981, the visitor count reached 40 million; three years later it had soared to 54 million – more than one tourist for each and every inhabitant of the country. According to the World Tourism Organisation, based in Madrid, the Spanish tourist market is forecast to grow 5 per cent, year-on-year, over the next ten years, reaching 75 million foreign tourists in the year 2020. But, by then, the industry itself might be untenable, as a UN report on the future of the Mediterranean recently predicted, with another 4,000 kilometres of hitherto virgin coast-line destined to vanish under the concrete tide, and the region as a whole nearing total environmental collapse.

Indirectly, the impact of tourism on the nation's food habits has been hugely beneficial, since the income it generates has allowed more people to eat more and better. At one end of the scale, there is no doubt that tourism has provided an audience for the new Spanish cuisine of the 1990s, which it might have lacked if it were left to local tastes to appreciate and local pockets to pay for it. At the package-tour end of things, however, poor cooking in hotels, the greasy paellas and insipid gazpachos (paella and gazpacho were found to be perfect hotel dishes, since both could be made in enormous quantities), perpetuated the bad historical reputation of Spanish food in general.

In his novel *Un Artículo de Encargo*, Miguel Sen has his principal character, chef Eudaldo Manera, describe the unsavoury culinary practices of the 1960s in the hotels of the Costa Brava – from whence, says Manera, comes the Spanish saying 'among the bad builders are the good cooks', since kitchen staff in the tourist hotels often found work on building sites when the season was over. The picture of package tourists drinking themselves into oblivion in 'hotels that were built in four days and are now falling apart', is convincing, if depressing. The hotels had fixed times for lunch and dinner, and, if anyone was late, they were required to pay a supplement. So the hotel managers got together and arranged for their guests to go on long boat rides around the bay of Lloret de Mar, ensuring that their charges arrived late for lunch. Waiting for them in the dining room, says Sen's character, might be a slab of breaded meat, which he swears was *mortadela*, dipped in egg and bread crumbs and fried, 'for all I know, in engine oil'.

From Valencia, I set a course for the far north-east corner of the peninsula, where the Pyrenees meet the Mediterranean sea and Spain meets France. I was heading for Roses, a small coastal town at the northern end of the Costa Brava and which I knew nothing about, except that it possessed what was routinely described in restaurant guides and magazine articles as the most innovative and exciting restaurant in Spain. Only that Saturday the national press was full of excited reports on the fact that the *New York Times* had proclaimed it the most important restaurant in the world, and plastered a full-face portrait of its chef on the cover of their weekly magazine. I was due to have dinner at El Bulli on Sunday night. But there was a night and a day to go till my appointment, and, until then, food-wise, I was on my own.

Roses: the name of the town made it sound fragrant and floral and postcard-pretty. But, on a hot night in July, Roses smelt of sunflower oil and tinned tomato. I watched the tourists come and go through streets lined with gift shops and boutiques. They dined in waves: first the Brits, with their stodgy-looking suppers of spag bol and pizza, then the Germans and Scandinavians (grilled meats and chips), and, finally, the French (paella, fish, and plates of *fruits de mer*).

It was my strong suspicion that finding anything really good to eat in this heaving holiday town would be a challenge worthy of Hercule Poirot. Sitting down at a table on the sea front, I asked for a plate of ham, a bowl of gazpacho, and a side order of *pa amb tomàquet*, the Catalan national snack of bread rubbed with tomato, anointed with olive oil, and sprinkled with salt. The tomato was out of a jar, the olive oil nearly rancid, the sliced serrano ham as sweaty and pink-tinged as the trippers filing past on the prom. The gazpacho had a dull, lifeless taste, like something insufficiently seasoned that had been sitting around for too long in a crowded fridge.

This might have been the sad end of my night out in Roses, were it not for Carmen Casas, doyenne of Catalan restaurant reviewers, whose Bible-like guide to the restaurants of Catalunya recommended a little restaurant in the backstreets of Roses. It was quite off the beaten trail, family-run, and, according to Carmen, served nothing but locally landed seafood simply but perfectly cooked. I practically ran the few hundred yards uphill to a bright dining room with white paper tablecloths, wall tiles painted with romantic scenes of the Costa Brava, the fishing boats plying the coast, the unquiet sea, the wild cliffs and sinewy pines. Around the walls were team photographs of the Barcelona footbal club. Late on a Saturday night, the restaurant was humming with locals, and the rubbery tones of Catalan voices bounced raucously off the walls. Every so often, the decibel level rose another notch, when a blast of sizzling came from the kitchen at the back.

Senyor Magesté reeled off the menu for tonight, and immediately brought me a plate of rock mussels, their shells stippled pale green with lichen, their pale little bodies vibrant with intense sea-flavour. My spirits were lifted in an instant. Thereafter, a series of dishes arrived, each more sensational than the last. The prawns, locally caught, were plump, russet-red, incomparably fresh. The razor shells were chewily delicious strips of golden meat; the soles, the size of my outstretched hand, came with a greenish, gleaming lump of perfect *allioli*, the Catalan emulsion sauce of garlic and olive oil, as piquant as mustard. There were monkfish chunks and baby octopus and langoustines, all caught the night before in the deep sandbanks along the coast of Roses, L'Escala, and Palamós, and tumbled briefly on the sizzling *plancha*. And there was a bottle of fizzy white Blanc Pescador, the so-called 'needle wine' (*vi d'agulla*), whose acid bite and freshness is a perfect foil for the richness of Mediterranean seafood. It was all so good and so genuine, that it almost restored my faith in Spanish seaside eating.

The road to Cala Montjoi begins unprepossessingly among the suburbs of Roses, winding up into the rocks and stones of Cape Creus, becoming a dusty, roller coaster track of hairpin bends and wide-screen vistas, before depositing you, breathless and wild-haired, in the harbour town of Cadaqués. At the height of the high season, a permanent stream of cars clogs the narrow road, as visitors head for these barely accessible rocky coves in a vain attempt to leave the Costa Brava crowds behind. Cala Montjoi's claim to fame, unlikely though it may look to the casual observer, is that it harbours probably the world's most famous, not to say notorious modern restaurant – a place about which more ink has been expended than about any other single eating place in the Iberian peninsula. If 'paella' and 'gazpacho' are the first two terms of the international lexicon of Spanish food, then 'El Bulli' is probably the fourth or fifth.

Getting a table at Bulli is, in the world of international haute cuisine, something like winning the biggest cash prize on some high-paying lottery. The restaurant is open from 1 April to 1 October every year, but only serves dinner, and the dining room has a capacity of just forty customers on any given night. Except in the months of high summer, it closes on Mondays and Tuesdays. The number of diners El Bulli can serve in any given year is, therefore, around 8,000.

So much for supply. To say that demand outstrips it is putting it mildly. For those 8,000 dinners, the restaurant receives no less than 400,000 requests every year. The faxes, the emails, the anxiously hand-written letters begin to arrive not long after 1 October, when the restaurant closes and chef Ferran Adrià Acosta and his acolytes decamp to their workshop/laboratory in Barcelona to dream up new wizardries for the following season. Surprisingly, for a restaurant of such stratospheric world renown, there are no quotas at El Bulli, no PR invitations, no freebies, no tables kept spare in case Antonio Banderas should turn up one night with Melanie. Not even Adrià's closest friends and associates are guaranteed a table. Legend has it that when chef Juan Mari Arzak, the grand master of modern Spanish cuisine and who is held in deep respect by Adrià, was in the vicinity of Roses and enquired after a table, he was turned away empty-handed.

On the evening of the appointed day, a Sunday, after a long siesta and a long hot shower, I drove out once again from Roses. At this hour, the tourists had all gone back to their hotels, and the sinuous road was empty. Down below, the sea was laid out flat, coloured a silvery grey from the evening cool.

El Bulli has a curious history going back to the earliest days of tourism on the Costa Brava, when a German couple called Hans and Marketta Schilling set up a bar in their new house catering for the divers who were drawn to the crystal-clear waters of Cala Montjoi. (The name of the place derives from that of the couple's bulldog, Bulli.) The house stands at the entrance to the *cala*, still undeveloped so far, apart from a few holiday chalets built in the free-for-all days before a law passed in 1969 put a stop to any and all building within fifty metres of the water. The low white house stands between road and beach, but almost nothing could be seen through the protective curtain of cypresses and Mediterranean shrubbery. The name was stencilled on a rusted iron plaque.

Finding a back gate open, I walked down towards the kitchen. A group of young guys in black shirts and trousers were lounging by the kitchen door, sitting on upturned fruit boxes, smoking cigarettes. A pile of empty wooden crates bore witness to the fact that the restaurant gets its melons from Valencia, its asparagus from Navarra, its lettuces from Barcelona. The building looked rather plain, a whitewashed Spanish seaside house with terracotta roof tiles and a terrace out front looking down to the beach through white arches. Closer to the sea, a wall of plate glass gleamed like a mirror. Beyond the glass was the sanctum sanctorum, the kitchen of El Bulli, a place of alchemical mystery and magic, where even now my dinner was being conjured up.

I found the man himself sitting at a table on the terrace, the arch behind him framing a view of the *cala*'s modest arc of sand and water, an image of calm after the frenzy of a summer's day at the seaside. He was scribbling something in a small pocket-book.

Not since the days of Escoffier and Carême has a chef scaled such heights of fame and admiration. Yet the details of Ferran Adrià Acosta's early life hold few clues to his eventual gastro-stardom. He was born into a working-class family in Hospitalet de Llobregat, a dreary suburb of Barcelona, in 1962. As such, he represents the generation whose knowledge of life under the dictatorship is almost entirely second-hand: in the year of Franco's death, he was just thirteen. His generation is that of the Transition; it bridges the gap between black-and-white TV and the MP3-player, between one-pot chickpea stews and molecular cuisine.

Adrià has a well-fed, lived-in sort of face, shortish brown hair mussed up so that you can't tell, at a glance, whether it is naturally curly or straight. He is neither thin nor fat, tall nor short, good-looking nor ugly. As he sat in front of me in his whites, he looked entirely neutral: neutral and normal.

'Mine was just a normal family,' he said mildly. I had asked him to tell me about his background. 'What did we eat? Normal things; the same kind of normal things that millions of people normally eat. My mother cooked. But the fact that I ended up devoting my life to haute cuisine had nothing to do with the way things were at home. Normal families have twenty or twenty-five regular dishes: ours were rice, a baked fish, tripe. My mother wasn't big on casseroles; our thing was more vegetables, fish *a la plancha*, fried fish. My family is mainly Catalan, but with ancestors who came from Andalucía and Murcia. So we had gazpacho, which is not from Catalunya. Except that, nowadays, you find it everywhere.

'I remember, from my childhood, four or five things. One was something they used to shut me in the toilet for not eating. Whenever we had lentils, I would refuse them point-blank. I was quite a fussy child when it came to food. If there was one taste I hated more than anything in the world, it was Dalky brand strawberry ice cream.' He made a pouting face, a child's expression of disgust. 'To me it's anti-flavour, like anti-matter. I've never got over my hatred of that taste. The other thing was green peppers, and I still can't bear them even now.'

A kitchen hand came striding across the terrace to show him something. I caught a flash of it, a dark little pillow of something on a plate.

'Yes, fine. But don't let it dry out too much. Let's present it with a little of the stock. OK?'

His parents, I asked him gently. What did they think of it all, his worldwide fame, the restaurant, and its extraordinary food, the cold soup of lychees and fennel *granizado*, the avocado sorbet with sunflower seeds, the electric milk?

He shrugged. 'Like any parent who sees his son succeed, that's all. They don't understand what you might call the international dimension. They know that something's going on, but they're not quite sure what. Maybe it's better that way?' He shifted in his seat. 'They are post-war people. They tell me that, after the war, they didn't exactly go hungry, but almost. The fact of having a tomato or an aubergine, was something you valued. So.'

Adrià's relationship with his background, his cultural surroundings, is interesting and puzzling. He is undeniably Catalan and Spanish, and identifies with both nationalities. On the other hand, he strongly resists the pull of place; he is a postmodern creator, picking up diverse influences from cultures all across the globe. This tension remains a vital element in his work; there's a sense of being rooted and yet somehow rootless – psychologically anchored, yet free.

'My surroundings are these,' he said quietly. Behind him on the water, a small boat pulled up to the grey sand. A first cool breath of wind came up from the bay. 'But I don't believe in *terroir*, not in that French sense of earth and roots. *Terroir* is feeling, the earth is nothing without people. Don't look around here too much, for, as much as you look, you'll see nothing.'

I told him about my curate's-egg experiences in the restaurants of Roses, and he gave a small shrug, as if to say, well, what on earth did you expect? 'Listen, I've been in Roses for twenty-one years, and I've never had a good tapa, a decent paella . . . People accuse me of lowering standards: "it's your fault there are so many young kids trying to do modern food, and doing it badly". Maybe, but isn't it much worse that there are millions of tortillas and paellas all over the country that are cooked so badly? Ordinary food in Spain is in a much worse state than haute cuisine, and that's a fact.'

Adrià started in ordinary food and crept higher and higher, to the very summit of haute. His professional journey has been a long haul. He has been at El Bulli since 1984: more than half his life. When he arrived at Cala Montjoi, the sum total of his work experience was a summer washing plates in Ibiza, a year in the kitchen of the military barracks at Cartagena, and another few months at Finisterre restaurant in Barcelona.

'I got here in April, and, in October, they made me chef de cuisine,' he said wryly.

The restaurant had already been functioning for twenty years, first under the Schillings, who upgraded the original bar into a grill-room with mini-golf, and, finally, with chef Jean Louis Neichel, who now has his own Michelin-starred place in Barcelona. At first, as he cheerfully admits, Adrià's dishes were far from the works of art we have come to expect from him. One of his earliest dishes was a salad of chargrilled vegetables, clearly rooted in the Catalan *escalivada*, which was common enough in simple restaurants but a radical novelty in haute kitchens, where vegetables were served in the French style, boiled or steamed.

His road to Damascus moment came during a chefs' conference in Nice in 1984, when Jacques Maximin defined creativity in cooking as *'ne pas copier'*, and the young Adrià sat up and took notice. The first fruits of that revelation were the early 'adaptation' dishes giving a twist to classic Spanish dishes and techniques, such as the lobster gazpacho and *ajoblanco* of langoustines. The early nineties saw the first of the apparently crazy combinations – bone marrow with caviar, rabbit with octopus, chicken wings with lobster. And, in 1994, Adrià brought in the big guns: the famous foams, a genial invention which involves impregnating a liquid with air for an ethereally delicate futuristic version of mousse. The foams were born in a juice bar in Barcelona, when Adrià noticed that the fruit-flavoured foam remained in the bottom of his glass and wondered if the effect could be reproduced. The notion of 'deconstructive' cuisine, separating the constituent parts of a given dish, modifying them and then putting them back together, in such a way that the result preserves the 'genome' of the original dish, was another of Adrià's immortal contributions to modern cuisine. Initially applied to the Spanish white-trash dish known as *arroz a la cubana*, white rice with banana and tomato sauce, the technique was subsequently applied to tortilla de patatas, gazpacho, vegetable *menestra*, and whatever other classic preparations seemed to lend themselves to Adrià's dazzling intelligence and wit. Thereafter, we had spherification, freeze-drying, and cooking on a cold *plancha* fired with liquid nitrogen; there was the new ravioli using milk skin or translucent-thin slices of prawn in place of pasta; the new aspic, using agar-agar instead of the traditional gelatine; the sponges, 'airs', and 'clouds'. Quite apart from the techniques, to date Adrià has created more than 1,500 individual dishes, fulfilling Maximin's maxim to the letter.

Success, when it happened, astonished even him. In 1993, Gault-Millau made El Bulli the first and only foreign restaurant to be included in their strictly French guide (they gave it nineteen points out of twenty). In 1997 Adrià won his third Michelin star. When Joël Robuchon, reigning genius of French cuisine, proclaimed Adrià his successor, it only confirmed what many foodies already suspected: that El Bulli was the most fascinating restaurant in the world. While Adrià has been happy to act as its public face and cover star, there are at least two other geniuses among his fellow-workers: Albert Adrià, *pâtissier* and brother of Ferran Adrià; and Juli Soler, business partner, restaurant manager, *éminence grise*.

Soler was the brain behind the amazing new kitchen at El Bulli, 325 square metres of high-tech wonderment carved out of the rock, with one whole wall of glass which floods the interior with Mediterranean light.

'Do you want to see my kitchen? Come.' Adrià got up, suddenly brisk and businesslike, and I followed him inside, my nerves of this afternoon now replaced by a bristle of excitement.

First things first. At some restaurants you are invited into the kitchen at the end of the meal, if you're lucky, when the service is over and startled sous-chefs look up from their cleaning at this tipsy stranger who has wandered into their realm. At El Bulli, the invitation comes before the meal, when the kitchen is firing on all cylinders – but firing with a gentle sort of streamlined power, like the engine of some fabulous Italian sports car. It is not your standard sort of restaurant kitchen, all harsh white light, noise and heat, but a calm, elegant space of generous dimensions with an atmosphere halfway between laboratory and monastery. And, indeed, the almost medieval aspect to the functioning of El Bulli, its blend of scientific rigour and alchemical fantasy, high serious-ness and holy fooling, has made it into a place of pilgrimage for idealistic young food-folk the world over.

From the kitchen, he led me to my table. The dining room was white-walled, warmly furnished in orange, purple, and red. The other tables seemed distant in space and time; similar things were happening there, but in another dimension. I could hear Italian voices, German, French. There was a hush, but it was not the solemn hush of chintz and velvet. There were smiles and giggles; I felt mischief in the air.

There are things that matter in the Bulli universe, and things that are passed over lightly. The menu is nothing much to look at, for instance. Nothing could be simpler, almost disingenuously so, than this folded sheet of paper, only a little larger than a postcard, with the retro publicity for El Bulli on one side (dating, I see, in the copyright small print, from 1964), and the menu for tonight on the other. There is a striking difference between this sober, cheaply produced document and the extravagantly decorated folders you find in most other high-end restaurants, which invite you to hold them aloft in both hands like a choirboy and study them as if you were about to read from St Paul's Epistle to the Corinthians.

Tonight's dinner would consist of thirty-two dishes, listed in small dark type with no capitals, like a piece of concrete poetry. Adrià was the originator of what came to be known as the 'long, thin' menu, a series of tapa-sized dishes over which the diner has no choice. Some of these dishes, like the home-made mozzarella, or the sea snails with crab, sounded like cooking of a more or less conventional kind. Others sounded like nothing on earth. I could only speculate on the nature of 'spherical melon caviar', and 'Tennessee infusion', to say nothing of 'popcorn cloud' or 'thaw 2005'. I knew that Adrià was given to tricks and humour in his work, and that he loved to bewitch his guests with theatrical flourishes, like the flowers handed round to be sniffed between mouthfuls, the natural essences sprayed into the air above the table. I reminded myself to be ready for anything. Three black-shirted waiters appeared beside me, smiling beatifically, like the Three Boys in The Magic Flute. I took a deep breath.

And the show began. A little green ball of tarragon paste, presented on a flat silver spoon on a delicate web of some other precious metal poised above a black plate. The tarragon ball was to be placed in the mouth and allowed to dissolve, flooding the palate with a powerful rush of herbal flavour: aniseed, spearmint, liquorice . . . Meanwhile, another black-shirted waiter was busy concocting a caipirinha with fresh lime juice, sugar, and Brazilian cachaça, using a bowl of liquid nitrogen at minus 40°C. Clouds of dry ice billowed out of the bowl as he stirred the cocktail, serving it up in a glass the size of an eggcup. After the cleansing flush of the tarragon, the cocktail's acid sweetness was an exhilarating assault on the taste buds, leaving the palate gaping. As an opener to the menu, it was a *coup de théâtre*, a spectacular curtain-raiser.

The meal's first act was a succession of 'snacks', recalling an innocent era of childhood pleasures. These '*tapitas*', as he calls them, give free rein to the playful side of Adrià's genius. A spring-like shape, made of spun sugar and olive oil, to be placed on the finger and eaten in a single mouthful. A pistachio caught in a shell of crystallised yoghurt. A cookie, made of black olives and cream, an exact visual replica of an Oreo cookie. I laughed out loud. A kind of communion wafer, made of air-dried mango, that vanished on the tongue with an intense burst of tropical fruit. Sensations, surprises. Chunks of air-dried and fresh melon, their jewel-like colours of orange and green, served on ice in a silver flower pot, with cool white fresh almonds . . . A white shivering cloud, which the waiter instructed me to convey to my mouth in my fingertips. The cloud seemed too big for a single mouthful; I crammed it in, laughing at the indignity, but it then seemed to melt away to nothingness and a distant, ethereal memory of cinema popcorn.

And it went on. None of the dishes on this *menú degustación* were bigger than a few mouthfuls, and some were virtually virtual, a single brushstroke or scribble of flavour. These little dishes were brilliant statements, essays, experiments, provocations.

The dishes gained in intellectual weight, if not in actual size. A tempura of samphire, perfumed with saffron, and a spoonful of oyster sauce: quintessence of oyster. Walnuts with walnut sauce: quintessence of walnuts. Tiny quantities; vast, echoing flavours. Miniature rock mussels like the ones I had last night at Can Campaner, here served with a multicoloured mini-salad of various types of seaweed. Strips of monkfish liver the size of your finger-nail, cooked at the table in a little pot of hot stock and then swiped across a spoonful of sesame sauce – delicious beyond imagining. There was almost no meat: it was all fish and shellfish, vegetables, fruit, and herbs. With a few exceptions, like the crunchy rabbit ear. Adrià blanches the ear, skins it, and fries it. It seems an outrageous idea. But why not? If there is one body part that identifies the rabbit more than anything, it's the ears. And it was fantastic, savoury and crisp, and somehow a throwaway gesture, like the best pork scratching in the world.

The 'morphings' are to the end of the menu what the *tapitas* are to the beginning. (More things . . . The excruciating English pun is purest Adrià.) They were sweet fun things, done on a kind of *plancha* filled with liquid nitrogen, so that the marshmallowy exterior actually 'cooked' on the ice-cold surface, and the steam rose into the air in big white cold sticky clouds. A draught came in from some open window, pushing across a dining room that, I realised, was now entirely empty apart from myself and the waiter with his Frankenstein dry-ice machine.

I turned on my mobile phone to look at the time: it was two in the morning. I had been the first to arrive, and now, five hours later, I was the last to leave. Feeling a little unsteady on my feet, I shuffled out to the terrace and sat down again at the table by the arch, the one with the neatly framed view of beach and sea. The warmth had gone out of the air; I wished I'd brought my thin summer sweater.

Adrià came out to sit with me, now that his night's work was over. He asked me what I thought of the dinner; I said I thought it was OK. He seemed tickled by this lukewarm response, and smiled indulgently. I told him I had spent much of the meal feeling I needed to laugh, or actually laughing, at the sheer zaniness of the food on my plate and the sensations it was producing in my brain.

He nodded. This is an important part of what he wants his customers to feel. The most wonderful of all the wonderful things about El Bulli, it might be said, is the exquisite balance it maintains between pleasure and science, between light-hearted enjoyment and a deadly serious approach to gastronomic experiment. 'Good, that's good. I do believe in a sense of humour in the kitchen. Food can be a way of having fun.'

Like a latter-day Marco Polo, he scours the world for strange and delightful novelties. On a recent trip to Japan, he had found a source of transparent rice paper, which he had been rolling and folding into a little *empanadilla*, stuffing it with berry fruits flavoured with eucalyptus. The bone marrow from the spine of the tuna. Fresh pine nuts, gathered in May before the nut is fully formed. From the Amazon basin, a series of strange fruits and stranger herbs, like the bizarre vegetable *jambu*, which briefly sends the mouth to sleep. Adrià's inspiration is childlike. It is based on a permanent sense of delighted curiosity about the world around him.

Curiosity, however, often depends on a deep-seated sense of security. A taste for the exotic springs from a profound knowledge of the familiar. And this is the central antithesis: the world, for Ferran Adrià, is both familiar and exotic, local and global, provincial and international, at the same time.

He has had offers from all over the place, and of millions of dollars, to set up shop abroad, in Las Vegas, Tokyo, or Paris. Yet, to see Adrià here with the sea behind him, sitting out under the stars, drinking a well-earned glass of white wine, the warm silence surrounding us both, insects clicking and whirring in the darkness, the smells of pine sap and rosemary and seaweed drifting across the terrace, you realise that he might not have achieved what he has in any other situation, any other context, any other landscape. Roots and family mean everything and nothing. Like the big black sea down there in the bay, you can't always see them, but you know they're always there.

CHAPTER FOUR

CADIZ & MALAGA

Zahara de los Atunes sat squatly behind a wild stretch of sandy beach at the southernmost tip of Europe, where the continents seem almost to touch, but then to change their minds. It was a rough-and-tumble, knocked-together sort of town, more of a village, that now lived off tourism in a small kind of way, but had not altogether shaken off the salty, stinky charm of a place whose life, if not whose livelihood, still revolved around the culture of fish and fishing.

After the gastronomic mountaineering of El Bulli, I figured, it would be good to breathe some less rarefied air. Back home, I had asked around about somewhere on the coast of Spain that had not been irredeemably spoiled, where the cooking would be simple, savoury, and unadorned. All of my informants had mentioned Cádiz, where the strategic importance of the coastline had kept much of the Costa de la Luz in military hands, thus saving it from destruction, and the popular fish cookery of Andalucía was still practised on a day-to-day basis. So it was that, on a Sunday afternoon in the dregs of late August, when the country has been in holiday mode for so long it is secretly rather bored with the lounging, languid life of summer, I was lying beside the pool of a three-star hotel on the outskirts of Zahara de los Atunes, where the probing tendrils of new development pushed ever further along the coast.

Zahara has always depended economically, and continues to depend in other ways, on the tuna that swim past the town in giant schools on their way through the Straits of Gibraltar, to spawn in the warm waters of the Mediterranean.

There was not very much to do in Zahara except sleep, walk along the windswept beach, and sit down to fine meals of fish prepared in the various forms of the local *cocina marinera*. The menu at the town's restaurants was a litany of andaluz coastal cooking. There were *tortillitas de camarón*, one of my absolute favourite things in all of Spanish food, essentially a batter with tiny shrimps and chopped parsley fried on the *plancha* in a splotch until it turns into a crisp little pancake. There was *cazón en adobo*, chunks of shark marinated in vinegar and herbs before being deep-fried in boiling oil. There was baby squid and sole and cuttlefish and anchovies, and a legion of little fish with names that sound familiar in Spanish and wildly exotic in English, all, or nearly all, prepared in the same manner. Which is to say, dredged in a mixture of chickpea and wheat flour, the speciality flour used in Andalucía for frying and nearly impossible to find outside the region, before being briefly plunged into boiling olive oil.

An oft-repeated adage holds that 'the south fries, the centre roasts, and the north boils'. It's a wild generalisation, but there's a generous helping of truth in there somewhere. The cooking of Andalucía, if the truth be told, makes the apparently simple act of frying into a pillar of its culinary practice.

Pescaíto frito, or mixed fried fish, in any case, has always been a

major element of life on the Costa de la Luz. In 1929, the gastronome Dionisio Pérez, in his witty and still relevant *Guide to Good
Spanish Eating*, believed the city of Cádiz and the villages along its
coastline to be 'the headquarters, the Olympus of *pescaíto frito*'. It
was true then, and it's true now. In Cádiz, and in the nearby Puerto
de Santa María, the custom is to buy a big paper wrap heaving with
freshly fried *pescaíto*. This wrap or cone, known as *el papelón* (the
big paper), is taken away for eating in the ozone-fresh air of the sea
wall, or conveyed to a bar or bodega, where the fish is eaten with
the fingers, washed down with beer, wine, or fino sherry.

In Zahara, there was no tradition of *papelón*, but plenty of
simple eating houses with upturned sherry barrels for tables, thin
paper napkins scrunched in drifts on the floor, and menus that
majored on fried fish in all manner of forms. After an exhaustive
investigation, I found that the Bar Paquiqui was the one I liked
best. It was hidden away in a flower-filled corner of the oldest part
of the village, in a pitched-roofed fisherman's house with Arab
roof tiles. Inside, the atmosphere was that of a proper village bar,
with the World Cup roaring away on TV and a tremendous noise
of frying from the tiny kitchen at the back. I found a table outside
and sat drinking *tinto de verano* ('summer red'), the iced refresher
of red wine and fizzy pop.

From inside the kitchen came a frenzied sizzle and clatter. A
round pink face in a white kitchen cap poked around the hatch in a
cloud of fishy smoke. A cry was heard: 'Table two, prawns, *cazón*,
tortillitas, on their way!' Antonia, owner of the face, stood in
charge of the fryer, and she was truly a master of her craft. She
called me in from outside to show me how she turned the pieces of
shark in the flour, shaking them from side to side on a special rack
to remove the excess, and then deep-frying them for just long
enough to form a crisp golden shell that sealed in all the tenderness
of the fish.

She had learned the art of frying from her father, Francisco, who
had retreated from the front line of the kitchen and was now
responsible for the backstage business of dealing with suppliers,

preparing the marinade for the *cazón en adobo*, and cooking up, in his own home, the menu's few long-simmered dishes, like *atún encebollado*, a delicious stew of tuna and masses of onions flavoured with oregano, sweet pimentón, bayleaf, and wine vinegar.

Francisco Martínez, known to the world at large as Paquiqui, had presided over the Bar Paquiqui in Zahara since the late 1980s, when he had finally given up the ways of the sea for the stability of a life on land. I found him sitting in his special chair at the back, making sure everything ran smoothly on this late-summer night when Spain was playing France and the atmosphere at the bar came perilously close to rowdiness.

He came out to sit with me, sipping a glass of wine while he watched me eat. Paquiqui had been a professional ship's cook, so there was not much he didn't know about catering for hungry and demanding customers.

'I worked on fishing boats, deep-water, for thirty-five years,' he told me. He was a serious yet amiable elderly gentleman, with heavy grey brows and a gaze that became solemn when he needed to concentrate on a recipe, a statistic, or a particularly intractable memory.

'The boats always left from Barbate, heading for the Canaries, Casablanca, or further south, the coast of Africa . . . We might be at sea for eleven days, twelve days, or, if we were going south, twenty-five days, or more. My salary was 1,000 pesetas a month. This in 1950. Life on board ship was hard. The boats had no bathrooms, there was very little water . . . You shaved once every ten days, when the boat got back to port.'

At least the food was good, or, at least, Paquiqui made it sound that way. I had heard about *cocina a bordo*, or 'on-board cooking', the particular genre of Spanish fish cookery in which so many classic dishes of *cocina marinera* have their origins. It is a genre that is fast disappearing, since big fishing boats these days have freezers and microwaves, and fishermen probably live off pizza and pasta like the rest of humanity, but Paquiqui was a living testament to its richness and variety.

'Fishermen, when they're working out at sea, want big meals at midday and in the evening,' he said. The repertoire ranged from soup-stews based on beans and vegetables, or chickpeas with cuttlefish, to rice dishes with cardoons (*arroz cardúo*), with hake tails, or with tinned tuna and red peppers. Paquiqui's speciality was a soupy rice based on monkfish with a *sofrito* of dried *ñora* peppers, tomato and garlic, using the liver of the fish and a piece of fried bread, mashed together in the pestle and mortar, to thicken the stock towards the end of the cooking. It sounded wonderful, and I told Paquiqui so, and he launched into a step-by-step description of the recipe, which I scribbled down on a napkin and still have somewhere, among my disorganised piles of Spanish kitchen notes.

Surprisingly, fish wasn't the only thing they ate on board. There was also meat, since the province of Cádiz is an important producer of beef cattle. 'We ate the beef until it ran out, then we started on the fish.' There might be *estofado en amarillo*, a beef stew with red pepper, garlic, bay leaf and pimentón, which he still cooked up for the workers at the Bar Paquiqui, though it never appeared on the menu. The name means 'yellow stew', though, from the red pepper and pimentón, you'd think it closer to a rich, dark red.

As for Zahara and the sea, they were like a divorced couple still living in the same house. Only a few old men still fished from the beach, more out of habit than necessity, bringing their boats in at midday to make a few euros from the sale of their meagre catch to friends and neighbours. In the last fifteen years, the town had thrown in its lot with the money-spinning businesses that had brought fame and fortune to the rest of the Spanish coast: tourism and construction.

'Since I retired, I haven't been back to the sea, I was that fed up with it,' he said. 'There is more work about. Life is better than before. There's no need for the youth to go to sea, and it's just as well. The sea is very bad.'

*   *   *

Steaming in the midday heat, Zahara had the feeling of a faded beachside outpost somewhere in Latin America: Cuba, perhaps, or the coast of Venezuela. It had flat-roofed houses with peeling whitewashed walls, and a sixteenth-century fortress that had once served as a store and factory for Zahara's tuna industry, but whose limestone walls were crumbling into the dust.

The market at Zahara was a humble affair, except when it came to fish, in which it would have seen off many a market in a town ten, twenty times the size. I picked one of the three stalls at random and stopped to talk to the attendant, a short, loud lady with short hair and thick black glasses. The range of fish, laid out in front of her in a kaleidoscopic arrangement of pink, orange, scarlet, and coral red, testified to the considerable biodiversity of the oceans off the Costa de la Luz. The quality was peerless, as it would be, when the fish had only come in a few minutes ago from the fishing port at Barbate, a few miles up the coast.

The fish lady pointed out the ugly *urta*, a fish that is much prized around the coast of Cádiz, where it is cooked *a la roteña* (in the style of Rota, a town famous for this dish and for its US naval base), with a sauce of tomato and peppers. I looked with cupiditous eyes at a group of red mullet, a fish I have always loved for its subtly flavoured, meaty flesh, so good when stuffed with fresh herbs (it goes particularly well with fennel) and slapped on the barbecue.

On the coast of Cádiz, neither of these species, however, could ever be the main attraction. At the top of the slab, crowning the stall's display, was a hunk of fresh tuna that had just come in from the harbour not half an hour ago. It was a large piece weighing at least ten pounds, as rosy as a cut of prime beef, and so fresh that it proudly kept its shape when the fishmonger gave it a hefty slap. At twenty-two euros a kilo, it was expensive, a good deal more expensive than the priciest rare-breed beef sirloin. You might imagine, in one of the least prosperous parts of Spain, that this fish would have few takers. You would be wrong: after me in the queue came three local women in blue and white aprons, the traditional uniform of the working-class housewife, and each took away a couple of juicy steaks, for cooking *vuelta y vuelta* in the frying pan, just a moment or two on each side.

'Around here, what we know about is tuna, tuna, tuna,' said the stall-holder, before sketching out, for my benefit, the basics of the local tuna industry – the four remaining *almadrabas*, the tuna-fishing installations founded by the Phoenicians and still operating in much the same way, though with catches that plummet every year to new and ever more alarming lows – and the habits of the species *Thunnus thynnus thynnus*, repetitiously so-called to distinguish it from the inferior Pacific sub-species *Thunnus thynnus orientalis*, as well as from tuna knock-offs like the albacore and yellow-fin tuna, both of which have the same family name, but cannot hold a candle to it in quality.

The *atún rojo* is a noble fish which reaches giant size. It spends most of the year in the cold but rich waters of the Atlantic, until early summer, when it heads south (like much of the population of northern Europe) in order to spawn in the bath-like waters of the Mediterranean. In order to reach its goal, these enormous fish must make their way through the straits of Gibraltar – where the *almadrabas* are waiting for them.

The etymology of the word is plainly Arabic – it is supposed to derive from *daraba*, to smite or hit, the *almadraba* being the place of smiting or hitting. The craft of tuna fishing by this system was invented by the Phoenicians and perfected by the Romans, before receiving its modern name at the hands of the Moors. The glory days of this traditional craft were the six centuries in which the *almadrabas* of the andaluz coast were controlled by the Duchy of Medina Sidonia, from the thirteenth century until the nineteenth. There were formerly *almadrabas* all along the Spanish Mediterranean coast, but now only four remain, and all are on the Atlantic side of the Straits of Gibraltar: in Barbate, Tarifa, and two in Zahara de los Atunes.

It is hard to imagine what an *almadraba* actually looks like without seeing a plan of its complex underwater structure of deep nets through which the tuna are led as through a maze, and finally corralled in a central net from which there is no escape. This net is then raised through the water – the so-called *levantá* – and the enormous fish, which can weigh up to 300 kilos or more, are left high and dry. The spectacle of the *levantá* is powerfully impressive. Those few outsiders that have witnessed it describe the scene as one of tremendous violence and danger, as the giant fish thrash about in their death throes, the fishermen jump into the fray to stab them with giant hooks for loading on board, and the water seethes with blood and foam.

The fish lady pointed out a picture on the white-tiled wall of her stall showing a *levantá* in full swing, a square of boats around the silvery mass of flailing fish, the fishermen in their uniform of bright orange and midnight blue.

'I've seen it once,' she said grimly. 'And that's it. I won't see it ever again.'

The tuna boats leave the harbour for the *almadrabas* at dawn, returning halfway through the morning. Sometimes there is nothing in the nets, and they come back empty handed. It hardly comes as a surprise to learn that the catch has dramatically declined over the last few years, to the point where it seems likely that the whole tradition of *almadraba* fishing, with its 3,000 years of history, will have disappeared before the decade is out.

I got to the docks at Barbate just as the boats were arriving. Today they had been lucky, and there was jubilation in the air. No less than fifty-four tuna had blundered into the nets. This was regarded as a fine catch, though, by the standards of an earlier time, when 300 or 400 fish per day was the norm, it would have been a meagre haul.

I stood on the harbourside and watched the proceedings, the grey-painted boats as they moored one by one, each with its cargo of corpses covered in grey winding sheets. A small crowd had gathered to see the tuna winched up from the floor of the boat, to be received at the door of the warehouse, where they would be weighed and checked. Their giant bodies swung above the crowd like futuristic sculptures; they were sleek and hard and gleaming, as shiny and cold as if made of solid steel, and their mouths gaped open in a tragic mask of horror.

Out on the dock, the heat was rising. There were shouts from the joshing fishermen, an excited noise from the crowd, and a mingled harbour smell of diesel fumes and fish remains. Inside the warehouse, the scene was very different. Computers clicked and beeped. Outside, the tuna had been a lump of meat, a dead animal. In here, it was science and big business. A slender, neatly dressed man with Oriental features was working away with some kind of clinical probe, designed to measure the body temperature of the fish and thereby determine its exact time of death. To the Japanese, who are the major buyers of *atún rojo de almadraba*, the freshness of the product is of paramount importance. In the sophisticated world of Japanese fish culture, there is no more exquisite delicacy than this. Their word for the belly meat of this tuna is *toro* – which is also, by coincidence, the word for 'bull' in Spanish. And this is not the only lexicological link between tuna and beef. Among the words for cuts of tuna, we have *solomillo* (sirloin), *lomo* (loin), and *espinazo* (spinal column).

It's in the form of salted and cured tuna, *en salazón*, that the *atún rojo* reaches the summit of excellence and value. Of the two remaining *salazón* houses in Barbate, most people you ask around the town will tell you the best is Herpac (the other is Salpesca). From the harbour, I walked to their shop and factory on the outskirts of town, where, at the back door of the building, the beep-beep-beep of a reversing lorry announced the arrival of three tuna from this morning's *levantá*. Inside the shop, a girl in a white coat explained the process behind *mojama*, the star product of Barbate's tuna industry and one of the finest of all Spanish food products. The tuna loins are salted and hung up to dry on the roof of the shop for a month, two months, three months, depending on the weather and 'what the tuna tells you', until they shrink and harden to the texture of a fine serrano ham. The firm's other top products were *hueva* – tuna roe cured in the same way, perfect for grating over pasta as the Sardinians do with their *bottarga* – and *atún de ijar*, the belly meat preserved in fillets under olive oil. The price of these goodies seemed agonisingly high, but I fought off the pain to buy one small piece of *hueva* and another small piece of *mojama*. Even as I left the shop, I was already thinking how I would slice it thinly, dress it with a little olive oil, and invite a select group of friends to a luxury *aperitivo* with fried almonds and a bottle of cold manzanilla from one of the sherry houses of Sanlucar de Barrameda, just a few miles up the coast.

By now it was lunchtime, and, in Barbate at lunchtime, if you want to eat tuna and are willing to pay for it, there is one restaurant above all that fits the bill. The parents of José Melero once had a bar in nearby Vejer de la Frontera, where locals went for wine and tapas and to play cards in the evening. In 1978, the family moved down to Barbate and opened a small restaurant called El Campero, which is still going strong, though it has mutated into rather a smart little joint with a striped blue-and-white awning and scary air-conditioning, where the rich land-owners and sherry barons of the province go to talk business over fino sherry and heavenly *cocina marinera*.

I sat a corner table and chatted to José, who was a short, stocky man wearing a neat moustache and a short-sleeved shirt, the garment worn by three-quarters of all adult males on a summer day on the Costa de la Luz. José was amiable and quietly spoken, but his voice registered an extra notch or two on the emotional Richter scale whenever he got on to the subject of tuna. 'The tuna is the great marvel of our culture, the culture of Cádiz, of Andalucía, and of Spain. *Es la joya del estrecho*: it is the jewel of the Straits.'

José was an expert on the traditional cooking of Barbate, which made cunning use of the less prestigious cuts of *atún rojo* in such homely dishes as tuna entrails with chickpeas, *mojama* off-cuts with tomato, tuna 'ears' with sauce, and casserole of tuna skin. There was also *facera* – the head meat and cheeks of the fish, cooked with potatoes in a classic of the local fishermen's cuisine – and *parpatana* – just behind the head, which was oven-roasted. Of all the various local tuna recipes, both the most elaborate and the most often prepared (since many of the others were falling rapidly into disuse) was *atún encebollado*.

But the menu at El Campero didn't stop there, not by any means. It was an exhaustive adventure in tuna cookery, running from the humblest tapa of tuna heart, served cold with a vinegary dressing, through to tuna sashimi and tuna tartare, to tuna in a bitter orange sauce (the analogy between the oily rich meats of tuna and duck does have a certain logic), and a slice of *morrillo a la plancha* with anchovy mayonnaise. The *morrillo* is long tubes of muscle held together with delicate fat, not unlike the finest sirloin of ibérico pork. Traditionally, this was a humbler cut, classified as *vísceras* (entrails). So was *galete*, a small piece of gelatinous meat located deep inside the head, which lends itself to long, slow cooking. José brought out a plate of *galete* to round off the proceedings: it was dark and meltingly tender in its rich concentrated sauce, more like *rabo de toro* than anything in the world of seafood.

What tricks history plays on us, and how dumbly we fall into the traps it sets. What are now luxuries were once common or garden staples. When things are abundant, they are scarcely valued, or even looked on with contempt. (Oysters, a poor man's food in nighteenth-century London, are the obvious example.) It is only when they become scarce and expensive that they are finally given the appreciation they deserve, by the minority that can afford them. But, by then, sadly, it is too late for the rest of us.

Marjorie Grice-Hutchinson is principally remembered today for her work in the field of economics: a disciple of Hayek, her 1952 opus *The School of Salamanca: Readings in Spanish Monetary Theory, 1544–1605* is a key text in the study of Spanish economic history. But she also wrote two books in a genre that might be known nowadays as 'the good life abroad'. In *Málaga Farm* (1956), now out of print, she paints a brightly coloured picture of life on the Costa del Sol in the last few years before tourism was to transform it out of all recognition, documenting local life with a curiosity occasionally tempered by a quiver of puzzlement.

She had arrived on the Costa in 1924, when her father, George William Grice-Hutchinson, bought the Finca San Julián, a farmstead just outside Málaga on the fertile coastal plain known as the *vega* (hence Las Vegas, the plains). In the pre-Civil War years, he and his daughter were well known in the area for their philanthropic work, in particular the school and medical dispensary they founded in the village of Churriana.

For a person who had lived so long among the Spanish, *Málaga Farm* reveals her as oddly squeamish about some of their habits. Describing the busy market, housed in the old Moorish harbour building known as the Atarazanas, she mentions the Arabic inscription over the entrance, 'There is no conqueror but Allah', and goes on to comment: 'The motto has not entirely lost its old force: for who shall arbitrate in the severe though bloodless struggles that are waged in the market?' Bloodless, or bloody: she found 'disagreeable' the sight of live hens and turkeys tied together by the legs, and wrote, 'I still feel revolted when I see a woman choose one of these unfortunate birds, look on unmoved while its throat is cut, and watch its death-struggles with detached interest.'

With her professional eye for the details of social reality, Grice-Hutchinson saw clearly that the lives of the working classes in the pre-tourist Costa del Sol came close to poverty. Housing for ordinary people was generally bad, and conditions often insalubrious. The diet of the malagueñõ farm hand, however, she thought 'fairly good'.

The typical breakfast of such a person would have been bread, leftover fish, and 'a beverage made from roasted barley and slightly resembling coffee.' Lunch might be soup, followed by a 'substantial stew' of rice, potatoes, and vegetables. And supper was fried fish, potatoes, and something called gazpacho, which she describes – it is clear that the dish would have been unfamiliar to British readers in 1956 – as 'a refreshing concoction made of garlic, cucumber, and tomatoes floating in a bowl of oil, vinegar, and water.'

Later on in the book, in the food and drink section, the author informs her readers that gazpacho is 'served as the first course of fashionable luncheons and dinners, and for the poor often constitutes an entire meal.' The recipe she gives for the dish hardly conforms to her image of vegetables bobbing in a bowl, and I have never heard of apples being added to the mixture. But the idea of the vegetables and bread being 'pounded' sounds authentic for a time before hand-held mixers and food processors, since anything that had to be mashed, crushed, or liquidised would have been worked at laboriously by hand in the pestle and mortar.

Few dishes in world cuisine are more rigorously seasonal than gazpacho. This is a dish which, for most of the year, is literally inconceivable, not just because the ingredients are out of season, but because the dish derives its meaning and *raison d'être* from a particular time of year: the season of summer. You would no more eat an ice-cold gazpacho in the frosty month of January than you would a mighty *cocido madrileño* with all the trimmings in the middle of August. During winter, the dish retreats into hibernation, only to emerge on one of those days in June when an early blast of summer heat takes the country by surprise, and you realise that everything you need for the dish is out there in the garden, minus one or two things which can be bought at the corner shop, and suddenly gazpacho is back on the agenda – where it stays, an irreplaceable staple of summer eating, until the first chilly days of autumn once more consign it, like Persephone, to another eight months of oblivion.

There are gazpachos that stick in the mind, along with places and people and moments. The first 'milestone gazpacho' of my life was one I made myself. As a child, I liked to cook, but more than cooking itself, what excited me was the business of planning the menu, setting the table, and creating the atmosphere around the food. I devised a series of dinners based on national themes, at which the guests were the members of my family. The Spanish

dinner consisted of gazpacho and paella – naturally enough – and
sliced oranges for dessert; the menu cards were typed up individually and adorned with motifs of Spanish flags, bulls' heads, and
castanets around the edges. I remember nothing about the paella,
though it was probably a travesty. But that gazpacho, oddly, has
stayed with me. I must have whizzed it up in my Mum's old
Kenwood mixer, the sort that required you to hold down the lid
with its rubber seal or whatever you were whizzing would end up
decorating the walls. It struck me then, not only as amazingly easy
to make for such a classic dish of world cuisine, but improbably
delicious. Which, of course, it is.

No one is quite sure of the origins of gazpacho, though the
idea of a watery salad goes back a long way, perhaps predating
the Romans. The word, however, has been traced to the Latin
caspa, implying small pieces or flakes – with which the modern
Spanish word for dandruff (*caspa*) off-puttingly shares a common root.

Until the tomato and pepper arrived in Europe, gazpacho would
have been made without either. Until the twentieth century, this
was not a well-known dish, and rarely figured in cookbooks.
Angel Muro's encyclopaedic *Practicón* of 1894 makes no mention
of it. Perhaps Muro thought it too embarrassingly primitive a
concoction to be worthy of inclusion. Yet it is odd that not a single
one of the andaluz repertoire of *sopas frías* makes it into his
culinary Parnassus: the only cold soup to be found in the pages of
the *Practicón* is an iced consommé, hardly representative, in any
sense, of Spanish regional cooking.

As the influence of France faded from the Spanish culinary
scene, which it had dominated for the whole of the nineteenth
century, the excellence of traditional cooking began to be seen for
what it was. For the great doctor and humanist Gregorio Marañón
(1887–1960), gazpacho was an inspired piece of popular gastronomy which anticipates a series of modern ideas about healthy
eating. 'The learned folk of a few decades ago marvelled at the fact
that, with such a light dish, harvesters were able to toil for so many

hours in the heat of the midday sun: they were unaware that the common instinct was many centuries in advance of the professors of nutrition, and that this emulsion of oil in cold water with the addition of vinegar, salt, pimentón, crushed tomato, bread and other ingredients, contains everything necessary to sustain workers engaged in the most tedious of labours', wrote Marañón.

There are gazpachos of all colours, textures, and aromas – some of which do not even bear the name. And the king of them all, in my book, is not a gazpacho at all, in any real sense. *Ajoblanco* (it means literally white garlic) is a soup of raw almonds with a little garlic, salt, olive oil, and water. It is one of those dishes that, primitive though it sounds in theory, becomes, in practice, a great deal more than the sum of its parts. *Ajoblanco* is often eaten with the inspired accompaniment of sweet Muscat grapes or chunks of ripe melon. It is a thoroughly traditional dish, yet it could have been invented last week. Cool and ivory white, with a creaminess that leads many people to the mistaken assumption that it contains a dairy product, the *ajoblanco* has a minimalist modernity that belies its age-old popularity in the city of its birth.

The culinary scene in the city of Málaga is not what you might call buzzing, but there is one address, at least, that is often cited as a point of reference. The Café de Paris. The name is terrible, but, after twenty-four years of existence and a shining reputation in the city, it must have seemed that there was little point in changing it. When José Carlos García's father ran the kitchen, it was famous for its French-style cooking, which ran to such things as beef Wellington and soufflé Grand Marnier. But, when José Carlos took over, fresh from La Cónsula cookery school outside Málaga, the menu underwent a radical change.

I first came heré in the mid-nineties, when José Carlos had just taken over in the kitchen, but his *ajoblanco malagueño* with a red wine and cinnamon *granizado* was already a firm fixture on the menu. As a dish, it made so much sense, not only because the silk and ice of soup and sorbet made for a fabulous combination, the deep red on ivory white a dazzling visual contrast, but also because it tapped into the traditions of the city, breathing new life into a recipe as old as the hills.

Now I was on my way back along the coast toward Málaga, sitting in sluggish, angry traffic on the motorway linking Cádiz and Algeciras with the Costa del Sol. I was already late for my two o'clock table, and I was also running out of gas, feeling my anxiety levels rising with the temperature inside the car. As I crawled past the endless shopping centres and car dealers, I noticed a turn-off for San Julián, the finca where Marjorie Grice-Hutchinson had lived and written until her death in 2003.

Few times in my life have I needed more urgently a cold gazpacho, or an *ajoblanco*, for that matter, with or without the red wine *granizado*. I conjured up the thought of cold, and of refreshing and relaxing, as I limped the last few miles into town, found a space in the ferocious sun beside the bull ring, and dashed for the door of the restaurant.

In a matter of minutes, my wish was granted. The dining room was silent, cool, and calming. The waitress brought me a gazpacho of red fruits, with marinated sardines in tight curls, and then a plate of José Carlos's famous *ajoblanco*. Then there was red mullet in fillets, arranged on a risotto of beetroot and chives. The bold use of colour, contrast, and intensity reminded me that the city of Málaga was the birthplace of Pablo Picasso.

Ajoblanco ran, so to speak, in the family. José Carlos's grand-father, who came originally from Rincón de la Victoria, a village a little way down the coast, had loved the dish almost to distraction. 'He ate it with grapes and a little fresh cheese,' said the chef, as we chatted in the kitchen after lunch. 'It was his dinner, almost all year round.'

José Carlos's parents had told him about the original, rustic gazpacho, which sounds more like Marjorie Grice-Hutchinson's description of roughly crushed vegetables swimming in oil, vine-gar, and water than the smoothly liquidised soup of modern times.

'My dad tells me that farming people used to eat it in the countryside as a working lunch,' he said. 'The women would bring it out to them in a clay bowl covered with a cloth. It must have looked pretty unattractive – everything just mashed up with a fork.'

The cold soups of Andalucía have turned out to be a rich resource for the new Spanish cooking, giving rise to modern classics like malagueño chef Dani García's gazpachos of cherry (with goat's cheese 'snow' and salted anchovies), of green tomato (with sliced sea snail), and his pine nut *ajoblanco*. Among Ferran Adrià's earliest inventions were a luxury gazpacho with chunks of lobster and a *salmorejo* of lobster and rabbit. Nowadays, it is no surprise to find a designer restaurant in Madrid serving tataki of salmon on a pool of *porra antequerana*. The fashion has even spread to Paris, where Joël Robuchon serves a tomato-based gazpacho with fresh almonds and basil oil at his chic new restaurant L'Atelier. *Sopas frías* are everywhere.

As for José Carlos, he has taken this central plank of his culinary heritage and fashioned it into dozens of curious and interesting forms.

'Gazpachos? I've made them out of everything!' he laughed, when I put to him the obvious question. One of his first variations on the traditional theme was *gazpacho de fresa*, replacing half the weight of tomato with the same quantity of strawberry. Raspberry works, so does cherry, and beetroot. I myself make a gazpacho with watermelon, which is hauntingly sweet and subtly perfumed. José Carlos's experiments have led him to try gazpacho with avocado, a thick greenish cream, and gazpacho with a garnish of roast scallops, or fried aubergines, or with marinated tuna from the *almadrabas* of Cadiz. His most radical creation was the *gazpacho transparente*, a normal gazpacho decanted and filtered again and again until nothing remained but the watery essence of the tomato and cucumber and green pepper. It was a long way from the English gazpacho of my childhood, further still from the dull tourist gazpachos of the Costa Brava – and a million miles from the harvesters with their scythes, among the dust and prickles of a cornfield in high summer, gratefully tucking into their midday meal of raw vegetables mashed in a clay bowl with vinegar, oil, salt, and water from the spring.

CHAPTER FIVE

GALICIA

Mediterranean and Atlantic. Two oceans, but also two cultures, two communities, two ways of looking at the same set of circumstances.

The peoples of the Spanish Mediterranean have turned their back on the special relationship they once had with the sea. Tourism and the construction industry have long since overtaken fishing as the principal occupations of Mediterranean society. Pockets of the old maritime culture still survive, it's true; I had found a few of them over the course of a summer's travels along the coast. To find this way of life in rude health, however, you need to look towards the north-west, and the great stretch of coastline abutting what the Spanish call the Cantabrian Sea, from Galicia in the west to Asturias and Cantabria and the Basque Country in the east.

Looked at on the map, the coast of Galicia is a crazed doodle, an intricate, madly complex tracery of estuaries, peninsulas, and islands. The region has a higher ratio of coastline to total surface area than any other of Spain's coastal communities.

Of all the regional 'autonomies' in the new Spain, none but Galicia has such a close and fruitful relationship with the sea. More than half of the Spanish fishing industry is concentrated here, and Galicia is unique in that fish still forms a pillar of its economy, despite falling catches, pollution, and European quotas. The community also has a greater consumption of fish and seafood than anywhere else in the country.

I stood on the sand in the weak September sun. On a calm afternoon in the Rías Baixas, the five sea-estuaries that push inland along the north-west coast of Spain, it is easy to kid yourself you are still in the South. Lemon trees and figs, orange trees and vines, thrive surprisingly in the mild micro-climate of the Rías. The sand on the beach where I stood, on a peninsula jutting into the Ría de Arousa, was made up of the crushed shells of cockles, winkles, and clams. The whiteness of this sand under the shallow sea, flat calm in the sunlight, gave the water a turquoise-pinkish hue that, if you half-closed your eyes and painted in a few waving palms, dared you to believe you had beamed down in some gorgeous atoll of the Caribbean.

The Pousa family were natives of this coast, gallegos to the core, attached to their origins like a limpet to a rock. Even when they lived in Madrid, on the fifth floor of a block of flats, they spent their August holidays here almost as a religious observance, the whole troop of eight children, parents, and grandparents decamping every summer to their stamping grounds in O Grove, a little town on a peninsula of the Ría de Arousa, taking fourteen hours by car along roads that, in the 1960s, were little more than winding asphalt-coated tracks.

Cold salt water ran in their veins. Even the eldest Pousa brother, CEO of a blue-chip company in Madrid, still came back for the occasional weekend to dress up in old clothes and potter about with fishing rods and baits and floats, feeling his stress drift out with the tide.

Julo was a sail-maker in Villagarcía, on the other side of the Ría. He showed me to my quarters, one of the original fishermen's houses in the tiny harbour at Rons, and then took me out to the beach again, where a soft drizzle had begun to fall. There, pulled up on the sand, was the family's pride and joy: a wooden fishing boat, one of three or four with the same curious, lean shape and a high curling prow. The *dorna*, as it's known, is a relic of Viking and Norman incursions along the Galician coast in the early Middle Ages, and related to the Nordic *drakkar*. Proof of its origins, apart from that evocatively curling prow, can be found in the construction of the boat, which uses the Viking technique of overlapping panels – known in the Galician language as *tingladiña*.

The little *dorna*, named *Nuka*, had been in the family for decades. Julo ran his hands over its red-painted hull, showing me its primitive mast and sail, its special rudder (*timón orza*), and the fish-scale construction of its hull. He remembered how, as children, they used to fish for octopus, attaching a stick and a hook to a live crab, tossing it over the side of the boat attached to a line and buoy, and coming back next morning to haul up the flailing beast.

We repaired to a bar behind the beach, owned and ruled by a fierce-looking lady with a sweet nature. Joaquina poured us glasses of Ribeiro, the gallego table wine whose clean green fruit and thirst-quenching acidity is like stuffing your mouth full of ripe white grapes, and a couple of her home-made *empanadillas*: little turnovers stuffed with mussels in the mild pickle known as *escabeche*.

The conversation turned around the Festa do Marisco do Grove, a ten-day fiesta that was just reaching its apogee this weekend, in a series of giant tents erected for the purpose in the harbour. The Seafood Fiesta had been celebrated in O Grove every year for the last fourty-two years, and was one of the great *exaltaciones*, the orgiastic homages to various foodstuffs, from potatoes to leek to octopus, which have become a characteristic element of the Galician festive calendar. According to the *Faro de Vigo*, the local newspaper lying on the bar, the Festa do Marisco had turned O Grove into nothing less than the 'world capital of seafood'. The full-page article was a potpourri of statistics: a quarter of a million visitors, 125,448 servings of seafood, more than half a million euros in takings.

The recent history of the town was closely caught up with the story of the Festa. When the Civil War ended, O Grove was just a small seaside town that subsisted, and only just, on what it could catch in the sea, dig up in the Ría, and grow in its orchards and vegetable patches. The humblest townsfolk, when they had noth-ing else, survived by eating clams and cockles scratched out of the mud at low tide. In Galicia, right up until the 1970s, it was an index of a person's truly desperate financial state that he was reduced to eating *marisco*.

There was nothing very desperate about the scene that met my eyes in the port of O Grove when I turned up there with Julo and his little son later that evening. A series of marquees had been put up around the town's fish market, trestle tables stood in serried ranks, and stalls around the edges of the tents offered a compen-dium of all that is best in the universe of Galician seafood: shrimp and Dublin Bay prawn and razor-shell and crab, mussels in vinaigrette, and octopus in the Galician style, dressed with olive oil and salt and pimentón, and a rice dish with local shellfish which, with admirable restraint, the organisers had refrained from describing as 'paella'. There was plenty of good gallego bread, chewy and crusty in a way that no other Spanish bread quite achieves, and a mighty quantity of Ribeiro, fresh and bracing as the breeze off the sea. Between the tables, the various stalls, and the computerised cash-desks, milled a huge crowd of fiesta-goers, filling the space with the noise of their happiness and greed. At the back of the tent was a stage on which a band of Galician musicians and dancers were currently performing, and the fast and furious music of bagpipes and tambourines, like a cross between Scotland and Andalucía, together with the intoxicating wine and the exhilarating seafood, was whipping up the atmosphere like the wind whips up the sea.

At the octopus stall, three big ladies in white coats were working with a slickness born of repetition: while one fished the pink, dripping octopus out of the bubbling cauldrons, another snipped the legs into slices on to a thick wooden plate like a medieval trencher, and a third busied herself with the dressing – a slosh of olive oil, a hail of rock salt, and a dusting of sweet pimentón. The *pulpeiras* are specialist octopus cooks who go from fiesta to fiesta the length and breadth of Galicia, taking with them their great copper cauldrons, their octopus scissors and tins of pimentón, and their years of experience in the art of *pulpo a feira*: octopus 'in the style of the fair', which is the style in which Galicia, as a whole, most enjoys its octopus. (The wooden plate adds nothing to the taste, though it certainly looks nice and does make it easier to spear the octopus slices with the toothpicks usually provided. I am told it dates from the days when the *pulpeiras* travelled by horse and cart on some of the bumpiest roads in Christendom, making the transport of hundreds of china plates severely impractical.)

Beside us at the trestle table, an elderly gentleman in a black beret had laid out in front of him a bottle of Ribeiro, a large hunk of bread, and a pile of paper napkins. He was either awaiting the arrival of a person bearing plates of *marisco*, or preparing to tuck in to what would be, given the circumstances, a deeply frugal

Sunday supper. Images caught in my retina as I stood at the table: a small child with a big drum; a cohort of housewives with identical perms and cardigans on a night out; a svelte young dancer in a long black gallego skirt, worn specially for the whirling, bagpipe-fuelled dance called the *muiñeiras*, hurrying past with a heaped plate of steaming mussels, the shells of the shellfish the same glossy jet-black as her long satin skirt.

The rain now thundered on the roof, dripping off the edges of the tents into the plates of food being ferried to and fro, mussing up the hairdos of the *señoras* in their Sunday best, reducing the floor to a mess of soggy serviettes and mussel shells. Rainfall in Galicia being a fact of almost daily life, however, there was no way the seafood-scoffers at the Festa were going to have their party spoiled. If anything, it made the whole thing even more fun, since now, with this driving rain, you were here for the duration, and what with the noise on the roof and the shrill music of bagpipes and drums, you had to shout even louder to be heard above the din. As long as the Ribeiro lasted, in any case, there seemed little point in being anywhere else. And the seafood kept on coming – plates and plates of it, juicy clams *a la marinera* and huge lanky langoustines, their crackable claws with nuggets of dense white meat as big as your thumb, fat lobsters split down the middle and flash-grilled *a la plancha* with olive oil and garlic, octopus *a feira*, more mussels *a la vinagreta*, and yet more octopus. Julo and his son tried a few steps of the *muiñeiras*, while I fell into the heightened state of mild hypnosis I remembered from another great seafood feast, in the port of Santander, years ago. The wine and the squalling bagpipes and the noise of the fiesta all seemed to coalesce into a single element of collective sensory experience, a feeling that was pleasure and well-being and forgetfulness all rolled up into one.

In the slow morning of the following day, I looked out of my window over the quiet waters of the Ría, only to find that they had disappeared. The low tide, not a feature of Mediterranean life, had left a landscape as messy as the floor at the Festa, brownish mud and rocks plastered with seaweed and the gurgling water of the outgoing tide. On the horizon was the isle of Arousa, shrouded in mist, and, beyond it, opposite the Ría, the town of Cambados, cradle of the Albariño vine and its gorgeously aromatic and perfumed white wine.

Examining the scene more closely, I saw that there were figures in this landscape: there were human beings down there in the mud, doubled over, slowly shuffling in rubber boots, some wearing headscarves and aprons, each with a bucket in one hand and some kind of tool, a small rake or pick, in the other.

I squelched out over the mud to speak to the nearest of them. Maruxa was a small woman with deep furrows in her face and a permanent stoop, a slight curvature of the spine, that seemed to suggest a lifetime of hard work, much of it bending down. In actual fact, Maruxa told me, she had been a *sequeira* – so-called because they operate during the seca, the 'dry' low tide – all her life, just as her mother had been before her. The craft, or profession, of shellfisherwoman often passes down the generations, sometimes along with the rights to work a particular stretch of beach. It always had been women's work; the men went out in boats.

'*Si senor*, I used to go out with my mother and grandmother when I was just a little girl. I used to come back with a few clams, even when I was tiny. There were more of them then. And there were more of us out here. It was what you lived on,' she said matter-of-factly.

She showed me the contents of her bucket, half full of big clams still begrimed in stinky estuary mud. Even in the 1960s, since shellfish had practically no commercial value, there was no control over who fished the stuff and how much they fished, and anyone could take home whatever they could carry. Maruxa said that those days were over. You needed a permit now, and there were no more being given out. *Marisqueo*, or the business of shellfish, was strictly monitored. You were allowed a maximum of three kilos per day, no more. The *sequeiras* were now so jealous of their harvest, Maruxa told me, that they even took turns as security guard on the best shellfish beaches, watching out for poachers.

The history of tourism in Galicia – not counting the Way of Saint James, which is one of the world's oldest forms of mass tourism, but was strictly confined to the interior – begins on the island of La Toja, just over the water from O Grove. Since the late nineteenth century, there has been a spa on the island and a grand hotel catering to its well-to-do clients. When, in 1908, the first bridge to the mainland was built, some of these wealthy folk began to venture daringly into the village, and their first stopping point was the small stone house just beyond the bridge, where Pepe 'O Coxo' (so-called because he was lame in one foot) and his wife, Doña Carmen 'A Andaluza' (so-called because of her glossy black hair and dark features, unusual for a gallega), ran a grocery store that doubled as a bar, where neighbours and friends could drop in for a glass of wine and a bite to eat. The tourists from La Toja were fascinated by this rustic set-up, and Carmen was happy to serve them a plateful of whatever she happened to be cooking up at midday, which might have been a succulent rib of local beef braised with onion, carrot and white wine, a piece of hake *a la romana* (fried in batter), or a fresh crab from the Ría. Before long, Casa Pepe was a fully functioning restaurant, the first in O Grove and the seed from which a whole dynasty of restaurants, run by Pepe's children and grandchildren, would subsequently spring.

There was a lot going on at Casa Pepe. Apart from the bar and shop, Pepe the Lame's main businesses were wine, which he bought in barrels locally and sold to the taverns of O Grove, and octopus. The family business had eight legs. Pepe went every morning to the fish market and bought up the best locally caught octopus. At the back of the shop, on a gentle slope leading down to the Ría, there was an octopus drying yard. Here the octopuses were beaten on rocks to tenderise their flesh – traditionally, three blows for every leg – then turned inside out and strung out on lengths of barbed wire like so much laundry. While the octopuses were drying, the whole family kept an anxious eye on the sky, and, at the first sign of rain, they would be whipped off the line and taken into the stone storeroom used for the wine, until the sun came out again. When they were dry and rubbery, but not hard, they would be packed in sacking and sent off to O Carballiño, an inland town famous for its mastery of *pulpo a feira*.

In the front room of her restaurant, Pepe's daughter, Marisol, brought out a framed photograph of herself as a young girl in a red-and-white headscarf, grinning at a thickset man with a jowly, imposing face, wearing a white shirt and a black tie that came halfway down his chest. The man was laughing at something, while the two of them leant on the marble bar top at Casa Pepe. He was her daddy, the paterfamilias, patriarch of the clan. She hugged the frame, caressed it with her hands, posed with it for my camera. She told me, 'He was the motor that drove our family. He was a kind man, a good man. Dear Daddy.'

Of his three children, all went into the restaurant business in their various ways. When the patriarch died, the business was split up between his offspring; his son Pepe took over Casa Pepe, and Luis married a woman called Lourdes, who opened an octopus bar (naturally) in O Grove. Like her elder sister, Digna, who started her own place down by the harbour, Marisol decided to go it alone, and opened Restaurante Dorna, just over the way from Casa Pepe, in 1959. She married a man from the next-door village, a seaman called Baldomero, and they set up home above the restaurant. But it was always really Marisol's show. She carried the torch.

She was a bright, breezy, good-looking woman with the easy charm that comes from years of attending to the public, and she was nicely turned out in a lime-green-and-white striped shirt and matching necktie, auburn hair cut short and neat, radiating a combination of perceptiveness, generosity, and restless energy.

While she busied herself with lunch, her daughter, María, my hostess in the house at Rons, gave me a tour of the family home,

which rambled up into the living quarters and beyond, into a
twilight zone of storerooms and attics. We poked around in a
darkened shed, finding boxes of the old china bowls that wine was
once served in, and piles of discarded clam shells which Baldomero
had been hoarding for years. At the top of the house was a fine
surprise – a proper backyard, following the slope of the hill
beyond, where giant pumpkins stood in rows and washing hung
out to dry, and, above that, a vegetable garden with cabbages on
high stalks, overarching vines, and a lemon tree at the back.

Down in the restaurant, a big table was laid by the open
window, with the Ría at low tide just across the street, and the
island of La Toja just across the water. It was a quiet day in the
restaurant, and we were to be the only table. It would be a big
family lunch with Mum: there was Roco, another of Marisol's
daughters, who had just opened a restaurant in her grandfather's
old storeroom at which, happily and not entirely coincidentally,
chargrilled octopus was the house speciality; and María and José;
and two other sons, Victor and Baldomero. First Marisol brought
us a delicious *empanada*, the Galician flat pie, filled atypically with
salt cod, a plateful of bright red shrimp, and a big dish of mussels
from the Ría with a proper Spanish *vinagreta* (which is to say, a
cold sauce of chopped onion and oil and vinegar and hard-boiled
egg), and then the grand second course: a real octopus *encebollado*, the excellent *plato típico* of O Grove and environs.

'Now this is *el plato rey de la casa* – the king of the dishes in our
house,' said Marisol, with a touch of solemnity, explaining how
she first simmered the octopus and then the potatoes in the same
water, before dressing both with a mixture of onions fried in plenty
of olive oil, with pimentón, salt, and a final topping of breadcrumbs. It was incredibly good: the potato meltingly savoury, the
octopus sweet and tender, the pimentón giving a hint of spice to
the oily, oniony sauce.

While her guests devoured the octopus, Marisol jumped up
again and moved behind the bar to roll up a platter of *filloas* – the
Galician version of crêpes, filled with a sweet pastry cream. She

wore two pairs of glasses, one perched on her nose, the other hanging around her neck. I asked her about the earliest days of the restaurant, the turbulent years when half of Galicia emigrated to Argentina, London, or Madrid. The 1960s and 1970s were years of massive emigration in Spain as a whole, but especially in Galicia, where times were harder than anywhere else.

'Yes, people did leave the town,' answered Marisol. 'But it wasn't because we were poor; we weren't really. People just didn't realise the possibilities we had, the richness of the Ría, the money to be made. At my wedding banquet, as part of the *aperitivo*, my father served oysters, shrimp, crab, spider crab, and mussels with *vinagreta*. And people were surprised: in 1967, it wasn't something you expected to be offered, at a wedding of a certain – how shall I put it? – social standing.'

She showed me a book documenting the growth of the Festa from a modest exhibition of shellfish down by the harbour, showing off monster specimens of lobster and crab, to the multitudinous *exaltación* it is today.

The background to the Festa is the policy of *desarrollismo* – the need to stimulate the national economy at all costs. In 1957, Franco's recently appointed cabinet agreed on a *Plan de Estabilización*, which would bring much-needed capital into the economy from three major sources: foreign investment, the money sent home by the million Spanish migrant workers, and, crucially, tourism. The latter, of course, was to prove a money-spinner beyond anyone's wildest dreams. The lion's share of the tourist deutschmark or pound or franc would be shared out between the various Costas: Blanca, Brava, and del Sol, while the Atlantic coast received almost nothing. Even so, on 5 October 1963, on the occasion of the first-ever Festa do Marisco, the *Faro de Vigo* touchingly described O Grove as 'the land of aristocrats of the sea', and predicted that its principal product, shellfish, would become the 'artifice of a new era, the era of the tourist, the dollar, and progress.'

*   *   *

North of the Rías Baixas, the microclimate changes. Just over the upper lip of the Ría de Muros, the landscape turns rugged and barren, and the sea, so benign in the Rías, becomes obstreperous and unpredictable. The Costa da Morte, as this stretch of coast is officially known, is a wild, windy corner of the peninsula, beautiful in a stark and sometimes forbidding way, and mercifully free (for the time being) of hotels and second homes.

I drove up there at five o'clock one morning, skirting the intricate coastline of the northern Rías, and arrived in the harbour of Lira in a sepulchral pre-dawn darkness. Figures in woolly hats skulked around the still-closed harbour bar – all of us dreaming of café con leche.

From the point of view of marketing, the Costa da Morte is at a severe disadvantage compared to the other Spanish coasts. Imagine the scene in the hairdressers: 'Going anywhere special this year?' 'Yes, we've got a week's package on the Coast of Death.' It is so-called because of the treacherous character of its ocean, which can rise up into a fury without warning, deep-sea currents pulling ships towards its fearsome cliffs and barely concealed jet-black rocks. More boats have gone down on this coastline than on any other in Europe, and mariners still live in dread of it. The area hit the headlines internationally on the morning of 19 November 2002, when the oil tanker *Prestige* sank 250 kilometres out to sea, discharging 80 per cent of its 77,000-ton load of crude oil, which eventually found its way onto the rocks and beaches of Galicia, Asturias, and Cantabria.

The port of Lira has a fleet of twenty boats, ranging in size from the tiniest *dorna* upwards, but most are after the same catch: *Octopus vulgaris*, *pulpo* in Spanish, *polbo* in the Galician tongue. After the *Prestige*, when their livelihoods were on the line, the fishermen of Lira got together to form a co-operative with some decidedly modern ideas. One was the online fish market, whereby anyone can order their fish over the internet and have it delivered by courier. Another was the notion of 'fishing tourism', along the lines of agro-tourism, a brave attempt to make the fisherman's craft more widely known and earn a few extra euros in the process.

The *Nuevo Perla* ('new pearl') was a pioneer of this brand new form of tourism. She was a traditional wooden fishing boat, the way one would ideally like all fishing boats to look, given the choice, with a square-ish cabin in the middle and a rounded prow, painted in classic fishing-boat colours of bright blue, green and red. The crew was three-strong, and all born and bred within a few miles of Lira: there was Jesus, known as Chuchu, the captain and owner of the ship; silent Cristino; and José, a sly-faced Jack-the-Lad, nicknamed Rápido for his quick efficient work. The three follow a well-worn routine. Leaving harbour in the early morning, they take up the octopus traps left on the sea bed the day before, remove any occupants that have just moved in, and put back the traps with new bait. They are back in the harbour in time for lunch.

At half past six in the morning, we chugged out of Lira towards the first of the catch sites, just a few hundred metres from the shoreline. A force 8 gale had battered the coastline the day before, and the *Nuevo Perla* had stayed in port. Today it seemed the storm had passed, though the sea was still unruly and threw the boat rudely to and fro. The stars shone in a cloudless, moonless sky.

As the sun rose, the coast came slowly into view: strings of sandy beaches backed with dunes and rising to sculpted moss-green hills; a wide bay stretching away to the hulking, shadowy cliffs of Finisterre to the north; and the straggling villages of Carnota and Corcubión, their plain, low, grey-painted houses seeming to huddle against the wind and sea-spray.

The smell on board the *Nuevo Perla* was the usual maritime cocktail of engine exhaust, which came at my face in belching clouds as I stood at the stern, and the reek of three big boxes of mackerel a little less than gleamingly fresh, just now being sliced for bait with a heavy, sharpened, wooden-handled fisherman's knife. The deck was slithery with fish remains; seagulls swooped and gaped, their squallings barely audible over the rattle of the

engine. The wind came in chilly and damp. I was grateful for the
green plastic wet-weather sea-suit the crew had lent me.

I sat on the coil of a thick rope, watching the three of them go
about their work. They had been on the same boat for seven years,
day in, day out, excluding weekends. 'If we hadn't worked
together for so long, we wouldn't be so well co-ordinated,'
reasoned Chuchu – and it was true. They were a well-oiled
machine. When we reached the catch site, marked by a pink buoy,
a primitive motor was set in motion, winding the rope that pulled
up the traps from the ocean bed. The traps, called *nasas*, were
drum-shaped iron structures lined with netting, with a hole for the
octopus to enter, attracted by the bait hanging in a bag, and a
drawstring at one end for its easy removal.

I looked over the side as the traps floated up through the dark
water. The crew of the *Nuevo Perla* dealt with them as slickly as a
factory production line, pushing the cages along a metal rim
installed on the side of the boat. They were quiet as they worked,
cigarettes clamped sullenly between their lips.

The traps came up full of writhing life. There were black conger
eels as thick as your arm – half a metre of twisting muscle – and big
orange starfish, huge sea snails, and twitching prawns. The octopus were harder to see, splayed like weeds against the side of the
traps in their doomed attempts to escape.

After years of close contact with octopus, Rápido knew a thing
or two about the creature and its ways. Pulling one out through the
drawstring hole at one end of the trap, he held it by the head in his
rubber-clad hand, and the beast did its best to break free, plaster-
ing a mass of tentacles over his forearm.

'See the suckers here, all up the legs? See that some are bigger
than others? That means it's a female,' he said, as, taking a
penknife, he made a deep cut at the base of the head. Out poured
a gush of black ink. The eight legs went limp; the suckers seemed to
lose their suck. And what was the oddest thing, the octopus
changed colour in an instant, its tortoiseshell brown and black
fading immediately to a dull grey.

'We have to kill 'em, or they climb all over the boat,' said Rápido cheerily. 'They're not as stupid as they look, you know. I saw a documentary once – there was a crab in a bottle, and the octopus had to get it out. They timed it. And each time it was quicker. Clever bastard.' And he tossed the dead octopus into a fruit box along with the rest of them.

A cold sun sparkled on the pewter sea. During the course of the morning, we had moved three times along the coast, edging ever further to Finisterre, and, in each of our three catch sites, the procedure had been the same: an exhausting process of pulling up, emptying, and replacing a total of almost eight hundred octopus traps. The results of such back-breaking labour would pay for the ship's gasoline and three big boxes of mackerel bait, and provide a living wage for each of the crew.

A few hours later, the four of us were sitting in the harbour bar, eating two wooden plates of *pulpo a feira* and drinking several beers. I fell into a tired sort of reverie, lulled by the soft gallego accents that I barely understood. Rápido was laying into the *pulpo* with a wooden toothpick, stabbing at the octopus chunks as if each one were a whole octopus it was necessary to kill before it slithered off the side of the plate. Plainly he, at least, hadn't lost his liking for the Galician national dish, despite the contempt that familiarity is meant to breed.

'It's good food, octopus. *Si señor*. Good food,' he said, through a full mouth, taking a large swig of beer to wash it all down.

By the next day, the cold front had come and gone. It was a serenely lovely morning in Rons, the shallow water beside the sands of my private beach misleadingly turquoise. It was to be my last day in Galicia, and I still hadn't seen at close quarters what has become one of the region's principal sources of wealth: the platforms called *bateas*, on which millions of mussels are cultivated on ropes hanging down in the plankton-rich waters of the Ría.

Down by the diminutive harbour, Alberto had just got back from a day's fishing and was cleaning up his boat before heading home. His box-like traps were smaller and lighter than the ones used for octopus, though, as he said with a grin, the odd octopus might easily find its way in along with the crab and shrimp he was supposed to be catching.

Alberto – Berto for short – was a young man who had spent all his life in O Grove, and, when he tried to speak Castilian, the roly-poly vowels of gallego came tumbling out. If he would take me out to the nearest *batea*, I cautiously proposed, I would invite him for a beer at Joaquina's bar. He looked at his watch, decided there was time, and said sure, come aboard. I jumped into the floor of his flat-bottomed launch the *No Hay Otra* ('there's no other'), and we sped away into the choppy waters of the Ría, the boat crashing among the waves.

Seen from the shore, the *bateas* are dark shapes crowding the surface of the Ría, and have a faintly sinister aspect, like some kind of top-secret military installation whose purpose can only be conjectured. The first *bateas* appeared in the early 1950s: now there are some 5,000 of them in this Ría alone. Each has a name and number and an official sign, staking the claim of its owner to a piece of this peculiar undersea goldfield. We pulled up alongside the first we came to and I climbed onto the edge of the raft-like platform, made from tree trunks bolted together with oil-barrel floats, the whole thing secured to the seabed with giant concrete weights.

A fishing boat fitted with a crane had pulled up at the platform and three guys stood on deck in orange plastic dungarees, sorting the mussels by pushing them through a rattling grille. The crane pulled up one of the ropes on which the mussels grow, depositing the clump on deck with the loud smash of a thousand shells scraping against each other. They formed a black mountain as high as your waist, mixed with mud and seaweed, stinking of undersea mud and rotting seaweed.

On the far side of the boat stood a row of net bags the size of small sacks. One of the three mussel men strode over and swung a bag over his shoulder, holding it out over the side of the boat for me to grab.

It was a present, a reward for coming to see them on their factory ship out here in the Ría. I could barely lift the sack, and, as I stretched out to grab it, ten kilos of mussels almost returned to their tranquil home on the bottom of the Ría. It wasn't the kind of souvenir that could be placed on your mantelpiece and forgotten about. I wondered how long a bag of mussels might last in a warm car before turning into a weapon of mass destruction. Twelve hours? Twenty-four? Thirty-six?

There was only one thing for it: I would invite my new friends María and José, daughter and son-in-law of the matriarch Marisol, to a mussel feast this evening. If there were three of us and we were hungry enough, we could easily dispatch a kilo each, or possibly two, given that most of the weight of a mussel is made up by the shell.

From the window of José and María's small apartment, I could see where I had just been with Berto. According to the theory of 'food miles', the ideal foodstuffs are those that have travelled the shortest possible distance from their place of production. Tonight, at least, by this reckoning, I was doing well. The Ría was like a vegetable garden where you might nip out for a lettuce or a bag of tomatoes in the afternoon and eat them as a salad in the evening.

The French may do theirs with parsley and wine and shallots, and, if it were me, I might have tossed in a little chopped onion, a glug of wine, salt and pepper. But Maria, bless her, had simply cleaned up the mussels, torn off their beards, and heated them in a big enamel cauldron until they opened, and somehow staggered to the table with the cauldron and left it in the middle, with a few chunks of lemon from the neighbour's tree to squeeze over them if we felt like it. The true simplicity of Spanish food is a kind of daring, a challenge to the diner that seems to say: 'Let's see if you can take this just the way it comes.'

On the face of it, there wasn't much to suggest that this very late lunch for three would be anything out of the ordinary. But, with two bottles of Ribeiro and a big round loaf of the best Galician rye bread, nutty and chewy and yeasty, and this big tub of juicy just-cooked mussels – fat pillows of a pale salmon-pink – it felt like we'd organised an impromptu seafood fiesta of our own.

Afterwards, I sat with my hosts in their glassed-in balcony and looked out at the sea. The tide was up and lapping at the beach below us. José was in an expansive mood.

'What do I need a satellite TV for, when I have a view like this? This is my TV screen,' he said, holding the vista in his outstretched arms. 'I see the boats come in, and I see the boats go out. I see the storm clouds on the horizon, and there's never a moment to get bored. See that guy in the orange suit? He's a friend of mine, goes out to fish for crabs. Works at night, sleeps during the day, and takes his catch to market in the afternoon. It's not a bad life. Though, I think mine's better somehow, sitting up here watching him work.'

The man in question was pottering about in a little boat under the single flickering lamp of the harbour wall, loading a heap of crab traps from the harbour to the deck. His fluorescent seaman's jacket shone out weirdly in the lamplight. As dark and rain began to fall, we sat in silence with our glasses of Ribeiro, watching him chug out of the little harbour and phut-phut out into the glassy waters of the Ría, his orange suit becoming a bright spot in the dark distance.

LAND

What must it be like to live in a rural society? I mean a really and truly rural society, one that lives off and understands the land. What must it be like not to think the countryside merely pretty or romantic? To look at a ploughed field, an olive grove, a vineyard, and see a piece of land either shamefully abandoned, poorly maintained, or correctly tended, its trees well pruned, its plantings neat, healthy, and productive? These are questions that have travelled with me for years, and I find that I am only now a little closer to giving them some kind of answer.

I finally left Ibiza in the year 2000, in search of a place to live that would be quieter, cheaper, and further away from the suffocating presence of the sea. After a series of serendipities, flukes, and unforeseen circumstances, I eventually found myself living in a small rural community in the deep interior of the country, as far from the coast as it was possible to go. On the far western edge of Spain, where it bumps up against Portugal, Nacho and I bought a small farm with olive trees and a vineyard, and set about restoring its long-abandoned water tanks and dry-stone walls. We bought a cow, pigs, chickens. Before long we were growing our own vegetables and fruit, as we had been doing for years, but on a bigger scale and with ever greater success. We were doing things we had never done before, like making wine and olive oil. And, for me, it was both a great adventure and a real education. I have learned more, in the five years we have lived here, about the way food is produced in the traditional societies of old Europe, than I would ever have thought possible when I first arrived in this country in my brown Mini all those years ago.

Modern western societies have created a yawning chasm between the realities of the country and the city, to the point where a recent TV programme in Britain revealed that children in an inner-city school in London were incapable of recognising an onion. In the Spain of the early twentieth century, the gap between one world and another was created not so much by ignorance, as by an abysmal disparity in the quality of life.

Spanish cities were beginning, by the 1920s, to enjoy the benefits of modern conveniences, such as electric light, the telephone, running water, and a functioning sewer system. Out in the villages, however, communications were still miserable, and rural society was permanently haunted by disease and starvation.

I have seen photographs of Spanish rural communities in the early years of the twentieth century, and the best of them are documents of a reality that, in the context of European history, lasted practically until the day before yesterday. The faces of the people – shy, suspicious, defiant, haunted – remind me of the faces of those vanished or vanishing tribes you see in *National Geographic* magazine: faces of the Third World, cruelly exposed to the curious, judgmental, or pitying gaze of the First.

In many respects, the rural Spain of a hundred years ago was more Third World than First. There were few houses, even in the cities, with running water or toilets; in the countryside, such luxuries were unthinkable. Doctors were a rarity, and, even when they were available, had to be paid for. Those without resources relied on folk medicine, herbal remedies, and traditional figures like the *curandero* (quack doctor) and *comadre* (midwife). Education in the villages was scant, mostly insufficient, and teachers were paid so little, often relying on donations of food from parents in order to survive, that a popular saying grew up: 'hungrier than a schoolteacher'. Children were put to work at an early age, often in simple tasks, like bringing in the sheep, picking fruit, or watching over a grazing pig. The routines of the *campo* took precedence over everything, including school.

During the first half of the twentieth century, Spanish agriculture was one of the most backward in Europe. Few of the innovations that had progressively transformed agriculture in, say, Great Britain, had reached the farmers of the Iberian peninsula. Timid advances in agrarian reform were made during the Second Republic of 1933, but the outbreak of civil war in 1936 prevented any further development, and agriculture during the 1940s more or less returned to the conditions prevailing in the nineteenth century: minimal use of machinery, and a labour force consisting mainly of landless *campesinos* hired on a daily basis, with no contracts and no legal protection. In the southern half of the country, the land was still largely tied up in *latifundios*, in which labourers and their families lived under the control of the *amo* or *señorito*, often in precarious conditions. Those who had access to their own land, the subsistence farmers, were scarcely better off: while a good harvest lowered prices and reduced their income, a bad one might mean they were forced to buy food at market, incurring a debt which they could barely pay off – or worse, the family went hungry.

In June 1922, the celebrated doctor Gregorio Marañón accompanied King Alfonso XIII on a safari to what was thought to be the most backward and isolated place in Spain: the region of Las Hurdes, in northern Extremadura. Marañón later wrote in his memoirs that rickets, *paludismo*, and other diseases associated with malnutrition, were rife. Some of the peasants of Las Hurdes, he recalled, came to him clutching their stomachs in pain. The gesture was not a symptom of dysentery, thought the doctor, but of 'Las Hurdes disease', otherwise known as 'acute hunger'.

During the 1920s, a Madrid newspaper published a series of 'Letters from the *Cortijo*', purporting to show readers the reality of life and work on a large, privately owned estate near Jerez de la Frontera. The agricultural year traditionally began on the day of Saint Michael, 29 September, when the fallow fields were prepared for sowing. Workers were paid twenty-one cuartos (a cuarto was a copper coin worth three cents) and a ration of food consisting of three pounds of bread and a cupful of olive oil to be shared between ten men, plus salt and vinegar. 'With these three pounds of bread and the accompaniments, they make three gazpachos; two hot ones for the morning and night, and the other, cold, at midday.'

The working day started early, especially during the ploughing season. 'Before dawn the foreman says: "Praised be Christ", and everybody stands up straight, and the labouring men go out and take hold of their ploughshares, and never let go of them till the sun sets, except for two breaks for food and a few moments to smoke a cigarette [. . .]'

During the winter, work at the *cortijo* was scarce and many of the labourers were sent back to their villages in Grazalema, Banaocaz, or Arcos de la Frontera. The picture the letters paint of these men's lives at home is pathetic. 'At this time of year, the thistles and sprue asparagus are just appearing, and many of the men are busy collecting them with their families for sale in the village, so as to earn a few cuartos, which aren't enough for bread, and they eat these thistles cooked in water and almost always without oil; never, for them, the convict's tasty and enviable ration of chickpeas and *tocino*.'

In the year 1900, around 70 per cent of Spaniards lived in the country. A century later, the figure had fallen to below 10 per cent. So, within one hundred years, Spain has developed from a predominantly rural society to an urban society living from industry and services. In time, the new metropolitan Spain will triumph over the old, the gap between country and city will become an abyss of ignorance, as in the rest of the West, and the rural environment will be entirely given over to agro-business and agro-tourism, a suburban zone that is neither urban nor properly rural, but something in between.

But the Spanish character was forged by its deep historical connection with the land, and, for the moment, the values of the old rural society are proving surprisingly resistant. Many city-dwellers feel a powerful emotional connection to the land. Most can trace their roots a generation or two back to some *pueblo* in the provinces, and they will say proudly, when you ask them where they're from, 'I'm from Brime de Urz, province of Zamora', when their only real connection to that minuscule village (population: 143) might be the occasional visit in the summer holidays, or a phone call twice a year from their last surviving elderly relative, who lives alone in a stone house without central heating, urgently in need of repair.

Spain is not a single entity, but a patchwork of identities cobbled together into a state. Each of the regions of Spain has its own distinct culinary tradition, and, for this reason, there is no such thing as a unified, definable national cuisine. Even so, the conditions of rural life unite more than they divide, and the lifestyle and food of a village in the province of Navarra clearly resemble those of an equivalent village in, say, the province of Córdoba.

More than anything, the cooking of rural Spain is a collective response to the realities of climate, weather, organised religion and its strictures and structures, and, above all, the need to provide the body with the calories needed for hard physical work. Manuel Vázquez Montalbán neatly defines the relation between environment and food as 'eating the landscape', implying a close connection with the natural world which, as (sub)urban habits invade the rural space, is fast coming undone.

The basis of the rural diet was always bread. Bread was a basic ingredient in such standard Spanish dishes as *migas* and gazpacho. (In fact, the Spanish word for bread, *pan*, is practically synonymous with food in general.) Protein came overridingly from pulses: chickpeas, lentils, and dried beans (*alubias*). Such meat as there was would have been predominantly pork, since many families kept a pig and fattened it for the annual slaughter. The coastal zones might have had access to fish and shellfish, but little of this catch ever reached the villages of the interior, unless it came in the form of salt-cured *bacalao*. There might be a rabbit or partridge or pigeon from time to time, if there was a hunter in the family. Vegetables were and are highly prized, and Spanish regional cooking is rich in dishes that give star status to humble ingredients like potatoes, broad beans, artichokes, Swiss chard, cardoons, spinach, peppers, tomatoes, and aubergines. Another crucial chapter of the Spanish rural diet is made up of wild foods. Without snails, asparagus, wild garlic and greens, and mushrooms, the traditional gastronomy of Europe would be much the poorer, and the Spanish rural poor would have been less well nourished.

If there is one word that captures rural Spanish food habits more precisely than any other, it is 'resourceful'. The make-do-and-mend habits of a people who never had a great deal of anything to spare have become part of the DNA of Spanish food culture. The ingenious use of leftovers is certainly a dying art, but it lingers on in the kitchens of the *pueblos*, where no one would ever consider throwing anything edible into the trash.

Economy comes naturally to the Spanish country cook. Nothing is wasted; as much as possible is recycled. Oil for frying is strained and reused time and time again, and finally turned into soap. From the leftovers of the Sunday *cocido* or *puchero*, for example, proceeds the *pringá* of Andalucía, the shredded meats and sausages transformed into a kind of pâté; *ropa vieja*, 'old clothes', in which the chickpeas and vegetables make their reappearance fried up with olive oil with garlic; best of all, the *croquetas* of leftover meat, creamy on the inside, crisp and golden on the outside, which the best Spanish home cooks still make from time to time. In traditional food cultures all over the world, it's often the case that creativity and parsimony go hand in hand.

As summer staggered to a close and the afternoons turned the hillsides a mournful shade of sepia, I got out the road map again. In my travels along the Spanish coastal zone, I had tried to understand the pressures that had come to bear on its way of life and its food: most obviously, a benign climate, access to the bounty of the sea, and the transforming presence of tourism. Now I planned a series of different journeys: inland, towards the rural heart of the country, as far away as possible from the *dolce vita* of the coast. I looked for destinations where the industry of mass tourism might not yet have distorted the economy or blighted the landscape, and where the roots of traditional cooking might lie more deeply in the ground.

I would be travelling in autumn and winter: low season on the coast, but the culinary high season of the interior. When temperatures fall and the days shrink and sputter like cheap candles, the true character of Spanish rural eating comes into its own. There would be rib-sticking stews of pulses and meats, fat-rich products of the *matanza*, bread-based soups, and slabs of chargrilled meat. After the bright, summery flavours of the coast, my taste buds would need to be retuned for bigger, stronger, heartier flavours, and my digestive system primed for generous servings of carb-heavy, protein-rich food.

I would start with a place I knew from hearsay as a land of good trenchermen, the northern kingdom of Asturias, and then make my way down into the flatlands of La Mancha, source of some venerable culinary, as well as literary, relics. I would need to think deeply about products, too, and especially the two great contributions to Spanish inland gastronomy, namely olives and olive oil, and the complex culture of the pig. From La Mancha, I might slip sideways to Jaén, world capital of olive oil production, then veer left towards the pork-obsessed lands of western Spain, close to my own home. My eyes would be open for history, and the way it leaves visible traces in the food customs of a people. For an insight into the Arabic influence on Spanish eating, I might revisit Granada. For a sense of the way medieval practices lived on in one of Europe's richest historical cuisines, I would have to make time for Catalunya. And, with that, I imagined, I ought to have my hands full – not to mention my stomach – until the spring.

CHAPTER SIX

ASTURIAS

While I had been racing up and down the coast, Nacho had spent the summer working on the land, processing car-loads of produce into every possible jam, sauce, pickle, and preserve for which recipes could be downloaded from the internet. Now he was due to leave for Jerusalem, where he would be working with the Palestinians to boost their nearly non-existent production of fruits and vegetables. When he departed at the end of September, I stayed on for a week to sort out the farm, then set off on the mission I had set myself: to track down the culinary roots of the Spanish interior.

I left home on a late-summer afternoon, when a pall of accumulated heat hung heavily in the air. The further north I drove, the further the temperature dropped, until I reached León, when I finally turned off the air-con and wound down the window. I pulled through the Pajares mountain pass with a palpable sense of relief: suddenly, and at long last, it seemed, the summer was over.

Coming from the south of Spain, or the Mediterranean coast of Spain, or anywhere else in Spain, for that matter, Asturias genuinely seems like another world. Where the rest of the country is a parched, scorched symphony in beige and brown, here the landscape is decked out in a dozen shades of green. Where there is not one drop of fresh water to be had from the riverbeds of Andalucía, here the streams rush heedlessly, one might almost say wastefully, down the mountainsides, sharing out their benefit in freshness and greenness with everything they touch.

To a Spaniard, the word Asturias brings to the subconscious mind one overriding image: rolling fields of green grass, dotted with Friesian cows. As children, Spaniards sit at the breakfast table sleepily examining the milk carton with its Asturian brand name and its symbolic imagery of cows in a pastoral setting, until the subliminal association is eventually made: Asturias = pasture = milk.

Asturias is dairy central. Some of the most familiar names in the Spanish fridge are those of Asturian origin, even if most of them are now part of massive food conglomerates. The milk lorries of Arias, Pascual, and Central Lechera Asturiana thunder by on the region's modest roads, rushing the milk to the central depots. In a country which has not traditionally been fond of dairy products, with the notable exception of cheese, this is one region that not only loves them unashamedly, but has almost singlehandedly managed to export dairy culture to the rest of Spain. Until the advent of modern distribution, Tetrapak, and fridges, most Spaniards never ate or cooked with butter. Yogurt, fat-free and fibre-added and vitaminised and flavoured in a myriad ways, fills whole aisles in the modern supermarket. Yet, it was virtually unknown until the 1980s. And all of it is traceable, by some means or other, to the pastures of the principality.

I had no particular agenda, beyond that of finding out just what it was that Asturians ate. Not being quite sure where to head for, I turned off the motorway at random and ended up at the town of Ribadesella, where the salmon-rich river Sella meets the sea. As the evening darkened, a gentle drizzle began to fall, sending locals hurrying home and emptying the streets like a bad DJ empties a dance floor. I pulled down the sleeves of my thin cotton shirt. Five hours of driving had left me with hunger pangs and my clothes were now clammy from the rain. It all seemed to point to an early dinner at some simple little place, where I could dry off and eat something restorative, *típico*, and tasty.

I headed straight for the harbour front and pushed through the door of the Sidrería Tinín, one of several simple cider houses in this part of town. It had wood panels and squat wooden tables, old photos of the town in earlier days, and two large amateur oil-paintings illustrating the art of cider-pouring. These depicted two guys in track suits wearing serious expressions and showing exactly how it's done: the bottle held at arm's length and a thin stream of cider splashing a long way down into the flat-bottomed glass in the other hand.

The cider house rules are simple enough. You can either pour the cider yourself, or you can ask your waiter to do it for you. You must only serve yourself a small amount, pouring from as great a height as possible, just like in the picture on the wall. Be sure to drink it quickly, and always leave a little cider in the bottom of the glass, which you may dispose of either on to the floor, or in a special receptacle provided for the purpose. At the Sidrería Tinín, a stainless-steel channel ran around the bottom of the bar and, in the corner, a sawn-off barrel held a white plastic container under-neath. The spillage of cider is a natural part of Asturian life and gives rise to one of the characteristically Asturian smells – a sweetish, slightly fermenty, moist sort of pong, mingling with the natural humidity of the air.

As well as the headquarters of the national dairy industry, Asturias is known as the cradle of Spanish cider culture. A region of the north coast around Villaviciosa is actually known as *La Comarca de la Sidra* ('cider county'), such is its commitment to the production of fermented apple juice. When Asturians have anything to celebrate, they crack open a bottle of fizz, just like anyone else. Not fizzy wine, but a carbonated cider presented in a thick-mouthed bottle to reinforce the association with real champagne made from grapes.

I sat down and ordered a bottle of cider and the waiter brought me a thick green glass bottle of an old-fashioned shape, with round shoulders and a generous lip, the kind of bottle you might send messages in. At a nearby table, a bearded old gent had finished his bottle and was murmuring quietly, lost in a reverie. The waiter cast me a glance as he opened my cider.

'*Ta cantarina*,' he said, with a smile of complicity – meaning, in the Asturian dialect, that this was the kind of cider that, if you drank enough of it, would make you sing.

I let my man pour the first glass, and the second, and the third. His technique was unerring, and impressive to watch: the cider fell a good metre in a steady stream, landing plum in the middle of the thin-walled, flat-bottomed cider glass, splashing a little and turning the cider cloudy with the oxygen acquired on the way down. (The process is known as *escanciar*.) On each occasion he presented the glass to me with a flourish and I swigged it down, remembering to leave the statutory mouthful as a polite symbol of my lack of greed, my willingness to share. It was a dusty gold colour, and so palate-scouringly dry it made me shiver. It tasted like the smell of apple trees in autumn, woody and spicy and fruity. When it came to the fourth glass, the waiter was nowhere to be seen, but, emboldened by the first three, I thought I would try my hand at the business of *escanciar*. It was not quite as easy as it looked. You needed a certain chutzpah to try it at all, being surrounded by locals who were used to seeing it properly done and would surely be scornful of your risible attempts. The stream of liquid tended to land on the floor or on your hand – anywhere but inside the glass – and this was not only embarrassing, but also highly wasteful. I cast a shy glance around the bar. If anyone disapproved of my efforts, happily, they were too polite to let it show.

Tipsy from the journey and the cider, I now had a raging appetite. Outside it was dark, and raining heavily. The food arrived on tin plates: crisp fried *morcilla*, the Spanish blood sausage, dark and delicious; and a bowl of fat clams swimming in a sauce that was nothing more or less than the juices released from their shells as they expired in the heat of the pan. Then came a plate of juicy sliced *lacón*, the salt-cured pork of north-western Spain, and, best of all, a platter of five Asturian cheeses in generous slices, each more rustic, farmyardy, and fabulous than the last. They were all distinct creations, but they all had the taste and fragrance of milk, the aroma of pasture, flowers, and (there's no other way to put this) warm cow. I thought of the sheep I had seen on the journey north, nibbling the dry herbs and stalks of the high Castilian plains. Here all was lushness and abundance, and you could taste it in these cheeses. There was a soft, yielding, fresh Taramundi, and a creamy, piquant Afuega'l Pitu (the name means something like 'fires in the throat'), a powerful, fruity blue Cabrales, and an Ahumado de Pria with a haunting suggestion of smoke. Cheese number five was the rare Gamonedo, which is produced in tiny quantities and rarely found outside the region. It was presented in a much smaller piece, and set slightly apart from the other four, as if to emphasise its rarity. Gamonedo is a cow's milk cheese and, like Cabrales, is veined with a delicate tracery of greeny-blue, but there all similarities end, because the Gamonedo has a dry, crumbly texture that looks rather alarmingly as though it'll gum up the palate, but actually melts in the mouth into a salty, creamy, almost Parmesan-like richness.

Asturias is a happy hunting-ground for cheese-lovers. With an estimated forty different cheeses produced within its borders, three of which have *denominación de origen* status, few places in the world – even in France – can boast such variety over such a modest surface area.

By morning, the weather had cleared, the air was sparkling, and the colours of the countryside were turned up bright. Thinking I would look for the sources of some of this cheesy excellence, I turned on to the old highway leading up the river Sella, then turned east into the sunlight, Ray-Bans on and the windows down, feeling like the king of the road. There was almost no traffic. Further inland, gentle hills rose inexorably to a wall of glittering, sugar-iced mountains: the Picos de Europa, peaks of Europe, so-called because their snowy caps were the first things mariners saw when they returned from their long expeditions to distant seas.

In the village of Poo de Cabrales, I screeched to a halt to take a photograph of the road sign – superbly appropriate, given the powerful odour of the cheese in question.

A few villages further on, where rushing streams arrived breath-less from the mountain range above, cramming the air with positive ions, I stopped at a small bar beside the river Grena, which doubled as post office, tobacconist, grocery, and general supply store, and also sold *raciones* of cheese. It was gloomy inside and the ceiling was hung with cowbells, harnesses, baskets, drinking-horns, and hams. Sacks of dry goods stood open-mouthed on the flagstone floor: I saw walnuts, hazelnuts, and *fabes*. The latter are the big white beans that go to make *fabada*, the Asturian regional dish numero uno. Behind the bar were edited highlights of the range of articles that locals might require in their work or leisure, from flick-knives and wooden clogs (still worn by Asturian country folk, for going about in the mud) to lottery tickets, fat cigars, and thick pairs of woolly socks.

At the Formica bar I asked for a beer and a serving of Cabrales. When in Rome, it makes sense to try the Roman speciality – after all, this is the region's most famous cheese, one of its most famous foods, and a justifiable source of Asturian pride. It is puzzling to me that cheeses like Stilton and Roquefort, though both wonderful in their own way, should enjoy worldwide fame while Cabrales, which is more than a match for either, should be so little known outside its homeland. The woman cut me a slab from a whole cheese she kept behind the counter, a big roundel covered in a green and red wrapping. At the centre of the label was a kind of heraldic shield showing two goats and a bear on their hind legs, robbing the fruit out of a tree. In the old days, Cabrales used to be wrapped in leaves from the plágamo tree, which grows beside the streams around these parts, but the EU health police was suspicious of the leaves, and banned them.

The Cabrales came on a square of greaseproof paper on a Pyrex plate. It was quite a cheese. Pungent to an incredible degree, with a blue-green veining that had nearly edged out the creamy whiteness. You needed a beer, or perhaps a glass or two of cider, to get it down without scorching the walls of the oesophagus. There was a spicy kick to it, with a touch of citrus fruit, and a potent aftertaste that stayed on your palate for ages and clung to your fingers for hours, however vigorously you washed them.

Cabrales shares its homeland with Gamonedo, the other great Asturian cheese, which is even less well known and considerably harder to find. There on the map I noticed the name, at the end of a meandering lane that seemed to head upwards, towards the peaks and mountain lakes and the famous monastery of Covadonga, birthplace and symbol of Christian resistance to Moorish domination (the so-called Reconquista) in the darkest days of the eighth century. I needed no encouragement to turn the car around and follow this lane, which ran along a valley dense with chestnut forests. From here, the hillsides plunged away steeply, losing themselves in dark ravines clogged with woodland and with grand stone ruins, farmhouses or churches, hidden in their depths.

Gamonedo turned out to be a pretty, if pretty basic, mountain village of stone houses and square wooden granaries with rough slate roofs, poised on four flat, mushroom-shaped stones at the corners to keep out the rats. Up here in the crisp mountain air, the granaries had a Tibetan look, like Buddhist pagodas. It was a quiet morning. Cockerels strutted in the street. I stood at the edge of the village looking out towards the crystal spires of the Picos. Brown cows grazed on steep slopes of thick green pasture sprinkled with wildflowers, their bells tolling in the distance. It is always reassuring to find the source of the product, there in front of you, before you buy it. And the source of the product did look particularly happy and fulfilled, working its way methodically through some of the tastiest pasture on the peninsula.

A lady in a black headscarf and clogs came shuffling past, and we spent a few minutes passing the time of day. It was very quiet up here in the *pueblo*, yes indeed. All the young people had left, though there were new people coming in. Buying up the houses for holiday homes. Outsiders, not people from here. A family of madrileños, a couple from Bilbao . . . She could hardly imagine what they saw in a village like this, so far from the city, with nothing, not even a school. She shook her head.

I was looking for cheese? In that case, I should come with her immediately to the house of a friend. We walked slowly through alleys spattered with cow dung, past the village washing post, now unused, half full of stagnant water.

'That's where I washed my clothes, for years. Now I have a washing machine. My son bought it for me,' explained the lady cheerily.

Her friend, Belarmina, lived in a large house in the lower part of the hamlet. Outside her front door, beside a flowerbed flaming with pink hydrangeas, stood a pair of clogs like the ones worn by my guide, and, next to them, their practical modern equivalent: plastic overshoes like sawn-off Wellington boots. Just across the way was a lovely old granary, one of the grandest I had ever seen, with strange, primitive designs, naïf symbols etched in whitewash on the weatherbeaten wooden panels. Behind these panels, up near the roof, cobs of maize hung in pale yellow bushels. I was reminded of the importance of this crop in the rural life of Spain's northern communities, from Galicia to the Basque country. Maize was food for chickens, pigs, cows, and people. A dense maize bread was even made from it, and, though the taste for *broa* has largely died out in Asturias, it continues in Galicia.

Belarmina González got up from her chair in the morning sun and ushered me inside, while the other lady clacked away down the street. The first room in the house was a sitting–dining room with a solid wooden table and, along the rear wall, a glass-fronted cabinet loaded with fancy silver cups in a variety of designs. But Belarmina did not run a football team: these were prizes for the Gamonedo cheese she makes with her husband and son.

To the right was a simple kitchen, its walls lined with bathroom tiles.

'We used to make the cheese in there,' said Belarmina, gesturing over her shoulder to the kitchen as she pottered about the dining room. 'But then they stopped us.' By 'they', I presumed she meant Brussels, or Madrid, or perhaps both.

She took me outside the front door again and pointed across the valley, high up towards the celestial landscape of the Picos, where a series of glacial lakes lie in mirror-like stillness beside the monastery of Covadonga. This was were the flocks were, with her son and husband watching over them.

There were few makers of Gamoneu, as the cheese is known in Asturian dialect, still in operation, she continued. This was hardly a surprise in itself, since all over Europe many traditional food products are threatened with extinction. But the reason for Gamoneu's decline is unusual, to say the least. It is due to the increasing numbers of wolves in the area, which are attacking flocks and making life impossible for shepherds. The Iberian wolf, *Canis lupus signatus*, is now a protected species in the Picos de Europa National Park, and its numbers have grown, forcing farmers into a vicious circle: the more of them sell their flocks and give up the business, the more the wolves' food supply diminishes and the further down the mountain they are prepared to venture in search of fresh meat.

Gamoneu is a seasonal cheese, made mainly in spring and summer, when the flocks are up at their mountain pastures. It is made from a mixture of milk from the Casina and Carreña cow, both traditional Asturian breeds, long-horned and big-eared, and with goat's and sheep's milk. Morning and evening milk are combined, lowering the pH, as milk acidifies over time. This cheese owes its character to the social history of the shepherding population. The shepherds of Asturias spent the summers in the high mountain, living in wooden shacks where, during the chilly nights of May and June, they might have needed to light a small fire to keep warm. Most mountain refuges in the north of Spain lacked a chimney, so the smoke simply lingered in the atmosphere, eventually finding its way out through the roof. Which meant, in turn, that the chorizos and hams hanging from the ceiling, and the cheeses left out to cure, would naturally receive their dose of smoke, preserving and subtly flavouring them.

Belarmina brought out a whole cheese, weighing three or four pounds, from a cupboard in the kitchen. It was three months old, but seemed much older; it was dry and hard to the touch, with an interesting nubbly rind that was coloured with an Impressionist wash of rust red, grey, and pale green moulds. She wrapped it in a page from the local newspaper, *La Nueva España*, with its stories about farming subsidies and local saint's-day fiestas.

'Now, when you get home, you must take a cloth and wet it a little under the tap, and you must wrap the cheese in it. That way it won't dry out,' she advised.

And she took my pocketful of euros, placed them carefully in a drawer in the cabinet groaning with all those silver cups, and went back to her place in the sun.

Asturias was never colonised by the Moors, and the Asturians are basically a Celtic people, light skinned and fair haired. The climate is mild in summer, but harsh in winter, with cold fronts that sweep in from the Atlantic. Crops that are common, not to say ubiquitous, in the rest of Spain, won't grow here – it is strange to see no olive trees, no vines, hardly any citrus fruit. The result is that traditional Asturian cooking is based on a different premise than most Spanish food: the natural frying medium, for example, would be butter or pork fat, rather than olive oil. The winter *matanza* or pig-killing is, or was, of vital importance in the nutritional and culinary life of this community. There is virtually no wine – Asturias, along with Cantabria, are Spain's only non wine-producing regions. Armando

Palacio Valdés, in his 1931 novel, *Sinfonía Pastoral*, gives the basic ingredients of the Asturian rural diet (whether in order of quantity, or of nutritional importance, he doesn't specify) as: maize, chestnuts, eggs, hazelnuts, walnuts, milk, lard, cider, spelt-wheat bread, *cecina* (dried cow-meat), pumpkin, cabbage, onions, potatoes, beans, pulses, and the products of the matanza: *lacón*, chorizo, *morcilla* and *tocino*.

Traditional Asturian cooking is solid, dependable, calorific, and fiercely loyal to its origins. There is variety here: each of the region's seventy-eight *concejos*, or councils, has some sort of edible speciality. But the local cuisine hinges on one great dish, which, for Spaniards as well as Asturianas, neatly sums up the region in one monumental edible symbol: the *fabada*.

The Castilian word *haba* tends to refer to the broad bean, which is generally eaten fresh. What *faba* refers to is what most Spaniards would understand as *alubia*: a bean that is grown specially for drying. There might be several dozen different types of *faba* grown locally – a whole hill of beans. We know from the diaries of Jovellanos, a central figure of Asturian literature, that, even in the eighteenth century, the *faba* was cultivated all over the principality, and in dozens of varieties. The *roxa* or *colorá*, a deep vermilion red, is like our kidney bean. The pale-green *verdina*, highly fashionable, goes nicely with rabbit, hare, or partridge. The *pinta* bean comes in extraordinary colours and designs, jewel-like, spotted and striped, so pretty they could be threaded on string for a necklace. But the king of them all is a big, flattish, longish, straight-sided bean, roughly the size and shape of the final joint of your little finger. The fame of the *faba de la Granja*, or *del Cura*, as it is variously known, is based on its smooth, melting, buttery texture when cooked, its fine skin, and its considerable capacity for absorbing liquid.

This is the best *faba*, and the favourite *faba* for making *fabada*. It grows best in a warm, damp climate in which the temperature doesn't drop much below 18°C or exceed 24°C – and exactly these conditions are those of Asturias during the months of May to

September, the bean's productive cycle. *Fabes de la Granja* were traditionally planted as a mixed crop with maize, so that the bean had the maize stalk for support. Nowadays, more than 2,500 hectares of agricultural land are given over to *fabes*, and the average yield ranges from 800 to 1,000 kilos per hectare. So that's . . . work it out – between 2,000 and 2,500 tons at every harvest. It's a lot of *fabes*. But then Asturias eats a lot of *fabada*.

Lentils, chickpeas, or beans, simmered for hours with a ham bone, a hunk of *tocino*, a chorizo, and a *morcilla* or two, and perhaps a vegetable: potatoes, turnips, or cabbage . . . Every region of Spain has its own variant on the Ur-dish of pulses and pork, or pork and beans, from the *cocido madrileño* to the *puchero* of Andalucía, the *olla podrida* of Burgos and the Catalan *escudella i carn d'olla*. Their common ancestor was possibly the *adafina*, a chickpea stew made popular by Sephardic Jews, who made it on Fridays for consumption on the Sabbath, and in which the meat was originally mutton or beef, until Ferdinand and Isabella made enthusiastic consumption of pork an article of faith. The *fabada* is Asturias's own version of the basic recipe. Its other main ingredient, apart from the *fabes*, is what is called the *compangu* – the accompanying stuff: salted *tocino*, *lacón*, chorizo, and *morcilla*. The beans and meats are soaked in cold water overnight, and bubbled together for several hours with no other extraneous element other than a few threads of saffron and a sprinkling of salt. It is not by any means a complex dish, but everything must be just right: the beans soft and creamy; the sauce not too watery, not too thick; the meats tender enough to be cut with a spoon; the sausages just maintaining their shape in the simmering pot.

On a chilly day when I had spent the morning thinking about *fabada*, it seemed only logical that I should find one to eat for lunch. I drove westwards and southwards, through landscape that varied between stark, bare moorland and leafy valleys of chestnut and oak woods. And at 2.30 p.m., zero hour for the Spanish midday meal, I found myself in the village of Pola de Allande, fifty miles or more off the beaten track, in a part of inland Spain as little known and unreconstructedly rural as any.

There was only one proper eating place in town, a hostel and restaurant that had practically been there for ever, but was nevertheless known as La Nueva Allandesa. The dining room was a big echoey hall, the TV news rattling away in one corner, and a host of tables with white paper cloths. It was a *comedor* like a thousand others all over the country, a place of big lunches for small money, unpretentious, brisk, and noisy.

As three o'clock rolled round, the customers were arriving in a continuous single file. I congratulated myself: this would surely be a good place. I ordered a bottle of cider and poured myself a glass, spilling only a little on the floor. The menu was *fabada* or *pote asturiano*, a variant of *fabada* which also includes cabbage, vegetables, pig's ear, and *chosco*. Unthinkingly, I ordered *fabada*, and they brought it to me on two steel platters, the beans on one, the meats on the other, in a serving of terrifying quantity, enough to feed four effete citydwellers, or one large Asturian countryman who's been out with the cows since dawn. The *tocino* had taken on a translucent, glassy quality, like a slice of caramelised melon; the chorizos were smokily sweet, the *morcillas* succulent and spicy. Best of all were the *fabes*, big fat white beans, so tender and fine-skinned they melted in the mouth, with a flavour so meaty it was hard to stop eating them until you were so full you wondered how your digestive system was ever going to cope. A politician in Asturias once invited Julio Camba, the famous journalist and gastronome, to a *fabada*. Six months later the politician happened to run into Camba again in Madrid, and asked him: did he remember that *fabada*? To which Camba replied dolefully, holding his hand to his belly, 'It's still here, my friend, it's still here.'

When I went to visit Nacho Manzano the next day, we talked about the vexed question of digestibility, and he nodded sagely. One had to be careful with *fabada*. When it was good, it was a marvel, a masterpiece, and, like all the greatest dishes of the Spanish rural repertoire, an example of what elegance there can be in simplicity. It was not, however, a dish to be taken lightly, nor partaken of heavily.

Señor Manzano – Mr Appletree – runs what is, undoubtedly, one of the most fascinating restaurants in Asturias. He represents a particularly southern European paradigm: that of the chef of a successful modern restaurant which was once run as a bar, or as a simple eating place, by the parents of the same man. (They are usually men.)

Casa Marcial, Nacho's restaurant, is a little place in a hamlet outside the village of La Vita, which, in turn, lies a mile or two outside the town of Arriondas. The first time I read about the restaurant was in a review by a Spanish journalist of a more delicate constitution than most, who loved Nacho's food but was primly disgusted by the bucolic details of the surroundings, particularly the cowpats in the driveway and the 'slobbering' dog that approached him in the car park. It was precisely this sort of detail that made me want to visit. Casa Marcial sounded like an honest sort of place that wasn't so dazzled by its own Michelin star that it failed to keep in touch with the reality of its rural context. And so it proved to be. The restaurant was a fine grey stone building among a group of cottages and *hórreos*, with a view of rolling green hills wreathed in downy mist. Chickens pecked in the hedgerows. Every house in the hamlet had its own vegetable patch: I could see potatoes, peas, jade-green onions with thick, juicy stalks, and the year's last beans, climbing in thick green garlands on strings hung from an A-frame of chestnut poles.

Nacho came out to meet me in his chef's whites. He was a small-statured, dry-humoured, quick-bodied young man in his early thirties, with dark hair, dark eyebrows, and a pale kitchen face, who spoke a rapid-fire Spanish with such a strong local accent I had to retune my ears to it. It was well before lunchtime on a weekday, and Nacho was in no particular rush to get back to the kitchen, so we wandered around the property chatting about food, family history, and the importance of staying true to your roots.

'I grew up here, in this house, in this environment,' he said.

The house had belonged first to his great-grandmother, who had passed it to his grandmother, who had sold it to her nephew, who was Marcial, Nacho's father. For a century or more, the house was a vital resource for the people of the neighbourhood: it was a bar, a shop that sold everything from shoes and socks to tinned sardines, and even had a dance hall on the upper floor. Mothers in the outlying farms would send their children down to pick up the bread every morning, and come down later themselves to do the daily shop. In what is now the restaurant's beam-ceilinged dining room, there was once a cider press, where, every autumn, the family produced its annual supply. It was a typical arrangement in the villages of northern Spain, where mountain landscapes and bad weather threw rural communities in upon themselves. There were no cars, so the place played a vital role in the commerce and society of the neighbourhood.

He left me in the dining room and retreated to the kitchen to prepare for me a nine-course menu that brought nicely into focus the contemporary sensibility that Nacho applies to his culinary origins. As I sat quietly eating, tractors rumbled back and forth outside the window, carrying bales of hay.

It began with a cream of Gamonedo cheese, lightly flavoured with sage and garnished with confit of tomato and fresh apple. I remembered the cheese I'd bought from Belarmina and its crumbly richness, laced with piquant blue, and the faint reminiscence of woodsmoke which also came through in this delicate cream. Nacho thinks Gamonedo the principality's greatest cheese, and the best for cooking, thanks to its dryish texture and salty piquancy.

Then he brought me his best-known dish, one of the flag-waving inventions of the new Asturian cooking, the maize *torta* with poached onion and scrambled egg. Thereby hangs a tale. Maize flour was the subsistence food of the rural poor; *tortas* were thick cakes of maize flour cooked on a piece of sheet metal over a coal fire: horribly indigestible, but with the advantage that they filled you up nicely. At the very least you could serve up the *torta* with a fried egg, and this was a popular combination. In the hard years following the Civil War, when half of Spain teetered on the edge of starvation, there was often little else in the storecupboard of rural Asturias.

Pondering the solid virtues of the *torta*, Nacho came up with his own version, trying hard to make it easier on modern stomachs. His *torta* is still made of maize flour from the maize that grows outside the window, but the doorstep of dough that took a day to digest has been replaced with a thin pancake, which, when fried in smoking-hot oil, puffs up into something miraculously light and airy. The onions Nacho uses are grown in the neighbourhood. Thanks to all that rain, Asturian onions are sweet and mild, and caramelise beautifully into a melting purée. The eggs are from the next door farm. 'The dish is no big deal, I suppose,' he shrugs, 'but it's harmonious, pleasant, easy to eat. Everyone likes it, even the highbrow critic I read the other day, who called it "delicate, featherlight, wholesome, and humble".'

The third dish was a more recent creation, also a product of the Asturian *terroir*: a crisp slice of salty *panceta*, sitting on a few finely sliced, almost-raw vegetables, with a light vinaigrette based on the perfumed juice of the *fabada*. A couple of tender *fabes* served almost as a point of reference, a way of saying 'this is where it all comes from'.

It made me curious to taste Nacho's *fabada* in its complete form, which, he said, used *morcilla* and chorizo from the Arriondas area, and which he himself loves cooking almost as much as eating. But this would have to wait for another day, just as I would have to forgo Nacho's famous *pitu de caleya*, the cockerels he buys from a neighbour at a year or so of age. As their dialect name implies (*caleya* means country lane or track), these cockerels live in a semi-wild state and are fed on barley, maize, and wheat, apart from whatever they can find for themselves in the fields and hedgerows. Nacho casseroles them until their dark, close-textured, flavoursome meat has released all its goodness, and serves the *pitu* with a rice made with the stock.

But I was still only halfway through: still to come were courgette flowers stuffed with crabmeat, with peeled green peas on the side; fillet of grouper roasted for a few seconds, with peeled broad beans; parmentier of squid; and a stunning dish of simply roasted wild salmon from the wild waters of the river Sella, the best salmon I can remember tasting in a long time, the flesh a delicate pink, flaky, and almost completely lean, nothing to do with the greasy orange slither of farmed salmon. Looking back over the menu after a refreshing dessert, a jelly-like *tocinillo* of muscovado sugar with green-apple juice and rocket leaves, was like looking back over a long walk in the country. There was nothing attention seeking about this man's cooking: it was modest. Though contemporary in every way, with light sauces that gently underpinned the generous flavours of the main ingredient, it seemed to draw its strength from deep below the surface, in memory, personal and collective, in the sureties of home and family, and in the timeless world of country people, country cooking, country life.

CHAPTER SEVEN

LA MANCHA

Looked at on one of those oddly fascinating relief maps which invite you to run your fingers over their rumpled surface, La Mancha appears as a vast, flat table land, stretching uninterrupted across the centre of Spain roughly from Madrid southwards to the mountains of the Sierra Morena. There are no summits, no hills to speak of, yet this plateau has an average height of 1,000 feet or more.

Nowhere else in Spain has these wide horizons, these endless vistas, this unremitting flatness. The extremes of climate are brutal. Winters are cold and stark; summers are three months of staggering, blow-to-the-head heat. Rainfall, however, is hardly a major feature of the weather forecast around here. There are few trees on this high plateau, apart from the great plantations of olive and wine-vine. No wonder the Arabs christened it Al-Manchara: 'hard and dry'.

I travelled in an afternoon all the way from the humid forests of Asturias to the imperial city of Toledo – capital of the autonomous region of Castilla-La Mancha and, until 1560, of the whole of Spain. My hotel room that night had views over palaces and convents whose towers and steeples were inhabited by dozens of nesting storks.

A paperback copy of *Don Quijote* lay on my bedside table; a free gift from the management. This being the four hundredth anniversary of the first publication of Miguel de Cervantes' novel in 1605, the whole of Spain was in the grip of Quijote fever. New editions – illustrated, abridged, annotated, for children – were coming out every few weeks. The tourist board of Castilla-La Mancha had gone into overdrive, putting up special green 'Quijote Route' signs on the outskirts of every village, whether or not it could boast any real connection with the events of the novel. The Don, always envisioned as a scrawny figure with a thin face and pointy beard, was everywhere: modelled in porcelain in a ceramic store, in pewter in a jeweller's, and in sugar icing in the window of a pastry shop.

What *Don Quijote*, the novel, has to say about Spanish food is fascinating in itself. Lorenzo Díaz, author of *La Cocina del Quijote*, a disquisition on the role of food in the novel and manchego food in general, argues that no other cuisine in the world has been promoted so nobly in literature as that of La Mancha in Cervantes' novel. It is true, and famously so, that the very first paragraph of the novel presents a broad-brush portrait of its principal character in terms of the dishes he partakes of on a regular basis: 'a stew with rather more cow in it than lamb, *salpicón* on the other nights, *duelos y quebrantos* on Saturdays, lentils on Fridays, and the odd pigeon on Sundays.' (*Salpicón* was a kind of salad of leftover meats dressed with vinegar and spices. As for *duelos y quebrantos* – the term means something like 'harm and suffering' – we have no very clear idea about what they might have been, suggestions ranging from a kind of all-in stew made from the poorer cuts of a cow that had died of natural causes, to a stirred-up omelette of lambs' brains and fatty bacon.)

Food certainly plays an important role in the novel, but there is a sense in which the more powerful force in its depiction of seventeenth-century Spanish society is not eating, but hunger. The perpetual search for food, and the ingenuity this presupposes, is certainly the underlying theme of many Spanish novels of the time, especially those of the picaresque genre, including Quevedo's *Buscón* and the anonymous *Lazarillo de Tormes*, with their characters whose overriding obsession is to get themselves a proper feed. This was an era in which Spain, as a world superpower, was forced to spend enormous sums in order to maintain its explorations, its warring armies, and its established colonies. Meanwhile, the homeland went to wrack and ruin: crops were abandoned, villages deserted, and the streets of the cities invaded by legions of beggars. The blind man in *Lazarillo de Tormes* keeps his rations in a knapsack which he closes with a padlock, but his cunning guide, the book's narrator, manages to unpick the fabric and extract choice morsels of bread and fatty bacon. On one occasion, he even swipes a sausage the old man has cooked over the fire, leaving a turnip in its place.

I opened *Don Quijote* at the part where Quijote and Sancho attend the wedding of the rich hidalgo Camacho. On the morning of the wedding, Sancho, forever dreaming of food, awakes to an aroma which promises well for the Pantagruelian banquet to come.

'From the direction of this leafy arbour, if I'm not mistaken, comes a vapour and smell a good deal more of roasting bacon than of rushes and thyme; wedding celebrations that begin with such smells, by my life, must surely be abundant and generous', he declares.

Indeed, the banquet proves to be a magnificent affair. Sancho's eyes are on stalks, his mouth watering uncontrollably, as he beholds a whole steer roasting over the embers of a whole elm tree. Two piglets had been sewn into the stomach of the roasting steer, a technique which, comments Cervantes *en passant*, 'served to give it flavour and keep it tender'. Six bubbling cauldrons, each big enough for 'a marketful of meat', held chickens, hares, birds of various kinds, and whole lambs. There were two giant pots of oil for frying up sweetmeats previously drenched in honey; cheeses galore and masses of the whitest imaginable bread.

Though the feast has yet to begin, Sancho cannot resist begging the cooks to allow him to skim off the foam from one of the cauldrons and eat this with a piece of bread.

But this is, tragically, all that Sancho will eat that day. Don Quijote is in a hurry to meet his next villain, and his trusty swordbearer is destined to go hungry once again. The man's disappointment at having to leave without partaking of the banquet is poignantly described as a 'darkness' falling on his soul.

For such a harsh and barren sort of landscape, La Mancha produces a prodigious range of edibles. The cereal crops grown on a large scale throughout the region mean that manchego bread is far superior to the (admittedly lamentable) Spanish average. The huge flocks of sheep that roam the plains are responsible for Spain's most famous and marketable cheese. The region makes a splendid olive oil, especially in the gentle uplands of the Montes de Toledo, and the town of Las Pedroñeras, near Cuenca in the south-east, more or less keeps the world in garlic. Not least, the region, as a whole, is the world's single greatest producer of wine – 'great' in the sense of quantity, not quality, though the situation is definitely improving.

There is plenty of bulk production, then, but also exquisite things from particular places. Consuegra, Madridejos, Villafranca de los Caballeros, and a handful of other manchego towns, provide the saffron which perfumes the rice dishes of Valencia and Alicante, and, despite swingeing competition from large-scale

producers in Iran and China, can plausibly claim that theirs is the
finest in the world. The pickled aubergines of Almagro, pungent
with cumin and vinegar, are a delicacy that, once tasted, is never
forgotten. The list of *dulces*, the regional sweetmeats, is endless,
every town having its own speciality, which, it has to be said, often
closely resembles that of the town next door.

As for the cuisine, we need to distinguish between the two parts
of this 'autonomous community'. On the Castilian side, game and
roast meats are the order of the day. Partridge *a la toledana* is the
main dish of Toledo, and the northern part of the region is
obsessed with game birds. In La Mancha proper, meanwhile,
the cooking has its roots in the hardship rations of shepherds and
country people. The feast-day dish here is gazpacho manchego –
nothing to do with the gazpachos of Andalucía, but a stew of
mixed game with a crisp flatbread (the dough for which was
traditionally kneaded on a dry goatskin) crumbled into it. The
region's everyday dishes, *migas* and *gachas*, are simple preparations that can be thrown together using ingredients carried easily
in a knapsack without spoiling, such as dry bread, flour, oil,
garlic, cured or dried meat, and olive oil. If *migas* ('crumbs') is a
true subsistence dish, based on dry bread rehydrated with a little
with water and fried to a crisp with garlic (chopped chorizo,
tocino, and even red pepper are added in better-off households),
gachas is even more so. This is a kind of savoury purée, massively
protein-rich, yet horribly indigestible, made with the flour of the
almorta, a relative of the lupin, and a good deal of pork fat and
garlic. It belongs to that family of thick cereal sludges, like
porridge and polenta, and was principally designed to fill the
stomach and stave off the biting cold of a manchego winter. I
once ate *gachas* on a hot summer day, and paid for my mistake
with a muck sweat from head to toe, a thirst barely quenched by a
litre bottle of Vichy Catalan, and a coma-like state from which I
would only emerge, dazed and dripping, after three hours of deep
siesta.

Toledo is a handsome city, full of poignant reminders of a

tolerance and cultural interpolation among the three great faiths, Catholicism, Judaism, and Islam, probably never to be repeated. But the few inhabitants of its museum-like *centro histórico* seemed a little too serious-faced and sober for my liking. I busied myself with the task of visiting as many of the city's legion of pastry shops as I could in a single morning, and came to the conclusion that the apparently upstanding folk of Toledo were secretly in thrall to their addiction to sugar. If they scuttled by me like ghosts in the street, it was only in their haste to get home, stretch out on the sofa, and gorge on their city's near-infinite range of sugary goodies, the deep-fried honey-drenched *flores manchegas*, the pumpkin-stuffed *empanadillas*, the marzipans, *mantecados*, and *milhojas*.

Above the door of Saint Ursula's convent in Calle Santa Ursula, I noticed a sign in Japanese, English, and Spanish, advertising the sweet things made by the nuns of the convent. I ducked inside and, there, in the gloom of the hallway, was a small window behind which were displayed the various speci-alities of the house, including *pastas de almendra* (almond biscuits), *yemas de Santa Rita* (egg yolk and sugar in a little cake), and the strange *anguila número uno* – literally 'eel number one', a snake-like form in yellow marzipan decorated with whorls of sugar icing.

There were footsteps in an adjoining room. Saint Ursula's being a cloistered convent of Augustinian nuns, all transactions with the outside world take place by the so-called *torno*, a wooden cylinder similar in concept to a revolving door. Clank, clank, as the nun unchained the *torno*. I caught a glimpse of black sleeves and the lily-white hands of an elderly lady, skin as delicate as crêpe paper.

She coughed, once. '*Ave Maria purísima*,' she said, in a flat, toneless voice.

I'd been briefed, and knew that, before buying at convents, just as when buying online, you need to log on with the secret pass-word.

'*Sin pecado concebida*.' Conceived without sin. Well, it goes without saying.

A box of marzipan and an eel, please. The *torno* clattered round, first to deliver the goods, then to convey the money, then made another half-turn to return the change. Finally, there was a moment of idle chatter. The recipes? 'Oh, we've been making these things for ever. World without end, Amen.' And I wouldn't have mentioned the plainly Arabic origins of a thing like marzipan, if Mrs Nun hadn't done so herself. 'They do say it goes back to the Moors,' she muttered, an audible frown of distaste in her voice.

She gave another little cough and busied herself with the cash box, padlocking the *torno* again.

'It's a shame we have to lock it. If we don't, they'll steal whatever they can lay their hands on.'

All that marzipan has to come from somewhere. South of Toledo, among the furniture warehouses and car dealers, I see the first almond groves. Then a couple of partridge farms, to satisfy the local hunger for *perdiz a la toledana*. The city straggles out into expanses of olive grove, and the earth around here is rust-red, the contrast with the grey-green leaves appealing to eyes tired of dust and flatness. Then the vines begin, hectare after hectare of low corridors, like a simple maze in which, nightmarishly, you could lose yourself for ever. Concrete vats stand like obelisks in the fields, discarded and forgotten since the wineries installed stainless steel en masse in the 1980s, begging to be considered for some alternative use – perhaps as an original shower-room for that urban pied-à-terre.

The roads were straight, flat, and long, furrowing the sea of vines. Hulking shapes in the fields moved slowly between the ripples of this yellow-green ocean: an army of grape pickers, some with the headscarves and dark faces of immigrants from Africa or South America. It was only mid-October, there had been almost no rain this autumn, and the countryside looked blasted, the tomato plants in the gardens browning, feeble, faded. What must La Mancha look like in August? What must the heat be like? No wonder the towns seem turned in on themselves, as if hunkering down until the first winter rains. Only the vine and olive stay green, giving a false impression of lushness when everything else has long since shrivelled away.

Lulled and slightly mesmerised by the hypnotic manchego roads, I wound up in Consuegra. The name, for some unconscionable reason, means 'mother-in-law'. Visible from miles away, a line of whitewashed windmills crowns the crest of hills above the town, and these windmills, with their quixotic overtones, provide Consuegra with its major tourist draw. Food lovers, however, have a more important reason to visit. This corner of La Mancha is the source of the world's most costly foodstuff pound per pound, worth more by weight, notoriously, than gold. During the months of October and November, the dun livery of the manchego countryside is suddenly scattered with patches of exotic colour, as the violet flowers of the saffron bulb, *Crocus sativus L.*, emerge from their crown of fine emerald-green leaves.

Beside a house on the edge of the village, I spied two women, down on their knees in the reddish earth of their saffron plot. They wore the *bata de casa*, a thin blue-and-white apron tied around the neck and waist. I stopped the car and chatted to them as they worked, watching them pluck the flowers whole into baskets, nimbly and at great speed.

There had been a heavy dew and a thick crowd of new flowers had come up during the night. It was what is known in La Mancha as *un día de manto*, when an extra-large quantity of saffron flowers are there for the picking and a mauve-coloured carpet or blanket (*manto*, in fact, means 'cloak') seems to hover a few inches above the ground.

'We always start early, with the dew still on the flowers. When they dry out, it's much harder, you know, to pick 'em whole.'

Dionisia, the first woman, had a husband and three grown-up children, but still tended her patch of saffron, which she shared with her friend María. The family economy had always turned upon her husband's work as a farmer of barley and wheat, but the saffron brought in a nice little extra income, which would be saved up. In the old days, saffron was kept in a safe place along with the family's other precious things, the bits of jewellery and cutlery, and, in the event of an unexpected expense, such as a wedding, a funeral, or a purchase of land, would be cashed in for the best price.

Few things in the world are more valuable than the blood-orange pistils of the saffron crocus, and few crops are more torturously labour-intensive. A single *celemín* of 235 square metres (the standard size of plot) produces just one pound of saffron, and every pound requires no less than 80,000 flowers. They must be picked by hand, since no machine has yet been invented to match the delicacy of the human thumb and forefinger. By hand, too, the process of removing the pistils from their flowers, known here as *la monda*.

'We sit around the kitchen table of an evening, with a pile of roses – we call the flowers roses – and we work away. And we chat as we work, and sometimes the neighbours come round to lend a hand. At the beginning it's not easy,' said Dionisia.

'But, over the years, you do get used to it,' put in María.

I leant down to watch the two of them closely, their fingers seeming to flutter over the ground, and the 'roses' piling up in their baskets.

'You have to be careful. The saffron, it's very light, it weighs nothing. When we're working in the kitchen, we keep all the doors shut. The worst thing than can happen is a breath of wind coming in and blowing it all away. It happened to my cousin one year. She was down on her knees for hours on that kitchen floor.'

Despite being one of Spain's most famous products and a spice with few rivals in its rich, exotic perfume, saffron has notably little presence in the national cuisine. Apart from paella, I can only think of two traditional Spanish dishes in which it features at all: *fabada asturiana*, and *gallina en pepitoria*, the classic casserole of hen or chicken thickened with ground almonds, pine nuts, and hard-boiled eggs. Now I understood why. In a rural society with limited resources, to use up the family capital in something as frivolous as cooking would have seemed a deeply reckless act.

We were a few days away from the town's big fiesta, which falls in October. The fiesta includes a saffron-plucking competition, at which local *roseros* compete to see who can remove the most pistils.

'I won it once, a long time ago,' said María, with a chuckle. 'I'm not so quick any more. The arthritis has got to my fingers, see.'

The sun was coming out, and the ladies would soon be setting off home for another morning's *monda*. The look of the two of them hunched over the ground like that, bent like wind-blown tree-trunks, made me wonder that it wasn't back problems she suffered from, rather than arthritis.

On a late Monday morning in Almagro, I sat in the Plaza Mayor and ate a fine Spanish brunch of *migas* with fresh grapes and a big glass of café con leche. Almagro was a collection of whitewashed streets around a perfect plaza, which was not so much a square as an avenue of balconied, columned arcades, the roof-tops above them irregular with history. Blank façades opened up to reveal a palace, a convent, a perfect patio.

Thanks, in part, to a sixteenth-century theatre that has miraculously survived – for centuries it was a kind of residential courtyard where plays were performed – Almagro has become a mecca for Spanish thespians who converge once a year for the Festival of Classical Theatre. In terms of food, the town's major point of interest is its unique recipe for pickled aubergines, which are eaten cold as a refreshing aperitif and are one of the most addictive of all Spanish delicacies.

Traces of the Moorish legacy are visible everywhere in Spain, if you keep your eyes peeled and your mind open. *Berenjena* is Arabic in more than one sense: the aubergine was introduced by the Arab and Berber colonists of Al-Andalus. The etymology of the word is also Arabic, and, before that, Persian: *bedinyena*. The Catalan alberginia and the French aubergine, then, come from the same root.

Wherever it comes from and whatever it's called, there is not much you can tell a person from Almagro about the aubergine. Especially a person like María del Carmen Sánchez Serrano, for whom aubergines are an indissoluble part of life, work, and family history. There is a word used in Almagro to describe Mari Carmen and her ilk. The word is *berenjenera*, or 'one who occupies herself with aubergines'. Around here, it's a normal trade, like being a butcher, a baker, a pharmacist, or farmer. I went to see her at the factory, a small warehouse on the outskirts of town with a sign outside reading Berenjenas La Jaula, which was the name of the firm. It was late afternoon by the time I got there, and Mari Carmen had just got back with her sister from a street market, where the company sells aubergines and olives and other cured goods by the kilo. I waited by the door for them to finish unpacking, breathing in the characteristic and quite unmistakable aroma of vinegar and cumin and pimentón, my mind suddenly transported to a Mediterranean beach and a grand picnic on a warm spring day a decade or more ago, when the crunch and sourness of these pickled aubergines, bought in a tin from the local supermarket, came as a new and surprising experience. A puddle of bright orange – the seepings from the pickling liquid – crept across the factory floor towards the drain.

No doubt about it, *berenjenas* are part of the identity of this town. The inhabitants of Almagro have always sold their pickled aubergines at fairs and fiestas all over the region. Their arrival was greeted, as one manchego writer remembers it, '*como agua de mayo*' (like May rain) – with delight, for there was no more refreshing and restorative food in the torrid heat of an August night than the vinegary crunch and spice of *berenjenas de Almagro*.

Carmen wore her hair tied back in bunches, and grey sweat-pants tucked into wellington boots. We sat in a small, dark office with peeling walls and grey old-fashioned office furniture. The way she sank into her chair made it look as if this was the first time she'd sat down all day, and maybe it was.

'I started work when I was eight, and I've never stopped,' she began, impressively. 'I know aubergines like I know my own family. When I was born, at the exact moment, my mother had a pot of aubergines on the boil. Funny, after forty years, I ought to loathe the things. But the fact is, I don't. I still love them.' Carmen gave a weary smile. Her face wore a colourless, early-to-rise sort of look.

'Where is the recipe from? Oh, it goes back centuries, to the Moors. That's what I've been told. We've been doing it for ever, nothing's changed, it's all still done by hand mostly. All natural, nothing artificial.'

The fame of the *berenjena* belongs to Almagro, but the special little aubergines, no bigger than a child's fist, are grown in the hamlet of Aldea del Rey, where the soil is better. The aldeanos plant the seeds in May and harvest from July onwards, picking the aubergines when they are still green and the rounded fruit has barely emerged from its spiny base. (The green parts are edible, surprisingly, and pickling makes them tender. In Almagro, even the stalk is peeled and eaten, though most Spaniards would leave it on the plate.)

The crucial part of the process is not the pickling, but the boiling. 'It's years of experience, years and years, that tells you how long to cook 'em for,' said Carmen.

We walked out into the factory to see the steel cauldrons where the aubergines are boiled until they take on their golden colour – a moment too long and they simply go black – and the vat where they are plunged into cold water. In the old days, they were laid out on cloths in the patios of the houses and sprinkled with well water.

Then comes the *aliño* – an important concept in Spanish culinary practice, associated mainly with salads (as in dressing), but also commonly applied to sausages like chorizo and *salchichón*, olives, and any other foodstuff that is flavoured after curing or cooking. The aubergines are opened, stuffed with a slice of red pepper, and closed with a fennel stalk cut from the wild plants that grow along the hedgerows and on fallow ground. Then they are tipped into terracotta jars with a mixture of water, wine vinegar, cumin seed, salt, and sweet pimentón. After eight or nine days, they are cured and ready to be sold.

Carmen slipped off the plastic covering of one of the jars and fished out an aubergine for me to taste. Anything you try in its place of production is always better than when you buy it in the shops, and this was a superb example of its type: fresh and crunchy, neither excessively vinegary, nor aggressively spiced. I peeled the stalk and ate that too, finding that it wasn't at all woody and fibrous, but perfectly toothsome.

It was delicious, but then Carmen and her family had had forty-five years to perfect the recipe. We stood in the storeroom filled with that special aroma and I wiped my hands with a paper towel (aubergines are messy things to eat) and we got to talking, and, little by little, detail by detail, a family saga unfolded before my eyes. Carmen was one of eight children, and her mother worked her fingers to the bone to keep them fed. Their education was not all that it might have been – Carmen's eldest sister was taken out of school at an early age because her mother simply couldn't cope on her own. The headmistress tried to remonstrate: it was a shame, the girl had brains and might go far, if it was a question of money she would see what could be done. But the woman insisted: the girl was needed at home.

Carmen shook her head, leaning her shoulder against the white-washed wall. 'We never knew hunger in our family, but there was hardship. I remember the neighbours' children, sitting on the steps with a bag of sweets. And us lot – well, we knew there was no way we'd be getting those sweets.'

Her father had grown up among seven children and no parents, his own father having been killed in the Civil War. Carmen's father was a survivor. First he worked in a flour mill, then he kept pigs on a borrowed patch of land, curing the hams at home and selling them. When this failed to support the family, he turned his hand to aubergines. He tried boiling them in a zinc cauldron his wife used for washing clothes, and curing them in a terracotta jar that had been the entire extent of her dowry. He had no very clear idea of the recipe, and the first three attempts were disasters.

'They went black on him!' laughed Carmen, her face colouring up a little. 'He got the timing wrong! They only came right on the fourth time, and he was furious, imagine it, all those aubergines gone to waste.' Her eyes glistened at the memory.

And so La Jaula was born. The name means 'cage', in reference to a proverb that was popular among the family, which went something like 'nice cage, shame about the birds'. And, from then on, it was hard work, and more hard work. She and her sisters, out on the road in the van with the aubergines, from village to village, setting up in the early morning, packing up in the raging heat or aching cold of the afternoon, back to base to wash up the basins . . .

I said goodbye before she stomped off to load up the van; tomorrow she had a delivery. We shook hands. Her arms were stained orange with pimentón – the permanent tan of the aubergine maker.

'*Berenjeneros, berenjeneros*, that's what we are. And it's too late to be anything else,' she said, with a smile of resignation and tiredness and satisfaction.

Manuel de la Osa has a restaurant in a village near Cuenca that has discreetly, one might almost say reluctantly, become known as one of the best in Spain. Señor de la Osa's surname sounds very like the Spanish word for 'bear', which pushes the mind towards a bear-like conception of the man in his physical aspect: burly, not to say hugely proportioned, bearded, with his charcoal-dark hair in a messy mane, and with fingers like thick game sausages and arms like serrano hams. But De la Osa's glance and smile are timid, sceptical, and free of fame-induced ego.

Manolo (everyone who knows him even slightly uses the familiar form of his Christian name) is not one of those chefs who spends most of his time away at conferences, workshops and guest appearances in other people's kitchens. He dislikes airplanes and finds travel generally tedious. 'If anyone wants to meet me, let them come and see me,' he says firmly.

Las Pedroñeras is a scratchy brickbuilt plains town with very little to recommend it to the tourist, with the obvious exception of Las Rejas.

A big sign as you enter Las Pedroñeras reads 'Capital of Garlic', which, in three words, neatly encapsulates what it is the town does best and on which its economy almost entirely depends. Warehouses on the outskirts are given over to thousands of tons of garlic, which lies in pale, lumpy piles and hangs in curtains from the roofs, and, in fact, a faint whiff of garlic hangs over the whole town, drifting into shops and offices, stealing into people's bedrooms and disturbing their dreams. The reputation of Las Pedroñeras hangs on the so-called *ajo morado*, streaked with pinkish purple, which is said to have a greater fragrance and subtlety of flavour, as well as fatter, juicier cloves, than the run-of-the-mill white garlic now flooding on to the European market, mainly from China.

It is hard to convey an impression of just how extraordinary it is to find a restaurant like this in a place like this. On a concrete wall, half obscured by the dust from the lorries that thunder past on the N301, a legend in big black letters reads: Restaurante Típico, Cocina Manchega, which makes it look like one among a hundred roadside joints that flash past at regular intervals along the roads of southern Spain, the kind where the ranks of lorries parked outside isn't any guarantee of a decent meal.

At midday, the kitchen at Las Rejas was a-simmer with activity, a theatre backstage alive with the sounds of chopping and scorching, the whizz of the liquidiser, the bubble of the stockpot. Through the back door came a constant stream of people carrying boxes, briefcases, offering samples, wielding forms to be signed, or simply dropping by to say hello. While Manolo gave a young commis chef a crash course in how to work the brand-new ice-cream maker just delivered from Madrid, I stood by the bar in the backroom and drank a café con leche with some of the suppliers who happened to be on their rounds that morning. There was a man who grew peas, a man who grew garlic, and a cheesemaker who had brought in his hand-made cheese, made from the milk of his own manchego sheep.

It was just coming up to one o'clock. Plenty of time before lunch, then, for a brief incursion into a region that is to garlic what Bordeaux is to the world of wine. My guide, the town's only producer of organic garlic, leapt into his Range Rover and roared off in a cloud of dust down a dirt track that wound away among an undulating landscape of vines, olives, and bare earth the colour of rust, all under the sun-roof of a cold blue sky. In the background, the town sprawled away, looking not unattractive from this distance, and the squat square tower of the church, with its pyramid-shaped roof, gave the view a civilised, picturesque aspect.

We walked out along the rows into the middle of the field and got down on our haunches to examine the crop. The water sprayers had been on all night, giving moisture to plants that, in the month or so since they had been in the ground, had seen no more than a day or two of rain.

Francisco pulled a fully grown bulb from his jacket pocket, passing it to me for inspection. I pierced the purple skin with my fingernail and punctured the juicy clove beyond: it smelt, not sharp and acrid, but mild and sweet.

Garlic and Spanish cooking would seem to be inextricably connected. The Spanish are supposed to love garlic, and to hurl it with abandon into every one of their dishes. It's a historical prejudice, the notion of the garlic-stinking Spaniard, reaching back at least to the time of Richard Ford, author of the great *Handbook*, who, in typically caustic fashion, declares: 'It is curious to see to what an awful extent the Spanish peasant on the eastern coast will consume garlic: we caution our traveller against the captivating name of Valencian butter, *manteca valenciana*. It is composed (for the cow has nothing to do with it) of equal portions of garlic and hogs' lard, pounded together in a mortar, and then spread on bread, just as we do arsenic to destroy vermin.'

To give him his due, Ford also says of garlic that 'the evil consists in the abuse, not the use', and, in this, of course, he is absolutely right. In point of fact, the Spanish do not use garlic in everything, and Spanish cooks are generally respectful of the power of the stinking weed, especially when used raw. An especially intelligent discussion of garlic and its correct use in cooking comes from the pen of the Catalan Josep Pla, who hated the way that, to paraphrase his words, any food cooked with garlic tastes only of garlic. Pla makes the important distinction between fresh new season's garlic, sweet and innocuous, and the thing it becomes after a few months' storage, which has 'such an expansive force, such a decisive presence, that it destroys all the flavours and all the delicate gradations of taste' in the food to which it's added. Interestingly, Pla suggests that garlic may owe its traditional popularity in Spain to hunger, since its powerful aroma created 'an illusion of nourishment' in those sectors of society whose diet was scarce and monotonous.

The traces of garlic juice were still on my fingers as I sat down at a table near the kitchen, where Manolo could keep an eye on me. At the next table, a dressed-up couple were each talking animatedly into their mobile phones, while the plates of food came and went beneath their noses. Opposite me stood an antique bottle rack in rough-hewn wood, with a row of terracotta jars standing sentinel as they had doubtless done for generations.

In the work of Manuel de la Osa, like that of other Spanish chefs working close to their particular regional traditions, taste and memory are intimately connected. Flavours and textures refer both backwards, to tradition and childhood, and forwards and outwards to the new worlds of multicultural and high-tech cuisine.

'As I see it, the kitchen isn't a laboratory full of test tubes, siphons, and other devices . . . A place for experimenting with flavours, sure, but, for that, the best tools are the tongue and the palate,' he said, as he stood at my table, looming over me like a human Mount Rushmore, holding in his hand a plate of lychee sorbet with caviar and olive oil – the first of three stunning little *aperitivos* preceding the menu proper.

It was certainly a most un-manchego kick-off to the meal, though the aromatic, refreshing lychee, the salty, rich caviar and the piquant, grassy olive oil formed a brilliant fanfare. Things got a little more rootsy with a rock mussel, with saffron foam, and fried cheese with quince and black olive, and a little more earth-bound with a cold garlic soup, one of Manolo de la Osa's most enduring inventions, presented in a cocktail glass with crisp wafers of ham poised above the egg yolk, parsley, and fried cubes of bread. Like the dish in its original form, this deconstructed version was satisfying and simple in equal measure. The garlic was absolutely discreet, subtle and sweet.

But now came the fireworks. A dish of roast squid with *pisto manchego* and a *raviolo* formed of a transparent slice of *tocino* filled with peeled baby broad beans, the sweet surprise of the bright green baby beans in their parcel of salty *tocino*, was amazingly good. So was the potato cream whipped up with sheep's milk, along with a pair of lamb sweetbreads and another pair of asparagus tips. Such wild and earthy flavours . . . By the time I reached the roast John Dory sirloin with rosemary, parsley oil and crushed potato, it was becoming obvious that the creator of these dishes was a man with perfect taste. I hardly knew what to do with the menu's final savoury dish, a suckling-pig confit with apple and quince sauce perfumed with vanilla and truffle, except to wolf down every last forkful of it and clean off the plate with a hunk of bread.

The clock ticked round to five o'clock, the well-to-do lunchers paid their bills, couple by couple, and left, toting their Prada bags as they prepared to cross the threshold into the prosaic, cash-strapped outside world, and still Manolo kept bringing me more and more dishes, pouring me glasses of curious and innovative manchego wines, and generally treating me with the kind of amiable generosity one doesn't expect, somehow, of a famous chef with much more important fish to fry.

His multiple desserts were a gorgeous blur, a farrago of ice creams and *granizados* of yogurt with spices, hazelnuts, white chocolate with fennel, coffee, saffron, orange and blackberry. A rich sponge soaked in red wine reduction, respectfully nodding to the importance of wine in the culture of the region, signalled the end of my capacity to eat, drink, or think, for the time being. And it was at this post-prandial point, as the afternoon turned snoozy, that Manolo appeared at my table once more and sat down to tell me something of his philosophy of life and food.

He called for two big tumblers of ice and a bottle of J&B.

'The story is as follows . . . Whisky?' Glug, glug, clink, clink. 'This is a farming town, 99 per cent of us are farmers. What kind of gastronomic activity is there going on in a town like this? Very little. Even so, my grandparents were already doing this sort of thing, they had an eating house, an old *posada* that stood in the main square, and they had an excellent relationship with the world of wine, with the world of manchego cheese, saffron . . .' He paused for a second to take a slug of whisky, his gaze losing itself momentarily in the empty space above the table. 'As a child, I was always interested in whatever my grandmother, my mother, and my aunts were doing in the kitchen. All my family have always been good eaters, and I loved food too. I began to realise that there were things you could eat that would make you happy: things from around the region, I learned what was meant by a good cheese, a good saffron, where there was good oil, good game meats, good vegetables. I have so many memories of the dishes of my childhood – memories of tastes, aromas, fragrances . . . The smell of cooking over an open fire . . .'

The restaurant was now deserted, its tables cleared and reset for the evening shift. From the kitchen came a sound of clanking pots and pans: someone in there was doing the nasty washing-up, whistling while they worked. It would be time in a short while for me to leave La Mancha and its idiosyncratic local cooking, and set forth, like Don Quijote, in search of new challenges. Manolo poured us both a final generous tumblerful of whisky, and lit himself a cigarette.

He leant back in his chair, which creaked a little in protest. A silence fell. Perhaps it was just the traces on my fingers as I lifted my glass to my lips. But just then, for a second or two, I caught another whiff of that haunting fragrance. It was the genie of the garlic clove, the poltergeist of Las Pedroñeras, sneaking into my brain and switching the synapses.

CHAPTER EIGHT

JAEN

From a table at a restaurant in Segura de la Sierra, a scrawny, stony village beside a mountain pass, I looked down at a distant plain that was coloured a dusty grey from the endless olive trees and the mist that hung above them. A thin river made its way awkwardly down the valley with a thread of bright green clinging to either side, while a neat forest of stumpy olives crept up the hillside almost to its craggy summit.

I was in Andalucía, but only just. Segura de la Sierra was backed into a corner of the country where three regions – Andalucía, Murcia and La Mancha – meet in a wild and lonely place.

To me, at least, what the waiter brought me as I sat at that terrace table tasted unmistakably andaluz, though I would be hard put to explain precisely why. There was *ajoatado*, a hearty mash of potato and garlic, and *ajopringue*, a pork liver pâté with red pepper, pimentón, and spices, and a roast leg of mountain lamb with a rust-red, smoothly oily sauce (known as *ajoharina*) made with tomato and potato puréed with chilli, cumin, and bayleaf. There was a simple salad, simply dressed. And then there were *enredos*, a fried dough paste in syrup. And *panates* and *flores* and *leche frita* – variations on the Spanish theme of flour-and-water dough deep fried and laced with something sweet. None of this would have been possible, of course, without recourse to the local olive oil, a limpid, greeny-yellow nectar which was brought to my table in a bottle, just in case I hadn't had consumed enough of it as an ingredient in the food. I sloshed some on a hunk of bread, chewed on it, shut my eyes, and emptied my head, and aromas came flooding in to fill my brain: freshly cut grass, standing in a pile beside a lawn; the milky sap of a fig tree; and, most surprisingly and unmistakably, the warm smell of tomato plants in a greenhouse on a summer's day.

That morning I had visited the offices of the local *denominación de origen*, of which twenty exist in Spain for olive oil. I had sat and listened obediently to a woman in a white coat extolling the virtues of extra virgin. 'Now, extra virgin, it may seem expensive. But let me tell you, with extra virgin, you can fry seven or eight times with the same oil. And with sunflower, it's only two or three times, then you have to throw it away. So, really, virgin olive oil is not only tastier, it is also much more economical,' said the woman.

I found myself feeling entirely convinced.

My gaze wandered to a wall map of the varieties of olive in Spain, with colours for each type forming a jigsaw across the lower half of the peninsula. Every olive-oil-producing region has its favourite variety, though a few are exclusive to a particular zone: Catalunya loves the Arbequina, with its small round berries and delicate oil; Toledo, Ciudad Real, and the central plain prefer the frost-resistant Cornicabra; while Extremadura favours the Manzanilla, 'little apple', whose oil is marvellously fragrant and long-lasting. Across the country, and especially in Jaén, the commonest variety is the Picual, which happens to combine the natural advantages of high yield, high oil-content in the fruit, and a wide spectrum of subtle flavours which often includes a spicy 'kick' as the oil makes its way down your throat.

Olive oil was, together with wheat, one of the economic pillars of ancient Iberia. The wild olive had always grown here and, according to food historian Manuel Martínez Llopis, some of the earliest tribes of the south of Spain may have made oil from its fruit. The cultivated olive *Olea europaea* (strange that the name of the tree has given us the everyday English word 'oil') was brought to the Iberian peninsula by the Greeks, or possibly the Phoenicians, but it was the entrepreneurial Romans, as ever, who first saw the commercial possibilities of olive cultivation on a grand scale. If, during the first centuries of Roman occupation, oleum had to be imported into Hispania from the west coast of Italy, before long the peninsula was self-sufficient in olive oil and even began to export to the rest of the Empire. The olive tree was planted throughout the southern half of the peninsula, reaching its northern limit in the mountains of what is now Madrid. The plains of Betica, as the Roman province of southern Spain was known, produced fabulous harvests of olives, from which was made an oil of high quality, and this oil was exported in enormous quantities to satisfy the sophisticated palates of Rome. By the second century AD, the olive was so much a feature of the landscape that the Emperor Hadrian (a Spaniard himself, let us not forget) chose an olive branch as the symbol of Hispania.

The Spanish word for olive oil derives from the Arabic *azeit*, which also gave rise, by a kind of reverse association, to the word for the olive itself: *aceituna* in Castilian. For centuries, olive oil was held in the highest possible regard, and lent itself to a wide range of culinary and medicinal uses, not to mention its ancillary role as fuel for lamps, a base for soap manufacture, and so on. The quality of much food-grade olive oil would have been generally lamentable: foreign travellers in Spain in all epochs testify to the mephitic reek of rancid, over-used oil that pervaded the atmosphere, and sometimes the food. In the northern provinces of Galicia, Asturias,

Cantabria, and the Basque country, where the olive tree doesn't grow, 'imported' oil would have been used alongside indigenous fats, mostly butter and lard. Generally speaking, however, the supremacy of olive oil as the Spanish cooking medium was never called into question – until the early 1950s, when it suddenly fell out of favour. As part of the American treaty of co-operation with the Franco regime, which established military bases in Spain in return for economic support, huge quantities of US-produced vegetable oil flooded the local market. The imported oil had to be consumed somehow, and official campaigns began a systematic denigration of olive oil. Rumours spread that it was more fattening than the new 'lighter' oils. Consumption plummeted. Many *almazaras* fell into disuse. Finally, in the early 1980s, the tide began to turn. The horror of the rapeseed oil scandal in October 1981, in which 1,000 people died and many more were permanently disfigured by a vegetable oil which had been adulterated with poisonous chemicals, sent many consumers back to the olive oil their parents had used, which was once again perceived as natural and safe. Successive studies revealed that, far from being bad for the health, olive oil was actively beneficial. Over the years, improved production techniques gradually removed the rancid tastes that had traditionally plagued it, so that subtleties of flavour and aroma could be appreciated as never before. For once, in the history of contemporary eating habits, the story is unique in having a happy ending, and the juice of the fruit of the olive tree, one of the great achievements of European civilisation, has returned to its rightful place at the centre of Spanish food and life.

Olive oil production in Spain is not what it was. Traditionally, the olives were picked off the ground, where they might have been lying for days, and packed into sacks for transport by donkey or mule-driven cart. The *almazara* (press) might have been many miles from the trees. Once there, the olives would be tipped into holding vats called *trojes*, where they might spend another few hours or even days before finally being pressed. There was often little regard for cleanliness. The whole process, in short, was guaranteed to produce an olive oil that modern palates would find simply repellent.

After lunch, I took the car up the deserted roads of the Sierra, winding up towards a crag with olives plastered along one flank. I walked for a while among the trees, letting my hands drift over the rugged grey trunks. These were mountain olives, so hardy as to be virtually indestructible, squeezing their nutrients from a soil so poor and thin that nothing else will grow on it except the vine, that other master of economical living.

The province of Jaén is dedicated in heart and soul to the cultivation and culture of the olive. There is nowhere on earth with anything like the surface area given over to olive trees, and nowhere on earth that works quite as hard to do things with them. Of the 220 million trees in the whole of Spain, almost a third are in Jaén. It comes as no surprise that the majority of Spanish olive oil comes from here, but the really impressive statistic is that this single province of Andalucía accounts for almost a fifth of the entire world production of olive oil.

The olive in Jaén is what is called a *monocultivo*. This means that there is only one crop, and what you see is what you get. Almost 85 per cent of the cultivatable land around here has olive trees growing on it. The plantations of Jaén, covering more than 600,000 hectares, have been called the largest man-made woodland in the world.

The city of Jaén has its own real cathedral – a neoclassical temple on such a monstrous scale that it dwarfs everything else in the city, the twin towers of its grand façade a landmark for miles around. But at ground level, just opposite the façade across the cathedral square, proudly stands an ancient olive tree, as if to say: I, too, have a claim on the souls of these people.

Taking the road out of Jaén towards Baeza, I launched myself into the sea of grey-green, turning off at the sign that reads: Cortijo de Nuestra Señora de los Milagros. Earlier that year, someone had given me an olive oil that had impressed me so much with its elegantly restrained aromas of cut grass and apples that I had copied the address in a notebook before setting out for Jaén.

Our Lady of the Miracles was a rare example of a privately owned farm producing and selling its own oil, since most of the land round here was worked by faceless agribusinesses. Luis, the guy who showed me round, was a scion of the Montabes family that owned the 850-hectare property. He was a big boned, pale-skinned, energetic young man, a Spanish businessman of the most modern kind, shiny with the American patina of marketing and PR.

The *cortijo* was a plain white building with bright green shutters on the windows, in the classic style of the andaluz country house. Ensconced in a niche in the hallway was a Barbie-sized figure of the Virgin Mary, she of the Miracles, sitting pretty in a long silk dress. Upstairs was a living room with a beamed ceiling, antique lamps and coloured tiles, and dark Spanish furniture against the white-washed walls.

There might have been a better time to visit, if I had thought about it properly, than a month of the year when the olive harvest is in top gear, when farm managers are scurrying hither and thither and the air is thick with activity and stress. As it was, Luis Montabes attended me with the affable courtesy I have become used to in the Spanish – particularly, for some reason, in those of them involved with the business of food.

Luis switched off his mobile and led me up a thin metal staircase to a walkway where we stood for a while, looking down on a giant hopper in which the olives, a blur of purple and green, looked more like a liquid than a collection of solids, churning and bubbling as the multicoloured mass moved slowly downwards. On a day like today, the factory was working at full capacity, humming in a controlled fury of trembling, rattling metal.

As an industry, Jaén's olive oil business is all about scale: quantity and scale. From the reception area where the olives are washed and sorted, we strode over to the bodega where thousands of litres of oil were stored in giant stainless-steel tanks that reached to the roof like futuristic silver rockets, and on to the *almazara* itself, where the old business of esparto-grass mats and hydraulic presses has long been replaced by Italian-made machines that pulp the olives and extract the oil by means of a centrifuge. There was little room for romance in this streamlined, neoteric process. One would hardly know what was being made in this room, were it not for the fragrance that hung in the air among the stainless-steel boxes that buzzed and whirred. That fragrance – and the thick runnel of golden liquid that just now emerged from one of the boxes, trickling out of a tube into the vat below. The olives used for the estate's finest oil, the one I had tried and loved for its grassy greenness, were being pressed at a temperature of 29°C, which, nowadays, passes for 'cold pressing', when the olives for most oil are subjected to much higher temperatures for maximum yield.

Climbing into the four-wheel drive, we set off at a great pace along the pitted dirt roads of the estate, twisting and turning into the labyrinth of trees. The *cortijo* has 85,000 of them, Luis told me nonchalantly. At the heart of this artificial woodland, we passed a gang of pickers, laying their green nets under a tree whose branches were bowed under the weight of fruit. A yellow machine like a tractor with a long arm advanced robotically, clamping its arm on the waist of the tree, and the trunk began to vibrate, the whole tree shivered violently from top to bottom, and the olives rained down into the nets below.

Up a steep slope, through a scrub of rock rose and lavender bushes, was the highest point of the estate, a little hill where wild olives grew – scrawny trees whose fruit was as hard and black as lead pellets. To the right was the barren ridge of the Sierra Maǵina, sparkling chalky white in the winter sun. In front of us, down towards the valley, was another vast estate with some 210,000 trees, making it one of the largest olive farms anywhere in the world. From here to the horizon, there was not a fig tree, not a vine, not a patch of vegetables or almond trees, nothing but an expanse of grey-green foliage. From a distance, a large olive plantation looks eerily like an restless ocean. The silvery leaves glitter slightly and, when the wind blows, currents sweep across the canopy of treetops.

'We're in a cold zone here, right on the edge of the sierra, and the Picual olive loves it here,' said Luis. 'Even in high summer, there's a cool breeze. It means our olives are generally healthier than those down there – and the oil is better.'

We tramped a little way further up the hill, startling a group of partridges into flight. Up here were secret remains of an Iberian burial site; treasure hunters had found the coins left behind by a Roman legion.

Back at the farm, we nosed about the installations, Luis showing me the little low whitewashed houses where the olive pickers stayed for the duration of the harvest. In the days before mechanisation, 200 people lived on the estate, which became, in effect, a temporary village, with a school, a bar, a salon for socialising, and a proper old knees-up on the feast of Saint John.

Strictly speaking, the *cortijo* had been a *latifundio*. The term, a crucial element in the historical makeup of rural Spain, implies a large property (*latus*, broad; *fundus*, estate) employing workers who lived and had their being on the estate. In 1930, in the south of the country (essentially Andalucía, Extremadura, and La Mancha), estates of more than 100 hectares occupied as much as 52 per cent of the rural space.

There is no doubt the *latifundio* system has been responsible for some dreadful instances of social injustice. At its worst, it was nothing less than a form of slave labour, under which landless, unsalaried peasants depended on their masters for everything from sustenance to education. In the novel *Los Santos Inocentes*, by Miguel Delibes, everyone's favourite horror story of the *latifundio* system, the miserable lives of ill-clothed, underfed and illiterate employees, are set against the lavish lifestyle of their *señoritos* (the owners), whose periodic visits to the estate to hunt and carouse only serve to exacerbate the shocking inequity of the situation.

Virgin of the Miracles was not that sort of *latifundio*. It was slick, efficient, and democratic. It was a thoroughly modern sort of country estate, the kind of place where the familiar *tu* was universal, the polite *usted* almost obsolete, and there was no doffing of caps.

Luis shook hands with a grizzled elderly man with a gappy grin and a grubby white cap planted squarely on his head. 'This is Paco Yeguas, the man who makes the food for us. His best dish is a rice with rabbit. A nice rabbit from the *finca*. And he's an absolute master of *migas*.' *Migas*, the national dish of the southern Spanish rural working classes – the triumph of artfulness over austerity.

'And what do you put in your *migas*, Paco? Apart from the bread? Chorizo, ham, garlic?' prompted Luis.

'That's right, a good few cloves of garlic,' said the man. 'I don't peel them, just crush them with my hand, they go in whole, and some red pepper, and fry it all up together, the breadcrumbs and everything, and maybe a few eggs from our hens. My *migas* are the way *migas* should be. It's all in the movement of the pan. You've got to keep 'em moving, otherwise they'll burn.'

'Good for you, Paco', said Luis, slapping him on the shoulder.

And we repaired to the *cortijo*, where my host had laid on an aperitif even simpler than Paco's fried breadcrumbs, though the context was a little more refined. In the sitting room, silent apart from a ticking carriage clock, a table had been laid with a white linen tablecloth. A large white plate was overlaid with slices of acorn-fed ibérico ham, so thin it was almost translucent, almost jewel-like in its ruby colour. There was warm bread and cold fino sherry. But the centerpiece of this miniature banquet was the family's finest olive oil, pressed a few days earlier at the Virgin of the Miracles. Luis poured it from the bottle in a thin, silent stream into a soup bowl, where it formed a puddle, the colour coming up bewitchingly against the white china.

Before I left, Luis gave me a five-litre bottle of his oil, and, over the following days and weeks, it would come to occupy an important role in my cooking and my life. The night I got it home, I fried up two eggs in the thick jade-green liquid: they were sublime. The next morning, I dribbled it on hot toast for breakfast; butter held no charms for me now. From then on, it was no holds barred – one minute I was cheerfully ladling it into a bowl of chickpea stew, the next I was mashing it with garlic and herbs to smother a leg of lamb, or beating it up with an egg yolk for a potent greenish-yellow mayonnaise. I made biscuits and rich shortcrust pastry, and an olive-fragrant Spanish béchamel, and a mint-green olive-oil ice cream. Between times, I caught myself drinking the occasional mouthful from a glass, as if it were fruit juice – which, in a way, it is.

But that oil didn't stop at the kitchen door. I found that it worked wonderfully as a moisturiser for scratched and chapped hands. When my neck hurt from sitting at the computer, I massaged it into my aching muscles. After someone told me the gypsies put almond oil in their hair, I even started combing a spoonful into my hair as a natural conditioner – until one morning I woke to find my pillowcase had greasy greenish stains on it, and that was the moment I decided this olive oil thing had probably gone far enough.

CHAPTER NINE

GRANADA

The week after the New Year, an Arctic weather system rolled in from northern Europe, leaving snow in all the right places and in some of the wrong ones. The festive season was officially over, and there was a sense of dyspeptic exhaustion in the air, a feeling that the whole country had simply crawled back under the blankets to sleep off its digestive overdose of shellfish, *turrón*, cheap cava, and late nights.

At Christmas time, Nacho had returned, bringing with him a Palestinian friend who was also his landlady. Haifa's family, an important dynasty of judges and intellectuals, arrived in Jerusalem in the eighth century, at around the time of the first Muslim settlement in the south of Spain. A natural cook in the purest Middle Eastern tradition, she found the simple, savoury dishes of the Spanish traditional repertoire not merely dull, but puzzling in their very plainness. Apart from the intensely pork-oriented nature of the local cooking, which occasionally repelled her (it was not the taboo so much, she claimed, as the excess of fat), what Haifa found hardest to understand was its studied avoidance of those piquant and stimulating flavours which, for her and her culture, were as natural as breathing. Some days, in my kitchen, she would cook up a storm of falafel and hummus and tabbouleh and ground-meat kubbeh, drawing on a rich palette of spices which she had wisely brought with her from Jerusalem, correctly guessing that she might not easily find them here. When it came to my turn at the stove, she would ask plaintively as I prepared a tortilla de patatas, an oven-baked bream, or a baroque *cocido* with ten vegetables and five meats, 'what spices will you use?', seeming to hope I would answer 'allspice, sumac, black pepper, and coriander', instead of 'just salt'.

It was Haifa's first visit to Spain, and she wanted to see the historic remains left by her Arabic forebears in the cities of the South. So we drove through Extremadura from north to south, and through Andalucía from west to east, ending up in the Spanish city which has known best how to maintain the romantic splendour of its Islamic past: Gharnata, in the language of its Arab and Berber colonisers, or, as it later became, Granada. While Haifa and Nacho explored the patios and gardens of the Al-Hamra (the red fort, as it was known by its inhabitants), I roamed the city below, hunting for the roots of modern Spanish cooking in the rich and strange aromas of its Muslim past.

On the face of it, the cooking of Granada didn't seem very Arabic at all. In point of fact, the reality of granadino food seemed about as far removed as possible from the kaleidoscopic, highly spiced dishes that would have been common fare in the city as recently as 500 years ago. The books of traditional cooking I looked at in libraries and bookshops were endless parades of *pucheros, cocidos, gachas, migas, sopas,* and *potajes,* flavoured with nothing more exotic than garlic, pimentón, oregano, and the occasional daring, faintly self-conscious foray into cumin, saffron, or chilli pepper. In the restaurants of the city, I tried *habas con jamón*, a sauté of baby broad beans with ham and garlic, and *tortilla sacromonte*, a rich omelette made with lambs brains and testicles, named for the famous district of Granada where hippies and gypsies live bohemian lives in cave dwellings sculpted out of the hillside. In the scalding summers of Granada, I learned, the city lived on refreshing gazpachos and crunchy salads. In the icy winters it fortified itself with monstrous all-in stews, like the *olla de San Antón*, prepared for the feast of Saint Anthony on 16 January, with dried broad beans, dried *alubias*, rice, and a compendium of pork products ranging from salted ribs and fatty bacon to the bones of the spine, the tail, ear, and *careta* (face). Notwithstanding the *alubias*, it is hard to imagine a less Arabic dish than the *olla de San Antón* – indeed, it almost amounts to a slap in the face, a deliberate offence against the exquisite code of Muslim sensibilities.

The Islamic adventure on the peninsula began in AD 711 with the arrival of 10,000 Muslim invaders under the leadership of Tariq ibn Ziyad, who set about founding Europe's first, and so far only, Islamic state, and ended with the final capitulation of Muslim Granada to Ferdinand and Isabella in 1492. The intervening years saw the flowering of a civilisation, known as Al-Andalus, which may justifiably be considered as Islam's most significant historical achievement to date.

When they first disembarked, however, the Moors can't have been impressed with the standard of living on the peninsula, which the Visigoths, never one of history's most dynamic peoples, had allowed to slip back to pre-Roman levels of penury. The land had been poorly managed in the absence of the Romans, so that the Visigothic diet, based almost entirely on cereals and meat, suffered from a chronic lack of variety. As opposed to the Christian triad of meat, wheat and wine, the Andalusians boasted a far more sophisticated culinary universe, in which vegetables and fruit formed a central column, spices were omnipresent, and the arts of *pâtisserie* and sweet-making were raised to the heights of exquisiteness.

After the Nordic blandness of post-Roman cooking, the food of Islamic Spain appears to us now as a brilliant starburst of colour and flavour. The newly irrigated land beside rivers like the Tagus, Guadalquivir, Guadiana, Turia, Júcar, Segura, and Genil, was planted with fruits like the watermelon, imported from Persia, the lemon, lime, and orange, the apricot and quince, the date palm, and the pomegranate, transcendental symbol of the whole enterprise of Moorish Spain. Perhaps the most significant of all the new crops, however, was the sugar cane, planted in the semi-tropical zones along the coast of what is now Motril, south of Granada, where it is still cultivated today (and an acceptable rum produced from its juice, by the firm of Francisco Montero Martín).

At the height of its development, during the twelvth and thirteenth centuries, the cuisine of Al-Andalus was believed to surpass even that of Byzantium in elegance and refinement. At the heart of this cuisine was the crucial importance of spicing, for, as the writer of an anonymous early-thirteenth-century Hispano-Arabic manuscript declares: 'The understanding of the use of spices is the principal basis of all dishes.' The most popular seasonings of the time were saffron, mint, lavender, cardamom, caraway, oregano, coriander, ginger, mustard, pepper, basil, nutmeg, rue, galangal, parsley, aniseed, thyme, cinnamon, cumin, and sumac. It's an impressive list, and one can't help but reflect on two things: one, the fact that the Spanish cooking of today has no use for more than a handful of them; and two, the absence from the list of pimentón, the best-loved Spanish spice of all, which the Moors had a good excuse for not using, since it didn't come into common use until several centuries after the discovery of the New World.

The Arabic influence on later Spanish eating is more a matter of suggestion, of resonance, than of particular ingredients or dishes per se. At least two specific dishes of the arabigo-andaluz repertoire have survived almost unaltered until the present day: *albón-*

digas, meatballs, a comforting staple of tapas bars across the country; and *alboronía,* sometimes called *boronía,* a summer vegetable stew of aubergines, onion, pumpkin, and garlic, made in the province of Córdoba with the addition of tomato and red pepper.

During the golden age of Al-Andalus, in which the three great faiths shared and learned from each other's foodways, Muslims were reported to be incorporating Christian food customs into their religious festivals, and vice versa. In the intolerant new world of the Reconquest, however, everything changed. A kind of ethnic cleansing was applied to the culinary arts: henceforth there was to be no more complex spicing, no more titillating combinations of sweet and savoury, no more perfumed sweetmeats. Any deviation from the official Catholic diet could be, literally, the death of you.

Either way, something happened to put a barrier between the cuisines of Araby and their assimilation and continuance in the post-1492 world. It is not only the history books that are written by the conquerors, after all, but the cookbooks as well. In food terms, what we are talking about is not so much a clash of civilisations as a gulf between culinary cultures. Only in a few places might you make the crossing. But the bridges are narrow, long-abandoned, and in poor repair.

José Luis Vázquez González, chef and researcher, was trying to make the connection. His restaurant, the Colina de Almanzora, occupied the top floor of a house in the shadow of the Red Fort, down by the meandering river Darro. The restaurant sat above a hammam and teashop, which had stayed open when the restaurant had closed after a legal row over wheelchair access. Señor Vázquez now had another place just off the Calle Recogidas, but the bourgeois patrons of the new town were not like the curious foreigners and free-spirited bohemians of the Albaicín. He would begin this new adventure with a classic Spanish menu, and bring in the old dishes stealthily, one by one, so that, by the time his well-to-do clients realised they were actually eating Arabic food, and enjoying it, it would be too late.

José Luis was born in Arcos de la Frontera, one of the famous 'white towns' draped like snowdrifts over the mountains of Cádiz. His culinary memories are rooted in such curious and now-forgotten foods as *meloja*, a dessert of melon cooked in honey, and *queso en borra*, a goat's cheese rolled in breadcrumbs and cured in the lees of last year's olive oil. He was trained as a cook in the city of Cádiz. When he married a granadina and moved to Granada, however, his perspective subtly changed. In a city with such a rich Islamic legacy, it made sense to consider the idea of serving traditional recipes from its era of greatest splendour – that of the Nazrid dynasty, who brought forth one of the wonders of the Western world and promptly disappeared in a puff of jasmine-scented smoke.

I stood in the kitchen and watched him prepare for me a dish that, in fourteenth-century Granada, would have been a familiar recourse. Its two main ingredients were aubergines, then, as now, probably the most popular of all vegetables in Granada, and a 'honey' that is really a kind of molasses, boiled down from the juice of the sugar-cane. This *miel de caña* was used both in sweet and savoury contexts: as a dressing and marinade for meat, and to drench sticky almond pastries.

The thin aubergine slices had been soaking overnight in a mixture of milk, honey, salt and pepper. Now José Luis drained them off, patted them dry, and coated them in a batter turned an amazing shade of bright orange-yellow by powdering a good pinch of toasted saffron threads and adding them to the mixture. The use of saffron, he explained, was limited to the houses of Gharnata's upper classes – as, curiously enough, was coriander, a much cheaper and more easily cultivated herb. Then he fried the battered pieces in thick green olive oil and heaped them on a multi-coloured plate, the rich saffron yellow standing out photogenically against the blues and greens of traditional andaluz ceramic ware. The sugar-cane honey, produced in the village of Frigiliana by the last practitioners of a craft established by the Moors, was dribbled over the fritters in a thin stream that dripped into dark puddles on the plate beneath them.

'Fátima, turn on the lights in the dining room, would you?' he called out to a waitress as he turned off the stove and we went in to eat.

CHAPTER TEN

CACERES

The anthropologist Marvin Harris has a theory that the human race can be divided into porcophobes and porcophiles: those cultures that flee from the pig as a taboo animal and want nothing to do with it, alive or dead, and those that make pork meat a central plank of their nutritional and culinary lives.

This being the case, there can't be much doubt about which side of the fence Spain comes down on. This is a nation whose love of pork in all its forms comes close to worship. There is even a popular saying: *del cerdo me gusta hasta los andares*, 'I like everything about the pig, even the way it walks'.

Yet the relationship is more complex than meets the eye. Even the most porcophile cultures have an element of love-hate in their love for the pig, but the Spanish attitude verges on schizophrenia. Of all the many Spanish words for pig – *guarro*, *cochino*, *marrano*, *puerco*, *cerdo* – not one is free from the taint of something gross, disgusting, or filthy. *Porquería* is dirt or mess; *una guarrada* is an act of physical or moral vileness. For a Spanish speaker, the worst kind of envy, *envidia cochina*, is that which is supposed to be experienced by pigs.

When I first lived in Spain, I was surprised at how seldom you saw pigs, given the fact that the country harbours half as many pigs as people (22.1 million of them, to be precise). I soon learned that you are never very far from one, it is just that their owners hide them away in hovels, in caves and holes in the ground, as if ashamed of their existence. In country areas, in the domestic context, the pig is nearly invisible. I have been walking past a high wall when a sudden sweet stink and a low kind of grumble betrayed the presence of a pig behind it.

One of my first neighbours kept a pig in a kind of underground cellar with no window. Her only contact with the animal was the moment, once a day, when she opened the door to hurl a bucket of kitchen slops directly into the ankle-deep muck in which it lived. This went on until the day of the *matanza*, when her attitude suddenly changed. Once dead, the pig was a thing of beauty, endlessly bounteous, and a source of delight. Thanks to the pig, the family would be nourished and fattened, deliciously, for the best part of a year. Why, then, had the animal deserved so little attention during its life? One Spanish writer talks about 'public shame and private honour'; the pig is a guilty secret, fêted behind closed doors, but socially inadmissible.

In any case, the roots of the pig problem lie deep in the strata of Spanish history. For centuries, if not millennia, the pig was an object of cultish devotion. The stone *verracos* in certain Castilian villages, while their religious significance is not well understood, are supposed to be primitive Iberian representations of boars or pigs. Porcophilia raged during the Roman era; the words *long-aniza* and *morcilla* come from the Latin; and the various *botillos* and *botelos* and *butiechus* of Galicia and Asturias all proceed from the word for its large intestine, *botulus*. The invasion of the Moors in AD 711 brought a first wave of porcophobia to the peninsula, though the Muslims of Al-Andalus were never too strict in their interpretation of Koranic dietary laws. (In a village of the Alpujarras, last refuge of the Moors after the fall of Granada in 1492, I have heard it said these last Muslims happily ate wild boar, a forbidden food, with a sauce made of forest berries.)

It was among the Jews, however, that the issue of pork became a matter of life or death. According to the ultimatum issued by the Catholic kings, the Jewish community faced a stark choice: conversion to Catholicism, or expulsion from the country. Consumption of pork was then a crucial outward sign of religious difference, and soon became a touchstone. Converts embraced the former taboo with an enthusiasm born of sheer terror. Perhaps, if they showed their liking for pork in no uncertain terms, if they festooned their kitchens with chorizos and laced their (hitherto pork-free) *adafinas* with bacon and sausages, and especially with *morcilla*, which, being made with pig's blood, was doubly offensive to the laws of Kosher, the thought-police of the Inquisition might leave them alone? If their repulsion ran deep, they would have to do everything in their power not to show it. Of course, there were those Jews who, while outwardly observing the forms of Christianity, continued to practise their ancient rites in secret, sometimes for generations afterwards. These secret Jews were given the scornful, as well as paradoxical name of *marranos*.

The annual ritual of the pig slaughter is of capital importance in the social history, as well as the culinary history of Spain. For a rural population living permanently on the cusp of poverty, in which every calorie had to be worked for, the pig killing had an importance difficult to overestimate. This was where people found the proteins and fats their bodies needed for their lives of hard physical labour.

At some point along the historical timeline, however, obligation began to be replaced by free will – and this moment is also the beginning of the history of gastronomy. The consumer of our time can choose from a complete range of meats, yet pork will always occupy a special place in Spanish hearts. I once saw a straw poll in a magazine in which participants were asked to name the single food they found most delicious, the edible luxury they wouldn't be without. More than two thirds of them said jamón serrano (a good proportion of the rest, by the way, said tortilla de patatas). But Spanish charcuterie goes a lot further than ham. Pork products in the form of *embutidos* (from the verb *embutir*, meaning to stuff, and hence meaning 'sausages') span out into an expanding universe of chorizo, *salchichón, morcilla, botifarra, morcón, chistorra, botillo, sobrassada, longaniza,* among others, each with its regional heartland and enthusiastic fan base. For older country folk, particularly, there is something succulent and special about a lump of *tocino* or *panceta*, crisped up in a frying pan or allowed to melt unctuously into the surroundings of a chickpea stew. Like Leopold Bloom in *Ulysses*, who 'ate with relish the inner organs of beasts and fowls', many Spaniards still have a thing for what is known as *casquería*: what you might call the offcuts of the pig, its feet and snout and heart and ears and tongue. Though losing its popularity as the modern squeamishness with regard to food takes hold, there are people in Spain who will still drive for miles to eat pork muzzle in a gelatinous sauce, or a pig's ear, sliced up small and flash fried with plenty of garlic. To say nothing of *cochinillo* – the suckling pig that, in the Castilian city of Segovia, is a branch of pork cookery in its own right, as well as an industry that gets through no less than 68,000 piglets a year.

I left Granada, and Andalucía, on the kind of bright, clear, sunflooded morning which anywhere else but the south of Spain would have trouble recognising as a winter day. There was colour in the landscape, and the afternoons were mild: it was shirtsleeve weather.

Back home in the far west, it was scarves and woolly jumpers. There had been a month's rain, then the temperature had dropped like lead, plunging the sierra into night after night of withering frosts. Nacho had left again for Palestine, and, in the absence of its principal carers, our little farm had taken on a sadly uncared for, wintry aspect. There were no more apples on the trees, no more olives, no more chestnuts. All that could be seen in the orchards were a few late persimmons, lighting up the leafless trees with their bright scarlet baubles. Meanwhile, in the vegetable patch, ranks of cabbages were the last crop to resist the relentless cold.

Here, in this outpost of deep Spain, life and work are on the small scale. My neighbours in the village are mostly farmers working tiny patches of land, with a patch of vines, an olive grove, herds of goats and sheep, and fruit and vegetables for domestic consumption. But a minority operates on a much larger scale, with cattle grazing on wide estates in verdant valleys.

The Téllez family belongs in the latter category. They run a ninety-hectare farm on the rolling plains a few miles outside the village of Villacolmena, a few miles from my own small-holding. Extensive beef farming is the family's main business, together with sheep, several thousand olive trees, and a guest house for the few intrepid tourists who make it to this western frontier country. Antonio Téllez is a villager who left for Bilbao to study and find work, in the post-war era when times in Extremadura were especially hard. There, in the Basque country, he met his future wife, and they returned with a son and three daughters to set up the farm on a property Antonio had recently inherited.

I left my house in the icy dark of a January morning, and arrived at the Téllez farm as the sun was coming up reluctantly over the sierra.

The Téllez parents and children were firm friends of mine, but unfamiliar faces loomed up out of the dawn light. The people who stood in the kitchen drinking coffee were villagers who had always helped out at *matanzas* in return for a daily wage and/or an armful of chorizos. Felipe, the farm hand, was also the pig-killer. Jesús would be the butcher, while his wife Petri was the main *matancera*, responsible for the processing of the meat. In the old days, the expert country women who came to work at *matanzas* were known as *sabias* – wise women – and were accorded a great deal of respect. One can understand why: if the *matanza* was mishandled, a year's supply of meat might be in jeopardy.

Petri was mopping out the *matanza* kitchen, a special room used only for preparing and storing the products of the day, and specially kitted out with a fireplace and a ceiling stuck with bent nails for hanging the sausages. Everything was quiet, but not for long.

'For three days from now, everything is the *matanza*. Nothing else matters,' murmured Petri. We were already on *matanza* time, and the routines and rhythms of normal life had ceased to exist. The *matanza* forms a whole world, a time and space of ritual and concentration. It has its own rhythm, a series of paragraphs that follow on one from another with the mysterious, ineluctable logic of a dream.

Out in the countryside, the holm oaks had a grey-green pallor, as if stricken by the cold night, and a deeper gleam of green towards the trunk where the cold couldn't reach. There is no more noble Spanish tree than the *encina*: half of the country is sustained by it. The pigs in their enclosure were already up, snuffling about in the short grass in the morning sun, vainly searching for any last remaining acorns, nuzzling the gate with their snouts. They were pure-bred ibéricos, floppy eared and long muzzled, with leathery skins of a dusty charcoal grey.

The ibérico pig is black and comely. It walks on the finest of elegant hooves, shiny and black and delicately formed, so that it seems to go about on high heels. One somehow expects a semi-wild pig to look more like a wild boar: fierce-looking and filthy, covered in thick matted hairs and crashing through the undergrowth. In fact, the ibérico pig is practically hairless, and has a rather statuesque and refined build.

The *cerdo ibérico* is a descendant of the wild boar *Sus medi-*

terraneus, which once roamed the forests of the Mediterranean basin. For centuries, it was the only pig breed of any importance in Spain, until the arrival of 'white' breeds, like the Duroc and Landrace from northern Europe, with their lean meat and adaptability to the new intensive farming. By the 1970s, the pure ibérico pig was virtually extinct, surviving on a few *fincas* that had failed to adapt to the changing times. The first *denominaciones de origen* in the late 1980s defined the breed as a crucial element of the finest Spanish hams, and eventually the *cerdo ibérico* has made a triumphant recovery.

The ibérico pig is umbilically linked to its habitat. So much so that writers on the subject habitually use the French term *terroir* to refer to the set of environmental factors which make *jamón ibérico de bellota* what it is. The pig and the *dehesa* were, almost literally, made for each other. The whole process, from holm oak to ham, is, in fact, as one Spanish writer wonderingly remarks, 'a system so perfect that it seems almost impossible that it was achieved empirically.'

The killers came out of the house, marching purposefully towards the pigsty. Toothy grins and glinting knives, a rifle loaded and ready, and a bucket to catch the blood.

'Let's go kill the pig,' said Felipe, looking like Hollywood's image of a serial killer with a black rag tied around his head and a dazed, psycho smile.

'Make sure you get the blood,' called Antonio from the house, 'or my wife will kill you.'

The next thing I knew, Felipe was right inside the enclosure. He raised the gun and fired, and the first pig was down. But Felipe had picked a bad place, right beside the frozen pond. The pig tumbled straight in, smashing the ice and flailing about, her blood dyeing the water bright red like a slaughtered whale. She's not dead yet, said Petri in her green apron from the Carrefour hypermarket, peering at the twitching body in the freezing water, while the menfolk swore blue murder. The second pig went better: shot clean through the brain, it dropped like a stone. Now, as her husband went for the jugular with his razor-sharp kitchen knife, Petri moved in with the bucket, stirring the bright hot blood with her hand. The blood and mud and cold of the *matanza* battlefield – this is the hardest moment of the day. When the others left to dispatch the third pig, I stayed on to watch the first one die, spasming there in front of me, her death rattle like a smoker's cough.

The three corpses were lain out on the green grass, crusted with mud and blood. Ready to have the hairs burned off them with gas burners, the first layer of epidermis blistered and scraped off with knifes and brushes. Jesús and Petri and Felipe and me, scratching and scraping the pig's body, our nostrils full of the slaughterhouse smells of burning hair, shit, and warm meat. This depilation was leaving this grey pig ivory white, like a posh lady at a health farm.

'Better make sure we keep the cheeks,' said Jesús, carefully shaving the pig's flabby chops. 'They're better than the meat!' he exclaimed, declaring there and then he would grill these leathery delicacies on the barbecue and share them even with those doubters who could not see quite where their attraction lay.

He was gearing up for the day's major task: the deconstruction of the three pigs, and their classification according to body parts and types of meat: lean, gelatinous, fatty, and bony. From now on the *matanza* would have a new scenario – a garage storeroom off the main farmyard, where the spare parts for the car, motorbikes, and powertools had been pushed back to make space for an impromptu morgue.

Jesús opened the pigs like treasure chests, revealing their caverns of pearly white lard, the steaming architecture of bone and muscle. He leant into them and pulled out a succession of bits and pieces: the liver, a hot shiny floppy thing, seeming to cling like an octopus to the butcher's hand; the long snake of the loin, a metre-long tube of flesh; the heart, kidneys, ribs, lungs. The noble parts are handled with care: the hams and forefeet, carved away from the rest of the body and neatly trimmed, to be hung overnight and buried in salt.

The ignoble parts, hauled out and flopped stinking into a sack, to be buried in the countryside and dug up by foxes.

What is this body part: spleen, thyroid, or pituitary? Distant memories of school anatomy classes came swimming back into my mind; little did my teachers suspect the uses I might find for them. A constant stream of banter flowed around the room: what goes where, how much fat to lean, what do we do with the tails – and what about the ears? (They are used, in fact, for the chorizo *de sábado*, an *embutido* from southern Extremadura, making good use of pig body parts that other sausages cannot reach.) There is meat for freezing, bones for stock, fat for rendering, leftovers for the dogs.

Like any other sort of collective creative endeavour, the *matanza* has a power structure and bureaucracy. Today, the absent patriarch, the unseen CEO, was the farm's owner, Antonio, while his wife, Ana Luz, was catering manager and chef de cuisine. Jesús was chief of butchery operations, while queen of the *embutidos* was Toni, a *matancera* in love with her craft and a cook of the old school who learned from her mother, worked firmly within the traditions of Extremadura, and wrote down her recipes in a girlish hand in an exercise book with the pages falling out.

Toni's frilly red-and-white polka-dot apron gave her a sunny southern look, like a Seville gypsy off to the fair. This morning she had painted her lips bright red, to match her apron and the general bloody, cheerful redness of the day. She was a robustly handsome, good-humoured Spanish woman, brimming with an old-fashioned pride in her house and cooking and husband and family.

'Remind me to give you the recipe for my lamb *caldereta*,' she said to me confidentially, as we worked side by side, knives separating lean meat for chorizo from fat for *morcilla*. 'It's the real and authentic shepherd's *caldereta*. My recipes are village recipes, the ones you don't see in books. You ought to try my way with lamb chops. What I do is: I crush up garlic, parsley, black pepper, and a little bit of vinegar, and I cover the chops with this, and I leave it for a day. Then I cover the chops in flour and beaten egg, and fry them in hot oil. It's a dish for a day out in the country. I take them with me in a Tupperware box. You can eat them hot or cold.'

Toni was now hard at work, trimming the fat off the long thick tube of the loin, slicing away with a practised hand. The loin would be rubbed with garlic and pimentón and stuffed into a casing, air-cured along with the chorizos, eventually becoming what is known as *lomo embuchado*.

I took a sneaky look at her exercise-book recipe collection, which was an anthology of extremeño cooking the like of which, as its author had intimated, you wouldn't find in any published book. The *perrunillas* and *dulces de chicharrones*, traditional biscuits made with pork fat and olive oil and almonds and anis, were not sweetmeats that anybody ate much any more, let alone bothered to cook. Here was a fine traditional dish made during Holy Week in Toni's home town of Almendralejo, composed of chickpeas with chard, flavoured with cumin, black pepper, garlic, vinegar, and pimentón. And here was Toni's famous *caldereta de pastor*. The *caldereta* was traditionally eaten in two parts, the thin sauce as a soup with slices of bread soaked in it, followed by the meat. Toni's recipe was a superbly authentic piece of local lore, and a powerful evocation of a farming society that has never quite forgotten from whence it came. In its big, strong flavours of pimentón, bay leaf, garlic, and wine, it seemed to sum up the hard-bitten, yet generous character of a region that, in the five years I have lived here, I have come to love zealously, possessively.

The name says it all: ferociously hot in summer and often miserably cold in winter, Extremadura can be an unforgiving place. For centuries, its people, of whom there are fewer per square kilometre than anywhere else in Spain, have left the region in search of work, ending up in Bilbao, Barcelona, Madrid – anywhere but here. Most of the great conquistadores of the sixteenth century, like Cortés and Pizarro, were extremeños, who presumably felt they had nothing to lose by taking on the perils of the New World.

This is cattle country first and foremost, which, in food terms, means three things: fresh meat, cured meat, and cheese. From the *cerdo ibérico*, the black-foot pig which feeds on the acorns of Extremadura's holm oak plantations, come the region's serrano hams, chorizos and *salchichónes*. The beef and lamb are of exceptional quality. And the cheeses are simply some of the very best in Spain. The Torta del Casar and its close relation, the Torta de la Serena, are luxuriously gooey Vacherin-type sheep's-milk cheeses which you scoop out of the shell with a spoon, or with pieces of toast or bread in the manner of a fondue; the Queso Los Ibores, from the hills around Guadalupe, is, to my mind, one of the three or four best goat cheeses in the country. Add to this the honeys of Las Hurdes, the cherries of El Jerte, olive oil, game, wild mushrooms, figs, asparagus, and some increasingly highly rated wines, and you have a larder pretty well stocked with good things.

There is one local product, though, which eclipses all others. The fame of pimentón has crossed both national and international boundaries. When the Emperor Charles V built his monastery-retreat at Yuste, among the fertile valleys of La Vera, Extremadura became a natural point of entry for the plants and products of the New World, of which none was to have such importance in the future development of Spanish cuisine (apart from the tomato, of course) as the pepper and its large extended family. *Pimentón de la Vera* is a spice produced by drying peppers over a smouldering fire of holm oak logs and grinding them to a powder. It has various gradations of heat, from *dulce* (sweet) through *agridulce* (bitter-sweet) to *picante* (hot), and gradations of colour from fiery blood-orange, to rust-red and ecclesiastical crimson.

Together with saffron, pimentón is the quintessential Spanish flavouring. (They are the colours of the flag, deep yellow and pomegranate red.) It is certainly the one that most Spanish cooks would not be without. It is ubiquitous in kitchens across the country, from Galicia, where life would grind to a halt without its presence in *pulpo a feira*, to the Balearic islands, where I have used catering bags of the stuff to make the raw pork sausage sobrassada (pimentón is a powerful natural preservative).

In my kitchen at home, I often use pimentón in summer gazpachos, in chutneys and pickles, even in the marinade for cured olives. My experiments have taught me that rubbing a leg of lamb with a pimentón, garlic, and olive oil paste before roasting gives the meat a tandoori-like fragrance and tenderness. Even a humble fried egg can be given a lift by whisking half a teaspoonful of pimentón and a little salt and pepper into the remaining olive oil and drizzling this sauce over the egg. A salad of cooked yellow French beans, chopped boiled egg, and yellow tomatoes is stunningly transformed by a blood-red pimentón vinaigrette – an idea I stole from chef Marcelo Tejedor at Casa Marcelo in Santiago de Compostela.

And it's pimentón, without a doubt, that constitutes the soul of the *matanza*. When Saint Martin's tide comes round in Spain, the pimentón factories of La Vera see their stocks dwindle, as *matanceros* all over the country buy in the big bags they will need for making their chorizos, their *sobrassadas*, and their *lomos embuchados*.

A shiny two-kilo bag of it stood on the sideboard in the *matanza* kitchen at the farm, ready for whatever use we might find for it. Now the wooden trough called the *artesa* came into its own. This traditional object persists in rural areas as a mixing vessel for large quantities of food, whereas, in the cities, it has already become a chic decorative item.

Now the *matanceras* from the village were down on their knees at the *artesa*, kneading the greasy mixture as if it were dough. They were up to the elbows in meat, their arms stained an unfeasible shade of radioactive orange. This would be the filling for the chorizos, flavoured with pimentón and mashed garlic.

'You always add a little water. The pimentón is dry, it takes in moisture,' said Petri, puffed from her energetic workout of the arms.

There are no recipes – it is all done, first by eye, then by taste. How much garlic, how much salt? *Lo que pide*, says Nieves: what it asks for. Nothing is prescribed. The measurements are a lot, less than that, a little, and a handful more. Experienced mixers can tell by the colour it leaves on your hands, when examined in the cold white light of a winter afternoon.

But the proof of the pudding, or of the chorizo and *morcilla*, is in the eating. In Spanish it is called *la prueba*. A little of the mixture is fried up in a small pan, and tasted for the balance of its seasoning. Is it short on garlic, pimentón, or salt? More of whatever is required is added to the mixture. If the *prueba* has its origin in the functional apparatus of the *matanza*, it has now become a popular dish in its own right.

A little more of this and that, humming and ha-ing over the various recipes. The *prueba* is always a rich seam of controversy and argument. This should be saltier, this can take a little bit more black pepper. This needs more pimentón; this has quite enough already! The sizzling spicy orange mixture is sampled direct from the pan, forks clashing together in the general eagerness to try a mouthful with a slice of bread. Somebody had brought their homemade wine in a two-litre Fanta bottle with the label still on, and we took big swigs from plastic cups besmeared with grease.

What with all that talk of food, and the appetite you work up over a *matanza* morning, the *prueba* serves as a fine excuse for a late-morning snack, but now the various mixtures were ready, and the time had come to wash our hands and arms, remove our orange-stained aprons, and sit down to eat a proper lunch.

In the old days, everything about the *matanza* was programmed with the precision of a religious rite. Even the food, which, in Villacolmena, was served and eaten according to a cast-iron timetable. The breakfast on a *matanza* morning was *migas* with glasses of *aguardiente*. Every porcophile village in Spain has its own *plato matancero* – the dish made at midday on *matanza* days. Here, in Villacolmena, it was kidneys and brains, with a pounded *majao* of garlic and breadcrumbs. And, in the afternoon, *roscas fritas*, an egg dough with lard and anis, fried until crisp in virgin olive oil.

'Before, when we finished in the evening, we had chocolate with churros, like when we finished with the olives, and we used to sing songs', reminisced Petri.

'How the old things come back into fashion!' cried Antonio. 'What I remember is the *mojo de naranja*, the orange salad with olive oil and onions, which nowadays you find in the best restaurants. I used to eat it for breakfast as a child, when my mother came back with the milk.'

Cooking is a reflection of personal circumstance, a codified version of everything you are in genes, history, and taste. Ana Luz grew up in Bilbao and the dishes she feels closest to are the classic pillars of Basque cuisine, salt cod *al pil pil* and *a la vizcaina*, hake in green sauce. A woman of substance and efficiency and a certain rough-hewn generosity, the way Basque women often are, Ana Luz doesn't just use her kitchen, she inhabits it. If I think for a moment, I can sum up in my mind the memory of her piquillo peppers stuffed with crab . . . a sumptuous flan made with milk from the farm's house cow . . . and a phenomenal dish of veal with artichokes, based on a *sofrito* of tomato and onion, a dish that anthologises all the organic, exuberant flavours of spring. Trays of *pinchos* emerge from Ana Luz's kitchen, as good as anything you might grab from a bar top in San Sebastián. Her *croquetas* are sublime nuggets of creamy filling, creatively deploying not only chopped ham and chicken, the essential traditional *croqueta* ingredients, but chopped mussels, *bacalao*, boiled egg, partridge meat, and, best of all, the shredded leftover meat from the Sunday *cocido*.

When Ana Luz married Antonio and made the move southwards, her cooking naturally responded to the change. In her new home, there was little seafood to be had, and a cuisine that has none of the refinement of Basque tradition, but a tremendous quantity and quality of meat. Now she was making *caldereta*, and rich sticky stews from the gelatinous cuts of pork and beef. Today, for lunch, she served liver with onions, and slices of goat's cheese in olive oil, and cuttlefish in an inky-black sauce, and *esparragao*, a hearty country dish of cabbage and potato quick-simmered with olive oil, garlic, and pimentón. It was the first time she had ever made this extremeño dish, but the villagers approved entirely. They nodded their heads as they ate: *si señor*, this was a good *esparragao*, even if Ana Luz's addition of thin-sliced fried *panceta* struck them as a sophisticated departure from the norm.

After lunch, there was coffee and walnut *turrón*, but no dithering at the table. With weary steps, we made our way back to the *matanza* kitchen. Outside, the afternoon was as cold and dark as lead. Our nerves were a little frayed, our senses a little dulled by the copious food and wine. But the last, trickiest, most important, and most longwinded of all the *matanza*'s panoply of processes now awaited us.

We stood around the table, each with our role to play. While one turned the handle of the big cast-iron meat grinder, forcing the mix down a spiral and into the skins, another tied the strings in a double knot, another pricked the sausages with a cork stuck with pins, to release the air trapped inside, and a gopher fetched the curling lengths of shiny sausage from the heap on the table and hung them up in ranks from the ceiling. How thoughtful of nature to provide, as part of the generous package of the pig, not only the meat for sausages, but also the containers with which to make them.

These are repetitive, fiddly tasks, and an atmosphere of quiet badinage develops, in which the subjects for discussion are the difference between women and men, illnesses, the gossip in the village, and, most commonly, the various ways in which the *matanza* is performed in the various villages of the region, and remembered *matanzas* of the past.

The timing of the event, earlier or later in the season, is a constant source of comment.

'Have you already killed? Yes, we killed last week.'

'On Monday my sister-in-law is killing.'

'We usually kill in the month of January.'

In an hour or two of purposeful stuffing and trying and knotting and pricking, we were finally done.

For the residents of the farm, there was still plenty of work ahead. The chorizos and *salchichón* turning slowly darker in the air, shrinking and hardening and drying. They would have to be checked on, and smoked a little with the coals from the grate if the humidity went too high, and sprinkled with pimentón if a crack appeared in the skin. Walking into the storeroom a month after the *matanza*, when the roof is garlanded with sausages and filled with a marvellous aroma of the curing meats, one has a moment of surprise at discovering that all that bounty has appeared there, as if by magic. There would be hams to salt and dry, bags of meat to freeze, lard to clarify, and, the best of all, the Spanish sausages to make. Ana Luz's family has roots in Villarcayo, heartland of the *morcilla de Burgos*, which she still makes at the farm according to the original recipe, with the pig's blood, poached onion, cooked rice, and a generous seasoning of allspice, clove, and black pepper.

But for the support team, the helpers, the *matanza* was over for another twelve months – and thank goodness, really, that it only happens once a year. I climbed stiffly into the car with a Tupperware box full of *prueba* to try some other time. My hands felt soft and supple on the driving wheel. All those hours with the pork fat had served as a luxurious manicure.

I turned on the engine, the heating, and the music. A profound tiredness had taken root in me, as well as a powerful need to steer clear of animal fats for a while. I may be a practising porcophile, but the *matanza* certainly tests the limits of your love for pork products, and pigs, and so on. What with all the bean stews, the *gachas* and *migas*, the dense country foods I'd been eating in recent weeks, I felt like one of those ibérico pigs, fattening up for slaughter.

Then and there, as I sat in the car with the engine running, I modified my travel plan. In my journeyings around Spain's wide interior, I had picked up rural essences galore – most of them based around fats and proteins, the basic building blocks of rural food. Yet Spanish country cooking is not all pork and pork fat. It is also vegetables, and, depending on the region, these play as important a role in the nourishment of the rural community as does meat. Now I promised myself a break from the hard core culinary culture I'd been immersed in of late. I would wait for spring to bring in its first fruits, and then I would head for a place that really knows its onions, and its lettuces, and its artichokes: the vegetable paradise of Navarra.

CHAPTER ELEVEN

NAVARRA

For most of the winter in most of Spain, the range of available greenstuff shrinks to a minimum of cabbages and other brassicas, chard and spinach and leeks, plus anything the resourceful house-holder has been able to bottle over the summer. Then, in February or March, a wave of early vegetables ripples across the country, beginning in the coastal zones of the south and east, where the first peas and beans, asparagus and artichokes are celebrated like homecoming heroes.

Six weeks had gone by since the *matanza*. In the mountains of the west, winter clung on, determined to sit it out till the solstice, leaving its nightly calling card of hoar frost on the fields and hedges around my house.

Driving east cross-country was like watching the year in

fast-forward. In Palencia, it was still arctic winter; there was snow on the roofs of the old town, and passers-by were swathed in fur and wool. Tractors were out in the arable plains around Burgos, sowing the first wheat under skies of a tentative blue. And, when I crossed into La Rioja, it was as though spring had arrived just that morning. As I waited by the traffic lights in Navarrete, I noticed an old gentleman pricking out tomato plants in his back garden. The lights turned green, and I thought: the whole of Spain will soon be turning green.

I only had one contact in Tudela, but, if you happen to be interested in vegetables, the King of the Vegetables is a pretty good contact to have.

Tudela is a good-looking medieval town with a distinguished cast of historical characters, chief among them being the twelvth-century mathematician and astrologer Abraham Ibn-Ezra, and the traveller Benjamin of Tudela, whose grand tour of the Jewish communities of the known world is recorded in his famous *Itinerary*. What had brought me to Tudela, however, was not culture or history or famous names, but salad. A sad sign of the times it may be, but, these days, Tudela is a good deal better known by the vast majority of the population for its *cogollo*, a sweet crisp lettuce, than for the life and works of its medieval thinkers.

I steered the car up into the dusty labyrinth of the old town, shuddered to a halt in a parking lot beside the cathedral, and called the only number I had at my disposal. Floren was out, but his secretary answered the phone, and directed me to a bar where, she said, I was sure to find something excellent to eat. The bar in question was the José Luis, just around the corner from the town's main square, where I ordered a beer and a selection of the bar's splendid *pinchos*, which had all won prizes in the local *pincho* contest. All were based on vegetables – as they would be, for Tudela is one of the great horticultural centres of Spain. I began with a miniature brochette, with tomato and prawn and fried leek all wrapped in a spinach leaf on a wooden stick; a nugget of soft cheese rolled in a thin slice of ham and another thin slice of courgette, the whole thing breadcrumbed and deep-fried; and a Swiss chard stem stuffed with thickly creamy béchamel and served straight from the kitchen, sizzling from the hot olive oil. I sat in the sun and watched the tudelanos go by, hurrying to get things done before the shops and offices clanged shut at two o'clock.

Now I needed a proper lunch, followed by a proper siesta to set me back on track. I made my way up to the Plaza de los Fueros and, finding a busy dining room where the lunchtime shift was well underway, headed straight inside with a dazed kind of conviction that this, for sure, would be a good place in which to sample the rustic cooking of Tudela.

The Hostal Remigio was a straight-down-the-line establishment which turned out to have two main things to recommend it: the interior decor, and the food. It had been functioning as a simple lodging house since 1936, and was now in the hands of the Salcedo Zabalza family, who had brought the old place thoroughly up to date, but had sensibly left its original wood-panelled dining room intact. The room was a fizz of activity on this Friday afternoon, black-trousered waiters darting around like wasps. One of them brought me a plastic-covered menu which I gazed at dumbly for a while, not quite able to believe what I was reading. Far from the standard Spanish eating-house fare, all brimming bowls of lentil stew and slabs of meat with chips and salad, the menu at the Hostal was a showcase for all that is best in the regional cooking of this southern corner of Navarra. For anyone who loves their vegetables, this was very heaven: there were broad beans and peas, and artichokes five ways, and little red piquillo peppers stuffed with spider crab, and asparagus and spinach and Swiss chard, and cardoons in almond sauce, and borage stems (*borraja*, the hairy-leafed vegetable unique to the communities of Navarra and Aragon), and scrambled eggs made with the season's first tender garlic. It sounded wonderful, and a small wave of content-ment rolled over me. I ordered a plate of *cogollos*, the crisp sweet lettuce hearts which had, after all, brought me to Tudela – they were draped with salted anchovies and dressed with olive oil – and a soup-bowl of white baby onions *a la tudelana*, simmered in their own juices with olive oil and black pepper until they were tender enough to be guzzled down with just one chew, and a medley of spring vegetables stir-fried separately and briefly bubbled up together: the *menestra* so characteristic of Navarrese and Riojano cooking. After all this, and most of a bottle of cold rosado, the wine that Navarra specialises in, I barely had the energy to pay the bill, enquire whether the Hostal had a room for the night, and haul myself up to the third floor and the siesta I had been dreaming of all day.

When I woke it was evening, and the day had embarked on the long preamble to a late, languid sunset. Just outside the walls of the old town lay an expanse of flatland called La Mejana, where the Arabs and Jews who populated the city in its glory days of the twelfth century kept their vegetable gardens in the rich alluvial soil of the Ebro valley.

The river Ebro is born in the mountains of Cantabria, and reaches the sea at the southernmost tip of Catalunya, where rice is grown among the sluggish waters of its oozing delta. Between Logroño and Zaragoza, it runs its course along a wide flat valley, a thick ribbon of green among the dry hills to the north and south. The town of Tudela, second most important in Navarra (the capital being Pamplona), sits directly upon it, with a stone bridge across its width. I walked halfway across and stood to admire this handsome river, swelling with khaki-coloured water, and thought about the benefits it brings to the vegetable farmers of the Ribera, as this riverine region is known, who irrigate their crops directly with these waters. To my left lay the sprawling Mejana, a district of *huertas*, all with their immaculate ranks of onions and lettuces and broad beans and garlic, their thickets of artichokes, their fig-trees flourishing in the quiet corners, and quinces clinging to the fences.

The *huertas* were a series of private worlds made intimate by hedges and high stone walls. Some had little pavilions for lazy

Sundays, and swimming pools and flower-fringed lawns. I found an open door and stepped inside, surprising an elderly man and his son, who were busy watering their patch, directing the river water down long channels between the rows. There was a little old house at the river end of the plot, on two floors, with whitewashed arches and a weathercock turning creakily above the clay tiled roof. These *casitas* would have been used for storing potatoes and onions, tools and paraphernalia; their upper floors were the architectural response to the Ebro's periodic bouts of flooding.

Here was a scene of rural Spain at its most bucolic. The old man stood with his shirt unbuttoned, leaning on the handle of his mattock. Beside him was an apricot tree, its branches bowed down with fruit. He handed me a couple as the water filled the channel around the tree: they were crisp and barely ripe, but sweet, a foretaste of summer. I wondered whom all this plenty was for: himself, or the market?

'For the family. We don't sell. All my daughters are married, so . . .' He left his explanation hanging in the air, leaving me to form an idea of the demand for vegetables this situation naturally implied. His nearest and dearest would be well supplied, in any case, by this grand *huerta* in which everything was huge and healthy, from the giant cabbages that squeaked when the breeze blew over their fleshy hearts, to the deep green glossy leaves of Swiss chard, wide and wrinkly as elephants' ears.

'In the old days, we used to take in all this stuff to market. I had a cart with iron wheels. The roads were dirt tracks. You should have heard the noise! The carts full of artichokes. Vegetables mean everything to Tudela, everything. Why, this town was built on them! Nowhere else has artichokes like ours, or lettuces, or chard. It's the river, you see, the river. Sweet water. Good water.'

He took up his mattock and swung it down into the earth, pulling open the channel which ran between two long rows of garlic plants. Their leaves were thick and fleshy, the white bulbs still forming in the warm soil.

'José, keep that water coming!' he called to his son. 'Never let it stop!'

In the prologue to her 1913 work *La Cocina Española Antigua*, Emilia Pardo-Bazán declares the central virtues of Spanish cooking to be 'its strong clear flavours, without the ambiguity of sauces and dressing; its picturesque variety according to the regions; its perfect adaptation to the climate and the necessities of man', and, last but not least, its 'vegetarian tendency, perhaps owed to religious ideas and heat'.

I admire the concision of her phrase 'religious ideas and heat', which nicely sums up two of the major determinants of Spanish eating over the centuries, and it seems to me she is right about the 'vegetarian tendency' – even though vegetarianism, in its literal sense, is little practised and still the object of puzzlement and/or hilarity among the older generation. Spain has no trouble whatsoever eating up its greens, and vegetable-based dishes account for a respectable percentage of the national repertoire.

If visitors to Spain are not often impressed by the range and quality of vegetable cookery, it is probably because they are not often brought into very close contact with it. Vegetables here tend to be associated with the honestly nutritive virtues of domestic cookery, as opposed to the kind of more elaborate or highly flavoured food you might want to eat outside the home. I would suggest that, though they might be ashamed of admitting it, many Spaniards have a secret love of *las verduras* that goes above and beyond the thrills provided by more superficially exciting foods.

Vegetables in Spain are most commonly fried or boiled, but you also often find them baked, chargrilled, or raw. The technique of *rehogado* – briefly sautéing a previously steamed or boiled vegetable with a little chopped ham or garlic – is often applied to Swiss chard or green beans. Chopped serrano ham is also a classic flavouring for broad beans (this is the essence of the granadino dish *habas con jamón*) as well as peas. Peppers, aubergines, and courgettes are commonly stuffed with minced meat, rice, or fish –

especially in the Balearic Islands and the province of Valencia, though the stuffed *pimiento de piquillo* is a classic of the Basque-speaking regions of the North (including Navarra). Root vegetables are most often found as ingredients of *cocidos* and similar pulse-based stews, or else in thick winter soups, purées, *cremas* and *potajes*. The tenderest green peppers, like Galicia's *pimiento de Padrón*, can be flash-fried in sizzling olive oil. When summer heats come round and the body craves refreshment, the southern Spanish repertoire of ice-cold soups naturally and gratifyingly comes into its own. But the best way of treating summer vegetables is surely the chargrill, which both brings out their natural sweetness and overlays it with the scent of woodsmoke. One of my all-time favourite vegetable dishes is the Catalan *escalivada* – the word derives from *escaliu*, meaning hot coals – which combines roasted peppers, aubergine, and onion, hand peeled and shredded, dressed with olive oil and vinegar, in a richly harmonious salad that sits perfectly alongside other chargrilled items, like lamb chops or fresh pork sausages.

An unmistakable aura of piety hovers over the vegetable kingdom, and this is partly the legacy of Catholic attitudes to nutrition and morality. Put simply, whereas meat excited the sensual appetite, vegetables were thought conducive to virtue. As Reay Tannahill points out in her *Food in History*, for much of Western history, meat, eggs, and dairy products were prohibited by the Church not only during the forty days of Lent, but also on Wednesdays, Fridays, and Saturdays – half the days of the year. For a great majority of the population, therefore, vegetables would have been a nearly constant presence on the family table, and especially from Ash Wednesday through to Easter Sunday. The important vegetable dishes of the Spanish repertoire, like spinach with pine nuts and raisins, and cardoons in almond sauce, clearly have their origins in the fast-day traditions of the Catholic calendar.

It is true, though, that, while sometimes accorded a supporting role, they are almost never the stars of the show. Most of the regions have at least one fetish vegetable, lusted after as something extra-specially delicious: in Galicia it would be turnip tops, in Catalunya spring onions, and, in parts of the Basque country, the long green chillis which are put up in vinegar and popularly known as *langostinos de tierra* (prawns of the earth). Only in a few places, however, is the vegetable kingdom as a whole given the respect it deserves.

One such place is Murcia, where, as we have seen, lettuces and beans are munched the way other people munch chocolate bars – as a delicious and self-indulgent snack. And another is the strip of land that runs along both sides of the Ebro river, especially in the one hundred or so kilometres from Logroño to Zaragoza, where the river is middle-aged and big-bellied and can afford to be generous with its waters. The Ribera del Ebro belongs, essentially, to two autonomous communities: Navarra and La Rioja. Here, more than anywhere else in Spain, vegetables not only aspire to the condition of meat or fish, but are actually valued more highly than either.

Floren was on a roll. It was a Saturday, and he was in his weekend mode – but then Floren's weekend mode was not perhaps especially different from his weekday mode. He sat squarely at the wheel of his black Mercedes, the music at top volume, cruising down the straight roads of south Navarra as if they were American highways, and shouting into the hands-free when the thing went off, which was every few minutes.

Floren Damenzain was what in Spain is known 'un personaje': quite a character. On the day I met him, he wore a pink T-shirt with a Caribbean palm-tree print, hair pulled back into a Status Quo ponytail, and scuffed black snakeskin moccasins with the backs trodden down. His wide wicked grin revealed a collection of teeth which appeared to justify the American view of European dentistry.

'Are you feeling cold? Thirsty?' he called. He flipped a couple of switches and a panel in the back seat folded down to reveal the in-car fridge with its stock of beers and Cokes. Another switch, and I felt a pleasant glow along my spine: the Merc's heated seats.

If Floren Damenzain tends to call a spade a spade, it must be because he knows better than anyone just exactly what a spade is for. He was raised in a farming family in the village of Arguedas, on the edge of the desert-like landscape of the Bárdenas Reales, a popular location for scenes in movies whose production budgets won't stretch to real Western deserts. There were six children in the family; Floren, the youngest, began a course at agricultural college, but his father's illness forced him to take over the family's one hundred-hectare farm with its mixed plantations of cereal and table vegetables.

'I had no idea about distribution or anything. I was a farmer, that's all. When the land started bringing in a bit of cash, I started up my business. At first it was all stuff from round here, peppers, artichokes, chicory, *borrajas*, cardoons, asparagus, *cogollo* . . . I was going around in a van, just me, with a load of artichokes and salad. And that's how all this started.' Floren made a gesture with his right hand in the air in order to indicate that 'all this' was not just the flash car and its heated seats, but 'my successful business'.

He scrabbled in the side pocket of the door and pulled out a thick folder lavishly illustrated with close-up photos of sexy veg in appealing poses, a pair of hands cradling the dirt. As a sales catalogue, it was an impressive document, with its lists of vegetables both local and imported, its fifteen different peppers, forty different salads, its azuki beans and arbutus fruit and kumquats. The inside cover was a collage of photographs showing Floren with some of the important chefs who, in the eighteen years since the birth of the business, had become his loyal clients. I recognized Nacho Manzano, Manolo de la Osa, Ferran Adrià. Some had added a tribute. Martín Berasategui, proprietor of the three-starred Michelin restaurant of the same name in Lasarte, outside San Sebastián, was pictured alongside the King of the Vegetables. 'Good cooking begins with the good raw materials of my friend Floren,' the chef had written.

We were on our way back to Floren's flat, through streets full of ritzy design shops and cover-girl hairdressers (Tudela seemed to be flush with money, much of it from agriculture), where he had prepared for me a special *menú degustación* based on the produce of the Ribera. Floren's skill in the kitchen is attested to by everyone who knows him – and not least by himself. Of all his brothers and sisters, he was the one who paid most attention to his mother in Arguedas and her loving interpretation of Navarrese classics, like *bacalao al ajoarriero* and vegetable *menestra*. He was a self-taught cook, but this had not stood in the way of his talent, nor his covert influence on chefs of worldwide renown. How many times had he received a desperate phone call from some chef, uninspired, at a loss, or bewildered by some exotic herb just arrived from Floren?

We pulled off the main road and down a dirt track among fields of artichokes, waving prickly heads above the jagged fronds of their leaves.

A structure loomed ahead, a polyhedral construction in wood and concrete. Building work was well under way for a splendid restaurant, no, more than a restaurant, a stately pleasure dome in which to sample the glories of the local produce as prepared by Floren himself. His restaurant would be called, with a logic that was hard to refute, 'The Temple of Vegetables'. The menu would turn around what was grown right here, in the *huerta*, from the giant red cardoons banked up with a miniature mountain of earth, to the salads and beans and *borrajas*, and, naturally, the artichokes, grown just beyond the plate glass windows separating the client from the countryside. Diners at the Temple would be invited to pick the vegetables themselves which they would later eat, just as you pick out your chosen lobster from the tank.

Half an hour later, we were sitting in Floren's flat, which was nicely done up with modern furnishings acquired in Tudela's most fashionable design emporia. My host disappeared to the kitchen and shut the door behind him, leaving me to chat with his girlfriend and an old friend from Zaragoza who wasted no time in inviting us all back to his place for a feast of snails on Sunday afternoon.

The kitchen door opened and out burst the chef, bearing the first two chapters of his special menu: a partridge salad made with his own buttery, crisp *cogollos*, a nest of tender borage stalks on a creamy potato and olive-oil purée; and a square white plate piled with the thickest, whitest, sweetest asparagus stems I had ever tasted, dressed with a fruity, uncomplicated local olive oil.

'You are eating the real, the genuine asparagus of Navarra. You'll remember this taste for many years,' declared my host.

Then, a bowl of fresh artichoke hearts, steamed until they were so tender they melted in the mouth. The flavour was intense, pure and concentrated. As was that of the next dish, tiny peas stewed quickly in their own juices, with nothing more than a spoonful of finely chopped *jamón ibérico de bellota* to offset their almost dessert-like sweetness.

'Just what is it that makes the vegetables of the Ribera the way they are?' I asked Floren.

He took up his catalogue and jabbed his finger at what has become his company's selling line, or slogan, or catchphrase: *Tierra, Agua y Sol* (earth, water and sun). It's obvious really: nothing influences the taste of a vegetable more than its natural environment. 'The soil might be clay-based, chalky, or sandy. Each has its advantages: chalky soil makes the best asparagus, clay the best tomatoes, *borrajas*, and peppers. Soil quality, plus fresh water. And there's something else: we have the best professionals. From the root to the flower and the death of the plant. From the foundations of the house to the pillars of the roof,' said Floren. He was sounding a little mysterious now. None the less, I got the point. It was a question of thorough understanding, of being close to the process from start to finish.

For the people of the Ebro valley, the vegetable kingdom is a fiesta all year round.

'If you were to knock on the door on a weekday lunchtime at any house in the Ribera, what would you find on the table?'

enquired Fernando rhetorically, the aragonese, while his friend
was busy in the kitchen. 'For sure, if it was winter you'd find
chicory, broccoli, cauliflower, cabbage, if it was springtime, asparagus and artichoke; if it was next week, the first *pochas*.' The
pocha is an entirely local phenomenon, a bean that is eaten neither
fresh, nor dried, but somewhere in between.

'Everyone around here has their own *huertá*,' said Floren, as he
came back with the coffee-pot. 'You might be a builder or
electrician, but you're bound to have some little patch to grow
your lettuces in, your *borrajas*, your beans.' Only about 10 per
cent of all the veg consumed in the Ribera is actually bought at the
shops, the rest being accounted for by a network of friends and
neighbours who might be happy to swap a kilo of *borrajas* for a
bagful of artichokes or a box of *cogollos*. We are not talking
economies of scale, or co-operatives, or even business as such, but
a return to appreciating things for the way they taste – with the
added thrill, irresistible to most Spaniards, of being delicately
poised on the edge of illegality.

Back in the Merc, Floren slammed a CD into the hi-fi. It was his
own group, Barricada, in the days when he used to play guitar with
what was, in the early 1980s, Spain's most notorious heavy metal
band. Track 1 came up on the screen, and from just behind my
right ear emerged a blast of grinding rock'n'roll, the bass sounding
like somebody moving furniture. Floren was up on stage again, his
ponytail flying as he nodded in time to the music.

We were heading out of town in the late afternoon. Our
destination was a secret, but I had an idea Floren meant to take
me to the house in Arguedas where his story began, the sprawling
village house where the family kept their fleet of twenty mules in a
stable on the ground floor, and Floren's mum gaven him his bottle
at intervals during her hard work among the artichoke fields.

He pressed a button on the panel and the sunroof slid open.
Floren pushed up his wraparound sunglasses, slid the gearstick
back into fourth, and we sped away through fields of artichokes
turning turquoise-grey in the setting sun.

CHAPTER TWELVE

CATALUNYA

When the Generalísimo Francisco Franco died in 1975 and his faltering regime finally crumbled, there were a lot of pressing questions that needed answering. One of the most urgent of these questions concerned nothing less than the geo-political organisation of the country in a future democratic state. How to give back to the Spanish regions the sense of identity and political autonomy which had been so rigorously suppressed by the Franco regime, while safeguarding the unity of the country as a whole?

The solution reached by the architects of the post-Franco administration was a brilliant one. The new Spain would be a federal state composed of individual regions, each of which would enjoy a measure of autonomy – the Comunidades Autónomas. The great virtue of the system was its flexibility: provinces with little sense of their own identity, such as Castilla y León or Murcia, would be able to exist side by side with regions with a long history of idiosyncracy that felt themselves actually to be nations, such as the Basque country or Catalunya. The Catalan and Basque 'statutes of autonomy' of 1979 were the beginning of an extraordinary process of national self-discovery. Regional languages and cultures, as well as political institutions, that had spent forty years in a state of hibernation, were quickly reborn in all their variegated glory.

By their very nature, the various regional cuisines of Spain had been harder for the dictatorship to suppress – you could hardly have a Guardia Civil watching over every Basque and Catalan and Galician stove – but they had certainly fallen into desuetude. Now they re-emerged as a proud assertion of regional identity. The Catalan nationalist Ferran Agulló (1863–1933) had once declared: 'Catalunya is a nation because it has a language, a legal system [*derecho*] and a cuisine of its own.' For Manuel Vázquez Montalbán, the novelist and *gastrónomo*, one of the major achievements of the new political status quo based on the devolution of power to the 'autonomies' has been the effort expended by each region to rediscover and celebrate its own gastronomic roots. 'The Spanish restaurateur has been obliged to bring back traditional cooking in response to the tastes of his avant-garde clientele, and it's thanks to that social pressure that Spain has not turned into a leathery hamburger, bordering on the quiche lorraine to the north and the couscous to the south.'

Which of Spain's regional cuisines is the best, then? It's a question which has caused almost as many arguments over dining tables as whether Franco actually did anything good for the country. The question really has no possible answer, beyond the equivocal, and boring, notion that each has its own strengths and weaknesses; each is remarkable in its own way.

Ask which is most highly developed, and the question becomes a little easier. Along with the Basque country, Catalunya is surely the region possessing the richest traditional cuisine on the peninsula – as well as the one that is, currently, taking most decisive steps to protect its heritage. Each of the four Catalan provinces – Barcelona, Tarragona, Lleida and Girona – has a distinct culinary personality, and that of Girona, as we shall see, is especially idiosyncratic. Unlike most of the other cuisines of Spain, this one has its basis not just in the rural context, but also in the urban reality of hostels, popular eating-houses, and the homes of the bourgeoisie. Its range and variety is enormous. Pepa Aymamí, of the Catalan Institute of Cooking, estimates there may be as many as 150 individual dishes in the local repertoire – even if the majority of them are little known by the population at large.

Of all the regional culinary traditions of Spain, moreover, there is no doubt which has the most distinguished history. *La cuina catalana* was basking in its first golden age at a time when the great modern cuisines of Europe were as yet unformed. During the fourteenth and fifteenth centuries, Catalan cooking occupied roughly the position in the international gastronomic Champions League as classic French cuisine does today. Some of the most important cookbooks of the Middle Ages were written by Catalans in their own language, and medieval Catalan cuisine enjoyed a reputation only equalled by Italian (with which it shared a number of dishes and techniques, including the use of pasta). The *Llibre del Coch*, written by Robert or Rupert de Nola, the Catalan cook at the court of Fernando, King of Naples, was first published in Barcelona in 1520 and, in its Castilian version, became a bestseller for the next hundred years. But the heritage of Catalan cooking goes even further back than this, into the murky prehistory of European gastronomy. As far back as one of the earliest surviving cookbooks written in a European tongue, the legendary *Llibre de Sent Sovi* of 1324, otherwise known as *De Totes Maneres de Potatges de Menjar* ('Of all manners of eating pottages').

A few years ago, I was lucky enough to see one of the two surviving original copies of this book, to carefully turn its parchment pages and attempt to decipher a few passages of its difficult language and calligraphy. It is bound together with several other medieval texts, has no title page as such, or apparent start or finish, and is composed of such a mass of black inky screed that you ask yourself whether this is really the document that you have come to see. Then, half-familiar words begin to swim out of the chaos. *Si vols fer*: if you want to make. *En altra manera*: in another manner. *Espinachs*; *macarrons*; *alberginies*.

There is a maddening vagueness and disorder about the way the *Llibre* is put together that makes you wonder how much genuine use it can have been to the cooks of the fourteenth century. Quantities seem arbitrary; timings are nonexistent. That said, it contains recipes that sound not only intriguing, but perfectly plausible. *Brou de gallines* is a chicken soup, given a touch of the Middle East by its spicing of ginger and almonds (spices like nutmeg, mace, coriander and hyssop were more freely used in European cooking during this period than at any time until the late twentieth century). You could use the *Sent Sovi*'s recipe for rice pudding with almonds and cinnamon without altering a word.

More than particular dishes, however, it's the techniques that have survived. Fundamental to Catalan cooking both then and now, for instance, are the *sofregit* and *picada*, the beginning and end of most Catalan dishes. The *sofregit* is essentially a sauté of onions and tomato (the *Sent Sovi* calls for onions and, occasionally, *cansalada* or fatty bacon) forming the base of a stew or casserole, while the *picada* is a mixture of various ingredients, including nuts, herbs and spices, fried bread, garlic, sweet biscuits, and even chocolate, which are pounded together in a pestle and mortar and added to the dish towards the end of the cooking time, to give texture and flavour to the sauce.

A great number of the 200 or so recipes in the *Sent Sovi* call for sugar or honey, whether or not the dish happens to be savoury, in our modern conception of the term, or sweet. The Catalan cuisine of today, too, particularly that of the province of Girona (known as 'old' Catalunya), confuses entrées and desserts with a nonchalance surely inherited from its medieval roots. We find pears and apples stuffed with spiced ground meat – the *rellenos* of the Ampurdán. The *botifarra dolça*, another Ampurdanese speciality, is a pork sausage made so sweet and sticky with sugar and spices that it almost crosses the line into a dessert. Compare this with the English mincemeat, which started as just that, spiced sweetened minced meat, and ended up as a pudding.

With the possible exception of Asturias, where every weekend of the year sees a fair or fiesta devoted to some aspect or ingredient of the traditional cooking, there is no region, like Catalunya, so thoroughly convinced of the need to celebrate the excellence of its own gastronomy.

The four provinces of Spanish Catalunya are so rich in gastronomic fiestas that the *Generalitat*, the Catalan regional government, edits a special agenda giving details of everything, from the Hazelnut Fair in Riudoms to the Gastronomic Days of the Potato in Palafolls, the Apple Fiesta in Barbens, and the Festival of Renaissance Gastronomy in Tortosa. The passing year in Catalunya is a dizzy whirl of celebrations of everything from turnips, peas, mushrooms, chestnuts, and snails, to chocolate, doughnuts, sardines and sausages. Such a celebration is often referred to as an *aplec* – a uniquely Catalan concept, combining revindication, workshop, and party, all in one. Almost every Catalan dish of note has its individual *aplec*, usually in the town or village most closely associated with the dish in question.

But the king of them all is the *calçotada*. The custom was born in Valls, outside Tarragona, but has now spread beyond its original homeland, reaching as far as Barcelona. It began, like many of the world's most succulent culinary inventions, as a way of making good use of an ingredient which would otherwise have gone to waste – in this case, the onions which the harvesters missed in the autumn, that remained in the ground over winter and, in January or February, gave forth green sprouts from the old bulb. In a wine-producing region where vine prunings were a traditional barbecue fuel, the idea of chargrilling these tender 'stockings' would have seemed logical enough. But the true stroke of genius lay in the sauce that, over time, became the natural accompaniment for grilled *calçots*. Essentially a kind of romesco, originally from Tarragona, *calçot* sauce is a rich *picada* of toasted hazelnuts and almonds, sweet *ñora* pepper, tomato, garlic, olive oil, and the flesh of a tomato roasted over the same fire on which the *calçots* are grilling. When the *calçots* are removed from the coals, their outer layers charred and blackened, they do not look espe-cially appetising. Peel off the burned skin, however, and the interior is pellucid, tender, and sweet. The idea now is to dunk the onion in the sauce and guzzle it, throwing your head back and dangling the *calçot* into your waiting jaws. The oily, nutty, faintly spicy sauce and the partly caramelised spring onion form a combination so strikingly delicious, that it almost comes as a surprise to discover that the recipe wasn't born in the mind of some modernist chef, but in the collective consciousness of a traditional rural society.

Masia Bou is where the *calçotada* experience began. The Masia was a farmhouse where the Gatell family specialised in growing onions. The earliest *calçotades* were gatherings of friends or extended families, during the months of winter and early spring when the onion sprouts from last year's bulbs were at their juicy best. Over time, the *calçot* fashion grew and grew, the Masia transformed itself from farmhouse into restaurant, and now the old place is a gigantic catering operation, a temple to the glutton-ous delights of the *calçotada*.

To get to Catalunya from Navarra, I had roughly followed the Ebro river down its long, broad valley, from its vigorous middle-age in Zaragoza, to its exhausted dotage in the sprawling delta where it finally meets the sea. In the hills around Valls, you could feel the closeness of the Mediterranean. In the first week of March, a cold snap had gripped the rest of the peninsula. But here the ditches were alive with frogs, and fronds of new fennel gave off a sweet scent at the roadsides. Cherry and almond trees, in sudden full bloom, made snow drifts of pastel pink and candy white.

On a Sunday during the months of early spring, the Masia Bou has to be seen to be believed. When I drove up one day on the stroke of two o'clock, tailbacks were forming on the road leading out of Valls. The restaurant was surrounded by car-parks – like at the airport, if you failed to remember in which section you had left your car, you would be left wandering round for hours on your return – with a gang of wardens directing the traffic this way and that. When you reached the front door, a committee of greeters holding clipboards came forward in a smiling phalanx. Once assigned a table, you were guided towards it by a red-waistcoated waiter barking into a microphone attached to his face. On a day like today, said a woman with a clipboard as we stood chatting by the door, there might be 1,500 people coming through the Masia, all expecting to eat and drink to their heart's content and possibly to its detriment.

The scale and slickness of the operation would be astonishing to anyone previously unaware of the Catalan lust for *calçots*. There was a fully equipped children's playground, there were gardens with tables and terraces, and a monumental stone frieze by the front door, in homage to the pioneers who made the *calçotada* what it is today. At the back of the house was the engine room, a covered enclosure where fires of vine prunings blazed on an earth floor, and the *calçots* were piled up in ranks on grills above the fire, filling the air with a thick, pungent smoke. I made a quick and easy calculation: if there were roughly twenty *calçots* per ration, and if 1,500 people would be passing through the Masia that Sunday lunchtime, we were dealing with a figure of around 30,000 *calçots* for every day of the season.

It was easy enough to believe. The various dining rooms were packed with families, and each table had its pile of blackened *calçots*, served on a roof tile, its pot of reddish, glistening sauce, and its big carafe of local red wine. Some of the tables were already finishing their lunch, the tables strewn with debris, the faces of the grinning children like Victorian chimney sweeps, black with grime. Just as well the Masia provides special paper bibs, for adults as well as children, or the dry-cleaners of Valls would be even better off than they already are. One couple had bravely ordered *crema catalana*, the caramel-topped custard that is the Catalan national dessert, but were struggling to finish it after their feast of *calçots* and grilled meats, dangling their spoons in mid-air as they gazed blankly into space. The volume of noise was prodigious. Even so, the grandfather figure at one long table had managed to sink into a post-prandial snooze, his head slumped over his chest while the storm raged about him.

Josep Pla (1897–1981) was Ampurdanese, a man of the world, and Catalan – in that order. His prose is regarded by some as the twentieth century's most elegant use of the language; his opinions on food and cookery are some of the wisest. It seems to me that Pla's *El Que Hem Menjat* (What We Have Eaten) is not only Catalunya's greatest work of gastronomical writing, but possibly the twentieth century's single most important Spanish contribution to the genre.

Pla was born in the town of Palafrugell, a few miles from Girona, and grew up in a house which backed on to a beautiful, sizeable and beautifully maintained vegetable patch. Pla never forgot that vegetable patch, which was such a permanent feature of his surroundings as a child. Indeed, he was to claim that his adult love of order and logic derived from the hours he spent gazing at the perfect arrangement of the rows of vegetables in his backyard *huerta*.

The secret of Pla's art was to treat simple things with attention and respect, teasing out of them all the subtlety and poetry hidden behind their modest outer shell. He defined cooking as 'an art which consists in metamorphosing things in an amiable and discreet manner'. Pla liked to eat with a knife, fork, and spoon, not with chopsticks or fingers. He fled from exoticism, freely admitting to a preference for the cooking of his own land, however poor and unglamorous it might have been, and positively welcomed its lack of variety.

When Pla was compiling *El Que Hem Menjat*, his two volumes of essays on everything from hare to mayonnaise, doughnuts to cigars, it seemed to him that the traditional cooking of his region had but a short time to live. 'In the country in which I generally live – the Ampurdán – there is a certain familiar cooking which is, these days, surely and inevitably disappearing. This cooking was good – or, at least, the inhabitants of the country thought it good. Now one eats well in a few private houses – very few. Before everybody ate well, poor and rich. Now, this cooking, ever more rare, is shut in behind the four walls of a private house.'

It's true that the twenty-first century has largely done away with that 'certain familiar cooking' of rural Europe. Even in the domestic context, it is rare to find Ampurdanese country cooking of the old school. Indeed, what Pla did not foresee was the role that restaurants, rather than private houses, would play in the future of Spanish regional food in general, and Catalan cuisine in particular.

In the case of *el niu*, Palafrugell's most famous local dish, it could not be any other way. Indeed, it was only a handful of restaurants, and the occasional lover of culinary archaeology, that had kept it alive at all. *El niu* – 'the nest' – is a dish so bizarre, so archaic, and so rare, that it has long since passed into a shadowy limbo of foodie legend. Few gastronomes, Catalan or otherwise, have ever heard of it, and even fewer have ever tasted it. Colman Andrews, in his pioneering English-language study of Catalan cuisine, calls it 'intense' and 'mysterious', with 'medieval overtones and a baroque sensibility'. Pla himself includes a chapter on the dish in his *El Que Hem Menjat*, describing it neatly, in a phrase that scarcely needs translating, as *una inexplicable i incomprensible combinació*. With his love of the simple and genuine in food,

Pla was unlikely to have much time for one of the maddest
mixtures of disparate ingredients that has ever occurred to anyone,
on any continent, at any time.

It is not the kind of dish you can walk into a restaurant and
order just like that. For a start, it can only be found in its true and
authentic form at the three or four places in Palafrugell where they
still know the secrets of its making – the guardians of the flame.
Even then, you won't find it on the main menu. They might only
make it on a few particular days each year, when the ingredients
are all in season and the kitchen can free up the five hours needed
to make the dish correctly. *El niu* is only ever eaten in winter and
spring, preferably on a day when the Ampurdán's wicked north
wind, the Tramuntana, howls across the landscape, striking a chill
into the bones of man and beast.

Together, Pere Bahí and Montse Soler, of the restaurant La
Xicra, probably knew more about the theory and practice of the
niu than anyone alive. Pere was the author of a book on food in the
work of Josep Pla which, by absolute coincidence, I had just been
perusing in the library of the great man's house. He was a jovial,
genial man, smoky-voiced and robust-figured, plainly a bon vi-
veur, the sort of restaurateur they don't make any more, but that
you rather wish they did. White-haired, he peered at me amiably
through wraparound dark glasses which he never removed, inside
the dining room or out.

Like all the great rustic dishes of the world, 'the nest' is the
expression of a particular landscape and a very particular culture.
It is a signifier of Ampurdán life at a time when work meant
something a man did with his hands, before tourism and industry
ushered in new ways of earning and being. In the old days, the
dense forests of cork oak around Palafrugell provided the corks for
some of the great wines of France. The men who cut the cork from
the trees and prepared it for export, known as *tapers*, worked in
groups of six or seven, of whom one took turns to read the
newspaper aloud (including the advertisements, it's said) *pour
encourager les autres*. It was the custom of the cork men to work

irregular hours, and, on their days off, to set traps in the forest for thrushes, pigeons, and other small game. In their free time, the *tapers* linked up with another social group which also worked irregular hours: the fishermen of the nearby Costa Brava port of Calella. When the time came to eat, each group contributed whatever it could to an impromptu, but no less extravagant meal. The fishermen brought dried stockfish and offcuts of salt cod (mainly the stomachs of the fish, which no one else wanted), plus the cuttlefish they caught off the rocks, while the *tapers* brought their little birds (hence, perhaps, the strange name: 'nest'), and a few fresh sausages from the *matanza*. From this menagerie, the *niu* was born.

As she opened the door to the restaurant, Montse's face was a picture of exhaustion and fury. 'Your *niu* has nearly killed us. Nearly killed us,' she said.

Whereupon her grimace dissolved into a wry smile. A week or so earlier, I had managed to persuade Montse, possibly against her better judgement, to have the kitchen prepare me a once-in-a-lifetime special edition of Palafrugell's major contribution to world gastronomy. A week, she had said, would only just give them enough time, since the *pejepalo*, or stockfish, needs to be soaked in water for five or six days to reduce it from the consistency of a baseball bat to something that can at least be cut with a knife.

I sat at the bar and drank a glass of beer, and Montse brought me an anchovy on a piece of *pa amb tomàquet* – the tomato-rubbed toasted bread that is practically the national dish of Catalunya. Outside in the street, the good citizens of Palafrugell were hurrying home for lunch. Whatever they were having, it surely wouldn't be what I was having.

Pere and Montse ushered me into the kitchen where the chef, Anna Casadevall, had been supervising the *niu* – feathering my nest, so to speak – for most of the morning.

There it was on the stove, a wide metal casserole of something dark and indeterminately coloured, still cooking after three hours on minimum heat. This was a serving for four people, said Pere brightly.

He reached out for a bowl with some leftover *sofregit* of grated onion and red wine, an extraordinarily dark, thick, sweet-smelling mass with the consistency of olive paste. It was this powerfully flavoured base, I surmised, that would form the common ground on which the whole crazy edifice of the dish finally rested.

Following the *sofregit*, related Pere, a long parade of ingredients had marched into the pot. First the stockfish, soaked for a week; the cuttlefish, in pieces; and the salt cod stomach (the swim-bladder, to be more precise), a flabby white flannel-like object with a frill around the edge. The *tripa de bacallà* was another of those items, like sea-cucumbers and *percebes*, that were once discarded, unwanted, poor men's foods, and are now fashionable and expensive. It would prove to be a cornerstone of the *niu*, releasing all its rich gelatinous juices into the sauce.

Then came the pigeons, the sausages, and the potatoes, and a little stock to keep it all moist during the further hour of gentle simmering it would need to create a close-knit relationship among the wildly disparate elements of the dish. We were in the home straight. All that remained to add, now, were some chunks of salt cod, de-salted and briefly browned in flour and olive oil, and some hard-boiled eggs in halves. 'It's a nest, after all, by God. And what good is a nest without an egg?' reasoned Pere.

El niu is a kind of *platillo*, or, as such things are known around the lower Ampurdán, *un cachoflino* – a throwing together of whatever you have to hand, however unlikely the mixture might seem. Next door on the stove, Anna was making another ambitious-looking dish, a *cachoflino* of Dublin Bay prawns, mussels, white beans, meatballs, and sausages, simmered into a rich stew with a final *picada* of hazelnuts, garlic, and fried bread. Yet another denomination of this peculiarly Catalan *mélange* is *mar i muntanya*: sea and mountain, the combination of fish or shellfish with meat or game. Local lore holds that Catalunya was born of the union of a mermaid and a shepherd, which may or may not explain the national liking for surf and turf.

I sat down at my table. First came a plate of Catalan slicing sausages, from the *matanza* at a nearby farmhouse. Then a dish of snails and prawns in a concentrated broth. Thoughtfully small, bearing in mind what was to come.

Slowly, holding the plate in both hands, Anna approached the table, her head lowered in an attitude of reverence.

'*Niu*,' she said simply.

It did look very brown. But that was normal. In Catalunya, you have to get over the brown food problem. It was a primeval soup of thick brown sauce from which the various ingredients could be seen to emerge as from a swamp: a bird's leg, a sausage, the dirty iceberg of a piece of cod.

With my first gingerly taste, my fears were dispelled. The *niu* was good. Not just surprisingly OK, but rich, concentratedly savoury, and extraordinarily good. What was fascinating was the degree to which the sweetness of the caramelised onion, the salty fishiness of the cod and stockfish, and the meatiness of the sausages and pigeons, had melded into a single complex flavour, with the potatoes providing unbiased proof, as potatoes do, of the balanced and powerful sauce. A cynic would say that any old assortment of ingredients would blend together eventually, if you let them cook over a slow heat for long enough. Perhaps that's true. But there would be no guarantee that the final result would be worth the effort.

I gobbled up everything on my plate – even the salt cod swim-bladder, which was so tenderly gelatinous it melted in the mouth.

In the last analysis, *el niu* remains a curiosity, a museum piece. But the *niu* is also more than just a dish, it's a monument to the ingenuity of a rural community that called on modest resources to create something truly grandiose. It is a triumphant piece of folk art; an example of subsistence cooking raised to the celestial heights where the air gets a little thin, and earthbound notions of logic and good sense begin to vanish into the ether.

Sils, in the county of La Selva, is a few miles south of Girona. A village like so many thousands across the length and breadth of

Spain – Three thousand six hundred people, and rising. Formerly, like all those other thousands of inland villages, a community that derived everything, wherewithal and sustenance and values, from small-scale agriculture. And now? Take a look at the village. The railway cuts the village in half, constraining whatever physical cohesiveness it may once have had. Now it fizzles out for miles in either direction into dull estates of chalets with neat gardens, interspersed with half-hearted woodland. Large numbers of Chinese and Africans have moved in to the area, attracted by work on the building sites and in a large abattoir behind the village.

If Sils is on the map in any other sense than the strictly topographical, it is largely thanks to the grannies.

Their story begins in 1992, during a dinner held by the town hall for the elderly folk of Sils. On the menu was a dish of stuffed *pimientos de piquillo*. The conversation turned around the various local recipes for stuffed peppers, and, by the end of the dinner, there were plans afoot. A group of the ladies agreed to meet up over the course of a year to record impressions, memories, and recipes relating to the traditional cuisine of the region. When the year was up, they had so much material that it seemed like a good idea to compile it into a book. The next stage was a tasting of regional dishes prepared by the ladies themselves. And, as these things do, the movement grew and grew. The initial group of seventeen grew as more and more women joined its ranks. By the turn of the century, there were sixty. Five years later, there were over a hundred. (The average age, by the way, is steady at seventy-five.) *Les iaies de Sils* appeared first in the local press, then the national, and finally journalists were turning up from the USA and Japan.

Llucia López had a big house in a residential neighbourhood some distance from the village centre. It was echoingly clean, neat and new, like a show-home, but comfortably furnished with big soft sofas and design-store lamps, a ficus in the hall, and Van Gogh-ish paintings on the walls.

Of my four hosts today, Rosa, Llucia and Rosa were real live grannies from Sils, while the fourth was the organiser of the group, Xicu Anoro. Xicu was just the kind of placid, imperturbable guy you would need to keep one hundred excitable elderly women under control. Rosa, Llucia, and Rosa had prepared, in my honour, a magnificent lunch, drawing on their years of expertise to produce three dishes, one made by each.

For most of these ladies' lives, the village of Sils was a community which, while not exactly grindingly poor, got by on modest rations of almost entirely home-produced and home-cooked food. There was a repertoire of day-to-day dishes, rather monotonous in nature, since it was based on the Catalan all-in soup-stew *escudella*, with its protein-rich combination of pulses and meat. There was also a hierarchy of special dishes, prepared on Sundays, on certain Catholic feast days, and during the village fiestas. In was in these *plats de festa major* that the true excellence of the regional cuisine took flight. The *platillos* of duck with salsify, rabbit with snails, octopus with potato and peas, meatballs with prawns . . . These were time-consuming dishes that required a great deal of skill and dedication. They could neither be cooked, nor eaten, nor digested in a hurry.

Some of the villagers plainly lived better than others. Rosa Brugué, on my right at the table, grew up in a big house in town. She was a forthright, straight-backed woman, somewhat grander than the other two.

'Even though we lived in the village, we had a nice big patio, and my parents kept two pigs – one to sell, to cover the cost of feeding the second, which was for the family,' she told me. 'We also had rabbits. Before, in the villages, everybody had their own *huerta*. And so did we. My father walked out in the morning and watered everything. He used to bring back grass for the rabbits. There were five of us, and the parents.'

'It sounds like we lived like kings,' cautioned Llucia. 'But there were bad times, also. Some of us did go hungry. There were days when there was nothing. We talked about that once, in one of our first meetings. One woman said, during the post-war, she had a speciality: tortillas for the whole family, made with just one egg!'

I joined her in the kitchen, where she let me nose around the cupboards while she gave the finishing touches to her chosen dish. Llucia had reddish hair, bright eyes, and a warm smile. She wore a black blouse with gold bits. She seemed like the ideal grandmother, with her big house and her smile and her cooking, but then they all did, really.

'I've made an *escudella*,' said Llucia.

I might have known from the unmistakable, evocative smell of long-cooked chickpeas, meats, and vegetables that had been wafting through the house ever since I set foot in it, that something of the sort was on its way. The *escudella* is the sister dish of the *cocido madrileño*: both are chickpea based, but differ principally in that the Catalans always add a large meatball, the *pilota*, and that they use no chorizo, so that the dish stays pale and wan. It has always seemed to me that the *escudella* was more comforting, and the *cocido* more robust (and the *fabada*, the Asturian contribution to the debate, robuster still), but these differences may be purely illusory.

Llucia's version was an *escudella* such as I have never tasted before or since: opulent, but not overpowering, subtly flavoured, but certainly not bland. You could taste the five hours it had slowly cooked, and the melding flavours.

'You wouldn't believe it, but, in the old days, the dish we're eating now was eaten every day,' murmured Llucia between mouthfuls.

'Not with all this, though, dear,' said Rosa Brugué. 'Not so much of anything.' She turned to me. 'You used whatever you had. My aunt made the meatball with *tocino*. I would have just a little bit, with potatoes.'

We sat around the lunch table, the five of us, chatting away like old friends. The grannies chirped away in Catalan, sometimes remembering to translate for my benefit, and sometimes forgetting, carried away by the undertow of memory.

Rosa Valls told me, 'Before, I was just sitting at home, and that was it. The cooking, the group, and everything has given me a new lease of life.' For years she had been the cook at the village school, dishing up huge pots of lentils, *macarrones* for 200.

Rosa V's dish of the day was a *platillo* of beef with wild mushrooms, cooked in a terracotta dish with a substantial *picada* of almonds, hazelnuts, garlic, and fried bread. The *sofregit*, she explained, was done with green pepper, tomato, onion, leek, and garlic. The meat was first roasted with *vi ranci*, a partly oxidised wine that is still drunk as an aperitif, then sliced and slow-simmered. It was such a purely, authentically Catalan creation, that you could taste it blindfolded and know where you were in the world from the taste alone.

When the dish arrived on the table, Rosa B hugged herself with pleasure. '*Quina meravella*,' she breathed. What a marvel.

The front door opened and a young woman breezed in, carrying a bag on her shoulder.

It was Montserrat, the daughter of Llucia, who had just got off work at the hospital. Like many Spaniards in their thirties, she still lived at home. What with the incomers from Girona and Barcelona, house prices in the dormitory town of Sils had risen way beyond her reach.

'Montse, come in here,' called her mother. 'Have you eaten?'

The girl sat down at a spare chair at the head of the table. She was pretty, fair-skinned, a modern girl, wasp-waisted, smartly dressed. 'Not really,' she shrugged. 'I didn't fancy what they had in the canteen. *Canelones*. I'd rather not know what they were filled with.'

'She doesn't eat much,' Llucia apologised for her.

'Mum! I eat little, but often. I'm trying to lose weight. At the hospital we're all on diets.' She patted her waist. I tried to picture her in forty years' time, with the low stature and thick-set figure of the three grannies around this table.

'Have a glass of cava and a piece of Rosa's cake, at least.'

Rosa B had made a superb sweet *coca*, more like a rich sponge

than the thin-based savoury *coques* I was familiar with. It was
studded with early strawberries. Montse took a tiny sliver and
nibbled it approvingly.

We sat side by side and exchanged opinions about the grannies
and their cooking club.

'I think it's fantastic!' she said. 'It keeps them busy. Because, as
we know, the devil finds work . . .' She winked at me knowingly.
We are of the same generation.

'She doesn't cook. It's a shame,' Llucia was telling Rosa V.

'Ah, my daughter does. She's a good cook. She makes everything. *Y eso que trabaja.* And she works, too. She makes an
escudella almost as good as yours, Llucia, except that she uses
a pressure cooker, which I don't. She leaves work at half past one
and gets straight into the kitchen.'

I wondered how many mothers in Sils could say the same.

'Not many, for certain, not many,' mused Llucia.

'No, it's true, we need to start teaching our grandchildren.
We've done what we can, but we need to pass on the message.'

'*Ay, señor,*' sighed Xicu.

We drained our coffee cups, pushed back our chairs. By un-
spoken consent, lunch was over. We dropped off Rosa B in the
village, then took the road out of town again, towards Rosa V's
small bungalow on the outskirts.

Rosa's husband, Jacinto, had long since finished his lunch and
had spent the afternoon working in the vegetable patch. For years
he had worked in a paper factory. Now retired, he could do
whatever he felt like, and he had, in a way, reverted to type. 'Type'
being a human paradigm of Spanish country life, predicated on the
values of simplicity, hard physical work, and a profound understanding of the ways of nature.

The two of them showed me round their little paradise. In the
backyard, he and Rosa kept chickens and rabbits in cages. Over
the street on a patch of rough ground, you could see cabbages as
big as footballs, and turnips and rows of bright green *calçots*. In
the front garden, lettuces and carrots and artichokes, Swiss chard

and salsify, broad beans and peas. Rosa never bought vegetables; they only ate their own, and lived according to the seasons. In late summer, when there was a glut of tomatoes and peppers and aubergines, she made tomato sauce and *samfaina* to last her through the winter. On high days and holidays, Jacinto killed a rabbit and Rosa made one of her *plats de festa major*, with pears, with prawns, with mushrooms, or with snails.

'We are country people, and we understand the country,' said Rosa. 'Our children, of course, have a different life. They do things differently. They eat different things.'

She gave me a look with her soft grey eyes. 'As for us, this is the way we always lived. And we still do.'

CITY

Cities represent demand; the countryside, supply. If cooking is about ingredients on the one hand, and the skill in preparing them on the other, the city only knows about the second half of the equation. It produces nothing. What it is good at is processing and transforming the raw materials that come in from the country. There is no doubt that cities are the seat of modern creativity, where taste and fashions are invented, traded, and paraded, and subsequently discarded. Most importantly of all, they are where we find the greatest concentrations of disposable income, and, without the cash nexus, frankly, there is nothing doing in the world of haute cuisine.

I have never lived in a Spanish city for any length of time, though I have frequently fantasised about it. I have spent the last fifteen years as a country bumpkin with email, whose visits to the cities have been, in Joni Mitchell's words, 'safaris to the heart of all that jazz'. I only duck into cities now, feeling awkward in clothes that looked clean enough when I took them down from the wardrobe in the dark of the early morning, but now, under the neon lights of the Metro, carry dog hairs and the ghosts of oil stains. There are callouses on my joints from digging the vegetables, dry dirt at the edges of my fingernails.

Where would I go, if I ever got bored of clear skies and an empty diary? Perhaps to a medium-sized provincial city, Lugo, Pamplona, Murcia, Cádiz? Or perhaps to a big busy metropolis, like Barcelona or Seville? Either way, my food life would undergo a major change. In my fantasy, I see myself as an urban foodie, flitting in hummingbird fashion from cheese shop to bakery, fishmonger to wine store. On Sunday mornings, I would join the aperitif round, grazing on regional tapas and sipping cold beers long into the lazy afternoon. In the evenings, I might meet friends for dinner in the casual-chic restaurant of the moment, or invite them round to my place, having previously shopped for a particular recipe rather than, as in the country, merely looking for new ways to use up a glut. I would be sure to have access to ingredients that don't exist within a fifty mile radius of my country home: soy sauce, ginger, grain mustard, green tea. Would my life be more satisfactory as a result? Possibly not. But I would relish the city's prodigal variety and *embarras de choix*.

I had spent the winter looking inwards and downwards – at the soil and the customs that spring from it, and the society that depends on it. Now it was time to look outwards and upwards – at the Spanish city and its peculiar way of life. Up to now, the object of my attention had been ingredients, raw materials, and the traditions that govern their use. Now I craved a taste of the metropolitan virtues: innovation, image, and technique. I wanted to see chefs at the coal face of contemporary cuisine.

I began by following this creativity right back to the source, San Sebastián, least Spanish of all Spanish cities, but the one which, in the twilight years of the Franco regime, witnessed the birth of a new kind of Spanish cuisine. I knew where I needed to go thereafter, in order to find out what Spanish food did next: to Barcelona and Madrid – or Madrid and Barcelona, if you prefer – the great rival cities where, in very different ways, the food revolution is polished and packaged for the world.

CHAPTER THIRTEEN

SAN SEBASTIAN

Ask any Spaniard, and he or she will tell you what San Sebastián is famous for: its festival, its jazz festival, and for its crazy fiesta of the Tamborrada, in which, for twenty-four hours, the whole place rocks to the thunderous sound of drums. Donostia, to give it its proper name, is also known as a hotbed of Basque nationalism, and as one of the few places on earth where Basque culture and language are able to flourish unselfconsciously.

But its major claim to fame, many would say, is cuisine. San Sebastián's proud boast is that it has not only the best food in the country, but the most sophisticated food culture of any Spanish city (and that includes Barcelona). No other city in Europe, with the obvious exception of Paris, has San Sebastián's constellation of

Michelin stars. Bryan Miller, erstwhile food critic of the *New York Times*, once declared that only Manhattan can top it for great restaurants per head of population.

But the city's food culture goes much further, and runs much deeper, than the bourgeois glamour of the fancy restaurant.

As a food-loving city, San Sebastián is nothing if not democratic, and this is true of the Basque country in general: there is good food at every level of society. Quite apart from the star-spangled gastro-temples, the range of eating places also runs to roast-meat *asadores*, rustic cider-houses (*sagardotegiak*), and simple menu-based eating houses where a three-course meal of plain, proper local dishes, such as *zurrukutuna* (salt cod, garlic, and potato soup, onomatopoeically named to suggest the action of slurping it, piping hot, from the bowl), *piperrada* (scrambled eggs with peppers), and *porrusalda* of leek and potato, will set you back no more than a few euros. Donostia is also known for its gastronomic societies, or *txokos*, some as much as a century old, where members go to cook, and eat, and talk about Basque food. There are more than sixty such societies in San Sebastián's old town alone, many of them historical foundations dating back to the early 1900s, and a good few of them obstinately resisting the admission of females to their ranks.

Perhaps its strongest suit of all, however, are the *pintxo* bars. The *pintxo* is essentially a variant of the tapa, the difference being mainly in the way these amusing *amuse-gueules* are laid out on trays on the bar top, to be grabbed at will, washed down with a glass of something, and paid for when you leave. The bars of San Sebastián have made the *pintxo* into a culinary art form in its own right, a superlative and splendid fast food, freely available to anyone who cares about such things, which, in Donostia, means pretty much everyone.

Every eating place here, every eating event, has its own menu and agenda. At a cider house on the outskirts of town, you will typically be given salt-cod tortilla and chargrilled lamb chops, the traditional vehicle for tangy local cider served foaming straight from the barrel. At the village fiesta pots of *marmitako*, the Basque fishermen's stew of tuna, potato, and tomato, stand bubbling on outdoor stoves, and stalls sell *bocadillos* stuffed with tender pork loin and roast red peppers. For anyone lucky enough to have access to a *txoko*, there will be rich old-fashioned dishes, like *bacalao al pil-pil* – salt cod in an olive-oil emulsion sauce, fiendishly tricky to make – and serious delicacies, such as *kokotxas de merluza*: highly prized morsels of gelatinous fish-meat extracted with some difficulty from the cheeks of the hake.

This is a place that cares about good eating and doesn't care who knows it. For donostiarras, the excellence of the city's gastronomic life can be a curse as well as a blessing. I have often heard people here ruefully declare that they hated travelling, because, wherever else you went in the world, the food was always worse than at home.

Marisa, the landlady at my *pensión* a few streets behind the beach, knew whereof she spoke. Taking a pencil and paper, she made me out a list of the places that, in her considered opinion, were worth the time of day. I was to avoid the new wave of fashionable, avant-garde, minimalist, nouvelle places like the plague. She couldn't abide that sort of nonsense. And I was to head for the sort of place that made a big deal of traditional Basque cooking with first-class raw materials – such as this well-known restaurant in the Parte Vieja. It was absolutely *de toda la vida*, insisted Marisa. I said I'd give it a try. Of course, traditional was best. Though I dared not tell her, I was far more interested in the avant-garde stuff, the restless creativity that had made this resort city one of the avatars of modernity on the Spanish gastronomic scene, effectively transforming the food life of the country in the process.

I left my bags with Marisa and made off along the promenade, making my way round the curve of the beach towards the Parte Vieja, San Sebastián's original old town, a maze of narrow streets all built in the same crumbly limestone. If anywhere has a serious claim to be the heart, the solar plexus, or perhaps the belly of good food in Spain, it's this square mile of medieval streets in which every other doorway seems to lead to a seafood restaurant, a simple *casa de comida*, a high-class *restaurante de autor*, a *pintxo* bar, where trays of goodies crowd the bar top in irresistible profusion, or the discreet headquarters of some gastronomic society.

On this cold March morning, the north wind came in bracing gusts off the sea. A few solitary figures came hurrying past me on the prom. Down on the sand, a woman was running with two dogs. It felt strange to be here, in these well-washed streets full of polite and well-to-do people, after the earthy charms of the Ampurdán. I puzzled over the street signs with their runic mixture of Xs, Ks, and Zs. (Basque is like a Scrabble game in which everyone gets to use the high-scoring letters.)

The Luis Irízar School of Cooking occupied a basement in a grand block of flats a few steps from the old harbour. It was run by a man who is often regarded as the founding father of the new Basque cooking and one of the patriarchs of the Spanish culinary scene, Luis Irízar. This maestro of maestros, as his numerous admirers call him, has been the inspiration behind several genera- tions of chefs, including figures like Arzak, Subijana, and Karlos Arguiñano, who have since become Michelin-starred master-chefs in their own right.

In the glass-walled basement office, Luis, a sprightly, amiable gentleman who looked a decade younger than his seventy years, was sitting with his two grown-up daughters, who work at the school. He got up from his chair and shook my hand warmly.

Beyond the office there was a Fame Academy atmosphere; attractive young people joshed in the corridors. 'When we first started, the pupils were mainly Basque. Now they come from all over Spain. But we also have French kids, Americans, Mexicans, Japanese. The foreigners tend to come with a point of reference, some Spanish cook they've heard about – usually Ferran Adrià,' said Luis, I thought a trifle ruefully.

In the small kitchen classroom, a teacher in whites was preparing to give a class on fine bakery, with particular emphasis on the croissant. The pupils chaotically found their seats, while their director looked on benignly. At the back of the room, a tall boy with curly black hair was flirting with a small girl in a bandanna, playfully pushing her with his hips against the stainless-steel wall of the walk-in fridge.

Luis and I walked out along the harbourside in search of a bar that might be able to provide us with a plate of good jamón ibérico and a bottle of fresh white *txakoli*. When we found it, Luis sat down gratefully, puffing a little. He had a neat grey moustache and a kind face with gentle eyes. When he was a boy, his parents ran a restaurant in San Sebastián called the Buenavista. The place had been in his mother's family for years.

'I was practically born in the kitchen,' he confided, sipping gratefully on his tumbler of white wine. 'My mother and my aunts were very good cooks; they had learned the trade in Casa Nicolasa, which, in those days, was the best in the city, and I, of course, learned from them.' At the age of sixteen, Luis started as an apprentice in the kitchens of the Hotel María Cristina, the grandest old wedding-cake hotel in San Sebastián, and so began a distinguished career that would take him to Biarritz, Paris, London, and finally Madrid, where he worked with the great Clodoaldo Cortés at what remains one of the city's poshest, plushest restaurants, the Jockey.

Don Luis is one of the last surviving witnesses of an era in Basque food, and, by extension, in Spanish food, that dates back to the late nineteenth century and the earliest days of San Sebastián as a resort town for the European nobility. There was no such thing as a native haute cuisine in Spain; it went without saying that, for elegance and refinement in food, there was no one but the French. So that, when the new grand hotels and casinos wanted chefs de cuisine and maîtres d'hotel, they naturally went to look for them on the other side of the border. But the lower rungs of the kitchen hierarchy were occupied by young Basques, who learned the art of cuisine from their French masters. Over time, a Basque–French

culinary tradition came into being, and it was in this context that
Luis Irízar, too, received his professional training.

Born in 1935, he grew up in the post-war period, when half of
Spain was living on the breadline. For the rarefied world of haute
cuisine, it was hardly an easy time either. Many ingredients were
rationed, and still more were simply unobtainable. Foie gras, then,
as now, an indispensable element of any grand restaurant menu,
was unknown in Spain. 'We used to pop over to France. There was
a border, and it was closely guarded, but we bought our foie gras
on the French side and brought it back. Here it hadn't been seen
for years – if ever.'

What was to be the New Basque Cooking of the 1970s sprang
from a combination of various factors, the most important being
the historic importance of good food, and the discourse of good
food within Basque culture itself.

Euskadi, the Basque name for the Basque country, is effectively
wedged between sea and mountain – like Catalunya – with rich
pastures and a mild, rainy climate, Atlantic along the coast,
Mediterranean towards Navarra and La Rioja in the south. Partly
as a result of this variety, the cuisine of this land has a wider, richer
repertoire than that of any other Spanish region (though Catalunya runs close).

It starts with history and geography, and moves into sociology:
the custom of the *koadrila*, the gang of friends-for-life who meet
on a regular basis to eat and drink together, is crucial to the Basque
way of being. The gastronomic societies grew up as permanent
meeting places where the cooking and eating of classic Basque
dishes could take place in a casual masculine atmosphere, away
from the structures and strictures of the domestic (i.e. female-
dominated) environment.

The final impulse towards the revolution was the nouvelle
cuisine. The food world of San Sebastián being umbilically linked
to France, its chefs were careful to pay close attention to a
movement which aimed at purifying and simplifying the country's
various regional cuisines, which had become so bastardised and

cheapened as to become almost unrecognisable. Many of the luminaries of the nouvelle cuisine – Michel Guérard, Paul Bocuse, the Troisgros brothers – were well known figures in San Sebastián, and, before long, the shock waves were beginning to ripple across the border. In 1975, a group of young Basque chefs set about creating a radical culinary movement of their own.

The year is significant. In 1975, Franco was on his death-bed. After forty years in which he and his cohorts had done everything they could to prevent the expression of Basque national identity, the time had come for Basque culture, language, and politics, to break out into the open. In a way, therefore, the new Basque cooking can be seen as one of the first acts of regional self-assertion to take place during the period following Franco's death.

Luis Irízar, who was one of the revolutionaries, remembers well the euphoria of those heady days. 'There were twelve of us. Let me see: there was Arzak, Arguiñano, Ramón Roteta, Pedro Subijana, Patxi Kintana . . . I think, of all the dozen, about ten were pupils of mine. We were all a bit fed up of seeing restaurants all over Spain that claimed to offer *cocina vasca*, *cocina vasca*, when really they had nothing to do with genuine Basque cooking.

'So we started trying to do what the French had done. Working together. For two years, we held a special dinner once a month, taking turns in each of our restaurants, and we invited journalists and knowledgeable clients, and, after each dinner, we held a forum and talked about the food we'd eaten. The idea was to preserve the authentic roots of the Basque repertoire, using genuine recipes, but giving them a touch of lightness and modernity. As we went on, we realised that we were indeed inventing a new kind of cooking, which was a paradox in a way. And that was really the start of the modern movement in Spanish food: everything that's going on now can be traced to what happened in San Sebastián in the middle of the 1970s.'

Irízar is right: the effects of those monthly meetings are still being felt thirty years later, and not only in the realm of food per se. In the old days in Spain, which is to say, practically until the late

1980s, the profession of chef de cuisine had none of the glamour it has today. The chef was never seen in the dining room: Juan Mari Arzak remembers that his father was once dismissed from the room by a client who felt it was beneath his dignity to deal with such a humble figure and asked instead to see '*la señora de la casa*' (the lady of the house). To be a cook was to be part of the working class: there was no social status attached to the job and the salary was poor. Luis Irízar and his friends gave the profession a cachet and respect that it had lacked before. The only thing lacking now was the possibility of a decent education in the trade – and this wouldn't be long in coming, thanks to the pioneering example of Irízar's own Cookery School.

It was midday, and Luis had people to see before lunch. 'I have an important date with my granddaughter,' he said, with a twinkle in his eye.

We took our leave outside the Bar Txepetxa in the Calle Pescadería and I dived inside for a *pintxo* and a glass of red wine. The Txepetxa is known locally as the 'temple of the anchovy', and its creative treatment of this little fish, cured in vinegar with a huge range of accompaniments, from sea urchin eggs to olive pâté, crabmeat and papaya, regularly wins prizes in the city's annual *pintxo* contest. There was quite a crowd inside the tiny bar, a mixture of business folk in suits and ties, dressed-up girls and boys, and the odd tourist couple, shyly nibbling in a corner. I tagged on to a gang of students from the city university, with Basque Nationalist leanings and the cropped haircuts of militants, and followed them on their *pintxo* round. Together we cruised the calles Fermín Calbetón and 31 de Agosto, the two main streets of this snack heaven, plucking *pintxos* from the counters as you might pluck cherries from a tree. Today, at Ganbara on the Calle San Jerónimo, there were hot crab tartlets and deep-fried asparagus, and chunks of marinated tuna roe with onions and peppers on cocktail sticks. At the bar Martínez, around the corner on 31 de Agosto, there were miniature croissants stuffed with fried baby artichoke hearts and a morsel of ham, grilled ceps with olive oil on toast, and pickled green chillies, long and thin and excruciatingly hot. I was pleased to see that La Viña, an age-old watering-hole in the Calle 31 de Agosto, was still serving its age-old *especialidad*, a crisp cone of flaky pastry stuffed with fresh goat's cheese. But there was new blood coming in, and new-wave *pintxos* I had never seen before. In the dank dark corner of two sunless streets gleamed a designer *pintxo* bar, a place of stainless-steel and polished concrete, brightly proffering salt cod tempura, baby squid stuffed with spring onion, and chilled crab soup with tomato compote.

My new Basque friends took it all in their stride. Their country had always been in the vanguard of everything, from industry to culture; it made Spain (they said the word España with a scowl of disgust) look primitive and old-fashioned. When they marched off to a meeting in the nearest Herriko Taberna, 'village tavern' and hotbed of ETA sympathisers, I invented a lunch appointment and said farewell to the whole gang, with kisses on both cheeks and promises to meet again someday in the future independent republic of Euskadi.

There is a case for saying that the truly important restaurants of Spain, the ones that will outlast the foams of fashion, are those that have been in the family for generations, where there is a continuum in the business and a well-established sense of roots. The paradigm is that of the humble or not-so-humble eating house where the son goes off to cookery school and comes back to run the kitchen with all his new energy and modern ideas, but still with the anchor of family and local tradition. Of the great Spanish restaurants of our time, it is rather surprising how many have followed this pattern. Las Rejas, Echaurren, Ca' Sento, Café de Paris, and Celler de Can Roca are a few that come to mind. And the mother of all the restaurants of this type, we might call them 'generational' or 'evolutionary' or simply 'family-run', is surely Arzak.

The Arzak saga stretches back to 1897, when Juan Mari's grandparents opened a wine shop, tavern, and eating house in the village of Alza, now a suburban *barrio* of San Sebastián. The restaurant is still to be found in the same house, on a busy road leading out of the city, and is now into its fourth generation of the same family: Elena Arzak, one of Juan Mari's two daughters, is the talented young chef who now runs the kitchen with her father and will take over the reins when he eventually retires.

The place is *sui generis*. The main dining room is small, over-stuffed, and cramped by modern standards, with the tables rather close together and lots of varnished wood and antique furniture. The waitresses are matronly ladies who have been with the family since the dawn of time, or at least the dawn of democracy, and wear curious grey uniforms with a minimalist, Yohji Yamamoto look. The menu was founded on the basis of classic Basque cooking as served by Juan Mari's parents and his parents' parents: *marmitako*, *chipirones en su tinta*, hake in green sauce. But the kitchen has taken note of all the newest tendencies, partly thanks to the influence of Elena, and now has a research department upstairs, where new techniques and flavours are cunningly developed, and the old restaurant is amazingly ahead of the game. When I was last there, I ate prawns cooked in apple-juice steam; poached egg with squid ink and parsley sprays; lamb subtly flavoured with coffee; and apple and black olive sponge with fresh cheese, turmeric, and orange powder. All tremendously and memorably good. Even if the effect of all that modernity, given the heritage of the place, is rather like the feeling you get when your parents are seen in public wearing the latest fashions, and looking surprisingly good in them. At first it's embarrassing, but you end up admiring them for the agility of their movement with the times.

Andoni Luis Aduriz represents the other side of the equation. A man who had no background in food, no family tradition, and no early aptitude for the kitchen. He was born and grew up in a suburb of San Sebastián, where his parents were simple working people. It had never occurred either to them, or to their son, that he might end up doing what it is he does now.

I first saw Andoni's photograph on the cover of a magazine, in an issue dedicated to the new culinary sensibility at work in Spain.

Andoni was pictured cradling in his arms a giant orange pumpkin, looking like the boy next door dressed up in chef's whites and smiling a toothy, faintly nervous smile.

Just a week earlier, the critic of the same publication had given Mugaritz, Aduriz's restaurant outside San Sebastián, a glowing review in his weekly column, calling him a 'real hot-shot of contemporary Spanish cooking'. 'He possesses the sensibility of an ecologist, the rigour of a cultural investigator, and the soul of an idealist with his feet on the ground. He has the sensitivity of a gastronome and the elegance of those who make simplicity into a way of life,' raved the man, awarding Mugaritz nine points out of ten, a score only surpassed by Adrià and Arzak.

I knew then that this was someone I would have to meet, if I wanted to take the pulse of modern Spanish food in all its scintillating novelty and brio. And now it seemed the time had come: I was within half-an-hour's taxi ride of the restaurant, they had a spare table for lunch, the chef was in the kitchen, and Andoni Luis Aduriz was looking forward to meeting me.

The history of the Basque country over the last century and a half is, at least in part, that of a rural society forced off the land by its own push for prosperity, yet still hungrily attached to its own, now semi-idealised, rural origins. Euskadi is the most densely urbanised corner of Spain, its valley floors scarred with heavy industry (the Basque country was the cradle of Spain's own industrial revolution), crammed with smoke-stained factories and identikit warehouses, and dark slabs of apartment blocks of an almost Soviet grimness. Yet the hillsides above this urban landscape are walls of luscious green pasture and bolts of dark pinewood, picked out here and there with the architectural forms of an earlier time: the rough dome of a hayrick, the isosceles triangle of a stone-built farmhouse that may remind you fleetingly of Switzerland. Nowhere else in the Spanish state do the industrial and pre-industrial, urban and rural values so intimately co-exist.

The word *caserío* describes the traditional Basque country property, the big stone farmhouse and its various inhabitants, both animal and human, constituting a practically self-sufficient socioeconomic unit. In one of these stone-built pitch-roofed farm-houses, just beyond the scrappy hard-work town of Errenteria, I found the place I was looking for. The house I was looking at now occupied such a sprawling surface area that two very different enterprises were able to fit comfortably under its low pitched roof: a dwelling occupied by the elderly bachelor who had been born in the house and still farmed the land, with cattle and chickens and vegetables and corn; and a restaurant said, by the few people who truly understand such things, to be among the four or five most fascinating and important phenomena in the whole wide world of Spanish food. The façade of the *caserío* – one side of it postmodern rustic, with plate-glass windows giving on to the dining room, and the other half proper, old-fashioned rustic, sharing the space under the wide arms of the clay-tiled roof – was neatly indicative of the curious convergence going on inside it.

In front of the house, a mighty oak tree marked the boundary between two suburban centres, once bucolic villages, Errenteria and Oiartzun. The boundary oak was the trademark of the restaurant, a tree in leaf straddling two halves of a rectangle, black and white reflecting in each other.

Outside in the garden, a group of white-clad figures crouched over flowerbeds, carefully plucking leaves into jars of water. The hillside above the restaurant was a sward of green pasture crowned with oak woods, the hedges fringed with hazel trees and apple orchards. Along the track that led beside the car park, a queue of brown cows plodded heavily through the mud.

The restaurant's interior was done out in a kind of 'rustic minim-alist' style, with beams and rough wood panels and big windows framing a voluptuous expanse of green. A long line of Ms, for Mugaritz and deliciousness, trailed mmmmmmmmmmmmmmmm around the walls.

Andoni Luis Aduriz came out of the kitchen, a small, quick, shy person in his mid-thirties, and introduced me to my lunch com-panion, a Basque girl called Nagore, who wore her hair in long shiny dark-brown tresses. She had known Andoni and Mugaritz ever since the confluence of man and restaurant; she had observed their development with admiration. A writer on Basque food, Nagore had grown up in San Sebastián.

'My mother lives in a big apartment overlooking the sea. She likes to shop at La Bretxa market and cook lunch for me once in a while. My ex-boyfriend runs the Urepel, just near the bridge where the river meets the sea.' What a coincidence: it was the old-fashioned Basque place that my landlady had recommended. Maybe I should give it a try after all?

Aduriz had prepared for Nagore and me a *menú degustación* which he hoped would provide a window on his world. The list of dishes, translated for my benefit into eccentric English, was an extraordinary document in itself. The descriptions of 'whipped mock lard', 'chilled liliaceous soup', and 'split crayfish royale upon a bed of plant roe' were pure Lewis Carroll. The 'squid and bread fisherman's gel with orchard shoots and simple grains of paradise' had a fantastical sound, like something you might dream you saw on a menu somewhere, and forget the minute you woke. A paragraph of his own writing, printed on the cover of the menu, loftily proclaimed the tenets of Aduriz's natural philosophy. 'Cultured and refined spirits are called to rediscover their relationship with nature. To this end, no better way exists than through the raw material, the only thing upon which, over time, human beings have never been able to improve. All the grasses, flowers, seeds and elements that you may find in any of our dishes are edible; the generous gift of a new world of emotions.'

Two small envelopes lay on the table before me. One read '150 minutes: submit', the other, '150 minutes: rebel'. I thought of the cake and the drink in Alice in Wonderland: one made you grow, and the other made you shrink. I chose rebellion; the card inside the envelope exhorted me to 'feel, imagine, remember, discover'.

The first dish to arrive was a mad mixed salad of 'raw and roast vegetables, shoots and leaves, wild and cultivated, dressed with walnut butter, dusted with seeds and petals, and generously seasoned with Emmental cheese'. The dish was clearly influenced in part by the wild-salad creations of Michel Bras, who shares Aduriz's romantic back-to-nature side. It was lovely to look at, in any case, and cleverly constructed, with bitter and sour notes from all those roots and shoots.

Next came a tempura-like fritter of artichoke pieces with a foamy sauce compounded of some kind of shellfish essence, grapefruit peel, and the juice of the mangosteen. And a dish of potatoes cooked in a crust of white clay, served with an 'unctuous cream' of *chipirón* (baby squid) and various squidlets roasted over coals. Then a comforting, almost homely creation with a strange and slightly sinister touch: eggs with crushed potatoes, perhaps a reference to the famous *huevos estrellados* at Casa Lucio in Madrid, and 'vegetable charcoal': pieces of purple potato smoked and dried until black and mummified. And a concoction of salt-cod stomach and *kokotxas* in a gelatinous sauce given a lift with parsley and tomato: in essence a traditional idea pared right down to the soul. And a fantastically fresh meaty fillet of red mullet with an elegant fumet tinctured with juniper, a comedy fish-bone on the side, all its ribs and vertebrae intact, fried in viciously hot oil until brown and crisp, a fire-scorched skeleton.

'You may eat the fish bone after the fillet,' graciously allowed the smiling waiter.

It was all very exciting, as well as wondrously original, and mysterious, and witty. Bursts of drop-dead flavour – the piquant herbaceous blast of curry leaves, the cool bitter crunch of earth nuts, and that strange-sounding fisherman's gel, which turned out to be an extreme reduction of squid ink, black and sticky as beach tar – punctuated the meal like the piercing notes of a trumpet. But Aduriz's isn't the kind of high-wire cooking you are invited to gasp in delight at or dissolve into giggles over. If Ferran Adrià's cooking is often described as surrealistic, this seemed almost hyper-real: there was an intensity born not so much of theatrical whimsy and conceit, as in a concentrated study of where things come from and just what they do to each other.

There were fourteen dishes in all. The card on the table had promised 150 minutes of feeling, imagining, remembering, and discovery. 250 minutes would have been nearer the mark. Even Nagore, who was used to the creative fireworks of the chefs of San Sebastián, was touched and impressed by the show her friend was putting on for us.

Under the neon lights of the kitchen, Nagore and I gave him our effusive congratulations – perhaps we were slightly drunk from all the food and wine and talk – and he blushed pink, shyness bringing out a tic at the corners of his mouth.

Later, we sat in the stone room where the chef and his team entertain their guests. The chef sat before me with a cup of green tea, talking quickly and quietly, leaning forward on the sofa. There was something monkish and ascetic about his rounded, delicate-boned face, pale from the hours spent in the kitchen, and his boyish haircut, fringe cut short along the forehead.

'I grew up in Egia, a suburb of San Sebastián. My parents had nothing to do with food, except that my mother was and is a marvellous cook. She is one of those women who always was a proper housewife, one of those women who cook twice a day at home, waiting for their husband – the sort of role that these days, for a young woman, is almost unthinkable. What did she cook? Simple things, good things: a lot of vegetables, pasta, stews, meat . . .'

Aduriz has done all the right things, and spent time with all the right people: Martín Berasategui, the businesslike but brilliant chef whose flagship place in Lasarte has three Michelin stars; and, of course, with Ferran Adrià, probably his true creative maestro and whose influence is undeniably present in his cooking, but whose work he now finds fussy and alienated. (He last ate at El Bulli in 1998, and hasn't been back since.)

Partly under the influence of the alchemist Adrià, Aduriz became drawn to the idea that scientific analysis could usefully be applied to the art of cooking. His research into the nature of foie gras, for example, led to a period of study in tandem with the pathology department of the University of Granada. Over the next few years, there would be further researches into salt cod, and into the nature and behaviour of meat. The conduit, in this case, between scientists and chef, was the gastronome and savant Raimundo del Moral, a man who specialises in opening the kitchen doors of famous restaurants to the curious world of modern science. The newest chefs on the scene are hard-headed, meticulous to the point of obsession; they are brain-boxes, fascinated by technique and process. At Mugaritz, a new dish typically passes a rigorous process of research and development, being rejected up to twenty times before it is presented to the public.

Yet there's another side to Aduriz. He is attached, like a forest fern, to the rock of his origins. He has roots. A child of Euskadi, with Basque as his mother tongue and his headquarters in a Basque farmhouse, how could he deny them? Bizarre and perhaps pretentious though it may sound, he even believes he is working in the tradition of Basque cuisine in its widest, most spiritual sense. Aduriz looks at a dish like *merluza en salsa verde*, with its emulsion sauce of parsley and wine – a totemic dish in Basque tradition – and decides that it is so naturally avant-garde, that he will keep it on the menu as a paragon of modernity. The boundary oak brings two sides together, tradition and zeitgeist, under the same overarching branches.

Casting about for sources of supply, he looks around the *caseríos* of the vicinity, bringing eggs from one farm, onions from another, potatoes from a third. In his stunning dish of espresso coffee grounds with chilled cocoa juice, chicory cream, and a skin of farmhouse milk, the farmhouse milk is provided by his neighbour's cows, those slow brown cows I saw go by as I parked my car.

Then there are the wild things. Historian Jean François Revel defines the dominant character of contemporary gastronomy as 'the return to nature'. Aduriz has found inspiration in the woods and meadows around the restaurant, and many of his ingredients now come straight from the natural environment. Like the *Poli-*

podium vulgare, one of his favourite of the wild herbs, a diminutive fern that grows among the forest moss and rocks, in the cracks of garden walls, and among the stones of cemeteries. In his book *Clorofilia,* a treatise on the cooking of herbs and grasses, he gives a recipe for foie gras escalope in a wood-fragranced stock with a liquorice and polipodium root infusion, Jerusalem artichokes, and muscovado sugar.

As much as a willed return to nature, Aduriz's work is a necessary redefinition of the idea of luxury. When so much about modern-day food has been cheapened and homogenised and spoiled, the leaf of some forest grass you gather at dawn with the dew still on it might be considered the greatest indulgence of all.

The chef leant forward on the sofa, fingertips touching to form a ball in the air. 'That's it. That's just it,' he said, conviction giving a tremble to his quiet voice. 'Society's values have changed. The man next door might think we're crazy, giving importance to these wild grasses he has known all his life. But, for the man from the city, those things might seem like the greatest treasures in the world.'

CHAPTER FOURTEEN

BARCELONA

It was getting late, and I was beginning to feeling awkward about taking up so much of the chef's precious time. Nagore had left for San Sebastián, cursing the afternoon meeting that would tear her away from Mugaritz. The office was almost dark and the lights had come on in the empty car park. In an hour or two, a new set of cars would be drawing up, bringing in the smartly dressed customers for dinner. And, the day after tomorrow, I knew, Aduriz had a major challenge on his hands: a banquet at the hotel Ritz in Barcelona, part of a four-day festival of fashion and design and the Sabatier-sharp cutting edge of modern European cuisine.

The chef led me back to the kitchen, where he was ready to bring out of the oven a piece of beef that had been cooking for the last thirty-five hours at a constant 70°C.

The kitchen was deserted. Its surfaces shone under the neon. It had the neutral smell, the non-smell, of absolute cleanness.

Andoni stood by the stove. He put a finger to his lips, turning over an idea in his head.

'Listen,' he said finally. 'As you know, I'm giving a dinner in Barcelona the day after tomorrow. It is a special celebration, something I have been working on for months. A lot of our friends will be there. I am sure there will be room for you. And, if not, we will make room. Come. It will be a fiesta.'

An invitation to Barcelona is never easy to refuse, and this one was impossible. The next day I was on the road again, crossing the peninsula at its slenderest point, skimming the southern slopes of the Pyrenees, via Pamplona and Huesca. And, by the following evening, I had arrived in the world's favourite Spanish city as well as my own, not to mention the most vibrant, the most questingly modern, and the one in which, together with San Sebastián, the new Spanish cuisine has reached arguably its highest pitch of development.

The banquet Andoni Luis Aduriz served for fifty friends at the Ritz in Barcelona has stayed in my mind as an expression of contemporary culture at its most challenging and exquisite. Some of the ten dishes Andoni presented were things I had eaten just forty-eight hours ago at Mugaritz. I recognised the crazy mixed salad; the toasted fresh foie gras with rosemary-infused soya cream; and the coffee grounds with cacao juice, chicory cream, and the skin from the milk of the cows that share the building with Andoni's restaurant. But the context had changed, and so, oddly, had the nature of the food. Taking it out of the Basque countryside and placing it within the velvet, low-lighted plush of a nineteenth-century hotel had made it seem even more radical, more dramatic, and more sophisticated, than it had the other day in the sylvan setting that inspired it.

If the food was memorable, the drink was almost more so. One might have expected a parade of fine Spanish wines, leading us through the meal with the comforting logic of sparkling, white, red, sweet. But Andoni, as usual, was one step ahead. He had created for the occasion a series of infusions, juices, and decoctions, each meant to accompany a particular dish. The drinks were poured from glass jugs into a series of specially designed cups and containers, some of them held in origami-like constructions that seemed to suspend the crystal in mid-air. We sipped and tasted, and murmured our surprise and approval. And, instead of an alcoholic crescendo, Andoni's banquet progressed in a hushed and reflective manner, and our senses were as twitchingly acute at the end of the feast as they had been at the start.

The very first time I went to Barcelona was as a student in the summer holidays. This was a decade or more before the *annus mirabilis* of 1992, when the Olympic Games transfigured the city into what it had always dreamed of being, a sparkling European capital and a design mecca to rival Paris and Milan.

The idea of Barcelona I held in my mind as I stepped off the train was as a murky harbour city, more Marseilles than Milan, a hotbed of anarchism and bohemian low-life. If Jean Genet had given the place his seal of approval (notably in his 1949 novel *The Thief's Journal*), that was all I needed to know.

The reality was certainly decadent, but not quite in the way I expected. I arrived in Holy Week to find everything shut: shops, banks, museums. I had so little money, however, it made no difference that there was nothing to spend it on. In the house of a friend who lived by Sants Railway Station, we ransacked the kitchen cupboards and sat down to a spartan Good Friday dinner, my first ever meal in Barcelona – tinned sardines, boiled spaghetti, and a handful of dried apricots.

Things could only get better. On my next visit a few years later, I stayed with Susan, another adventurous English friend, who had found herself a top-floor apartment with a roof terrace on the Carrer Joaquín Costa, in the Raval, for the not unreasonable price of forty pounds a month. The Raval was Barcelona's old red-light district, and an area described by the Catalan essayist Josep Maria de Segarra as one of 'great poverty, great dirtiness, a resigned and desolate humility'. In the late 1980s, the *barrio* was a bohemian dream: atmospheric, cheap, and shot through with an exhilarating undercurrent of sleaze. Immigration hadn't yet begun in earnest – there was just one Pakistani restaurant, the Shalimar (now there are dozens), and just two or three halal grocers selling basmati rice and catering drums of ghee.

The streets below hummed with life. One night there was a house fire a block away, and we leaned out of the balcony to watch the roaring flames. In the evenings, we went out to drink absinthe at the louche Bar Marsella, founded in 1947 and apparently undecorated ever since, followed by dancing at La Paloma, the working-class dance hall where an orchestra plays and couples turn under a huge chandelier.

Susan was a smart cookie, and there was no cheap restaurant in the *barrio* where she didn't know the price of the daily *menú* by heart. Together we sampled most of these cheapies, and never spent more than 600 pesetas on a three course meal, with a bottle of red wine so thin it was more like rosé. These restaurants were family-run places, noisy with clattering dishes and boisterous customers. At Cal Estevet, I see from my diary, I ate oven-roast artichokes and salt cod with *samfaina*, the Catalan summer sauce of tomatoes, aubergines and peppers; Susan had *macarrones* and *fricandó* of beef. 'Not bad,' pronounced my friend. 'But Can Lluis is cheaper.' So, the next day, we duly tried Can Lluis, on the Carrer Cera, then one of the darkest grimiest streets of the Raval, and it was even more rough and raucous than Cal Estevet, but the food was just as good: gazpacho, grilled rabbit with garlic and thyme, *gambas a la plancha*. For dessert we usually had one of two things – either flan, the eternal pan-Spanish favourite, wobbling above its pool of caramel, or *crema catalana*, the Catalan national pudding, yellow and creamy, with a hard crust of burned sugar to crack, satisfyingly, with the side of a spoon.

One of our few daring sallies out of the neighbourhood was to eat *arroz a banda* at a beachside *chiringuito* called El Merendero de la Mari, just below the fishing district of Barceloneta, above the beach. The *merendero* was one of a line of shacks that served ultra-fresh seafood and rice dishes at bargain prices, in an atmosphere of cheerful indifference to modern standards of construction and hygiene. Partly for this reason, and because the chic new Barcelona of the 1990s found them embarrassing, the shacks were eventually cleared away, and nostalgists for old Barcelona still lament their passing.

What would I have found to eat in the city at large, if budgetary constraints hadn't prevented me from moving very far beyond the cheap and cheerful ghetto of the Raval? The late 1980s were not, perhaps, a very remarkable era in Barcelona restaurants. The excitements of the new Catalan cooking were chiefly to be found elsewhere in Catalunya: at the Hotel Ampurdán in Figueres, and at Big Rock in Platja d'Aro. In Barcelona, the restaurants of note were classy places for the upper classes. Reno, Via Veneto, Windsor: the names almost say it all. For posh seafood, there was Butafumeiro, a Galician place where the seafood was famous, as well as famously expensive. The interior of what passed for a fashionable restaurant would have tended towards the frilly and over-stuffed, the carpeted and curtained. Colman Andrews, whose book *Catalan Cuisine*, first published in 1988, turned a whole generation of English-speaking food-lovers on to the fact that here, in the north-east of Spain, was a coherent and idiosyncratic cuisine which had hitherto been over-looked. In it he mentions Reno and Via Veneto, Florian and Petit Paris among 'Catalonia's [. . .] best contemporary-style restau-rants'. Which, at the time, meant that they were serving *canelons*, *bacallà*, stuffed pigs feet, and *mongetes amb butifarra* (sausage and beans 'raised to an art form'), hardly what one would describe today as state-of-the-art contemporary fare.

Another ten years were to pass, however, before I got up to speed on what exactly modern Barcelona food was all about. In the spring of 2001, I was sent on assignment by a magazine to research the restaurant scene, which was beginning to be talked about as one of the most varied and excellent of any European city.

Needing a second opinion, I called a Catalan friend who, exiled for many years in Alicante, never the less kept in close touch with the food scene in his home town. Yes, yes, confirmed Joan, it was true what they were saying: Barcelona was in the grip of a restaurant boom. He had been back recently and had been amazed by the quality and sophistication on offer, a massive improvement on earlier decades, and a world away from the old-fashioned rice dishes and *cocina marinera* of his adopted city.

Joan was the first to tell me about the restaurants that really mattered in the early years of the new millennium, and I was happy to follow his instructions to the letter. In the course of that four-day stay, I ate at Cal Isidre, where Isidre Gironés and his wife Montse have been dishing up their impeccable Catalan food for nigh-on forty years, and at Alkimia, where, at the time, chef Jordi Vila was offering rice with *ñora* peppers and salt cod and sautéed banana with ice cream of yogurt, cinnamon, and lime in a ragingly fashionable haute-industrial setting. At a place called Abac, down by the Born – 'it might be the best in town', Joan had told me – I ate a strange but unforgettable tarte tatin of eel with apples and foie gras. I also recall a restaurant, Espai Sucre, that served only desserts – but what desserts! There was so much variety, so much fizzing creativity, it was hard to get a handle on the nature of the scene.

When I began planning my year-long assault on the foods and food habits of Spain, I knew for sure I'd be coming back to Barcelona. And here I was, with the memory of last night's banquet fresh in my mind, and the prospect of another few days in a city that, whatever it offers you to eat, almost always leaves a good taste in the mouth.

I left the car in a parking lot and spent a few days revisiting old haunts, some of them more haunted than others. From everything my senses told me as I walked its familiar streets, Barcelona was still immersed in its twenty-year cycle of convulsive change. It was cleaner, neater, shinier, and faster than I had ever known it, and its inhabitants were more expensively dressed. It was no longer the shabby Southern harbour city I had once known; it was functional and efficient, prices for everything had soared, and it had smart hotels with interiors straight out of *Wallpaper**.

As for restaurants, there was more *disseny* – design – about than ever, and in the most unlikely places. In the dark and narrow Carrer Carretes, one of the last real grime-zones of the old Raval, a fusion-food restaurant had recently opened its doors. Over various days, I lunched on Japanese–Hispanic fusion food at Invisible, Catalan tapas in a converted convent called Carmelitas, and 'new global cuisine' in a design workshop that was once a church. DJ restaurants – the type where a man in headphones puts on electronic music while you attempt to make yourself heard across the table – were all the rage. Salsitas, on the Carrer Nou de la Rambla, had been around for years. But now this latest incarnation of the *restaurant de disseny* had gone forth and multiplied, and, within a few square miles, there were DJ restaurants with names like Iposa, Rita Blue, Nova ('Cuisine + Musique'), and Lupino, a so-called 'restaurant lounge' with a terrace at the back for schmoozing and boozing into the early hours.

I spent my first morning on a tour of the city's best food shops, fulfilling my out-of-towner's dreams of urban eating. My wanderings took me out of the Raval and all over town, into neighbourhoods I barely knew, each with its own distinct culinary personality. The Born, an old-town barrio down towards the port, was Barcelona's new high-fashion zone, its hyper-modern restaurants serving wild fusion cuisine with the emphasis on oriental flavours. Gràcia, a former working class neighbourhood turned boho central, was strong on middle-eastern bakeries and souvlaki bars. Deep in the Barrio Gótico, the city's medieval heart, I found cheese shops, coffee merchants, and new-wave bodegas specialising in the potent new wines of Priorat and Penédes. I spent a happy half-hour in an old-fashioned grocers called Gispert, hard by the church of Santa Maria del Mar, where I bought *ñora* peppers and dried *mongetes*, and watched a batch of toasted hazelnuts emerge from an ancient oven at the back of the shop.

Fired up by the morning's adventures, I had a quick lunch at a falafel shop on the Ramblas and climbed back on the Metro, letting myself be guided by instinct, curiosity, and the recommendations of various observant Barcelona friends.

This afternoon, the theme of my investigations would be sugar. Barcelona had always had a notoriously sweet tooth, and its *pastisseries* had always been an important ingredient of the city's gastronomic life. No saint's day or other religious fiesta was without its own special biscuit or cake or sweetmeat. At All Saints, there would be *panellets* – round almond macaroons studded with pine nuts; for the Three Kings, people rushed to buy the Tortell de Reis, a cake filled with marzipan which often hides a dried *fava* bean and a tiny figure of a king (whoever finds the bean in his slice must pay for the cake the following year, while the finder of the king is 'crowned' with a party hat in gold cardboard).

It was only two weeks away from Easter, and already Barcelona was gearing up for one of its most important fiestas. On Easter Monday, according to a tradition dating back to Roman times, godparents are supposed to give their godchildren a *mona de Pasqua* – originally a bread loaf with a whole hen's egg, shell and all, encrusted in its surface. Such primitive *mones* can still be found, but in Barcelona the ritual, like so much else in its food culture, has taken a radical departure. The modern-day *mona* is based around chocolate, either in the form of a rich chocolate cake or, in the grandest *pastisseries*, a figure moulded entirely out of chocolate.

Steering a course through the cross-hatched streets of the Eixample, I went to have a chat with Christian Escribà, scion of the city's most important pastry-making family, and to take a look at this year's *mona*.

The Escribà family are the aristocrats of Barcelona *pastissers*. The business was founded in 1906 and Antoni Escribà, the patriarch of the firm, is as famous in Catalunya as Ferran Adrià, and even has an entry to himself in the Catalan national encyclopedia. ('A man of great culture and sensibility,' declares the text.)

The window display at the family's flagship shop on the Gran Via was a stage set crammed with elaborate confectionery. I saw pairs of high-heeled shoes modelled in chocolate, white and black; spun sugar flowers at 150 euros the box; and multi-layered chocolate cakes as gorgeously decorated as abstract paintings. In the midst of it all was the *mona*: a metre-high representation of Harry Potter, complete with wizard's cape and wand, all moulded from an almost obscene quantity of chocolate couverture.

Inside the shop, well-coiffed Barcelona ladies patiently waited in line to be served their bread, cakes, and other sweet fripperies, all beautifully packed up to take away.

Christian is the Escribà brother responsible for the important business of made-to-measure fantasy cakes, which he has produced in honour of Pedro Almodóvar, Bruce Springsteen, and the Pope. When something is truly worth celebrating, it is worth talking to this man. When Ferran Adrià got married a year or two ago, it was he who planned the extravagant wedding party, using actors and lighting effects to create a cake-centred 'happening'.

'My job, really, is to make people's sweetest dreams a reality', said Christian, with conviction.

Together we stepped up a flight of stairs to an upper room that the family keeps as a kind of museum of the *mona*, where some of the masterpieces of Easters past are preserved for posterity. Around the room, on podiums under atmospheric lighting, stood chocolate sculptures of Gaudí's Sagrada Familia, and of Mick Jagger's guitar; there were dinosaurs and dolphins in chocolate, and a quarter-scale model of a Formula One racing car, made for Spanish driver Pedro Martínez de la Rosa.

The author of all this artistry stood and watched as, awestruck, I took in this shameless display of sugary kitsch.

'We in Barcelona always liked chocolate, but we never understood chocolate,' pronounced Christian. 'Now, finally, we are becoming experts. We have artisans doing really interesting things, and a whole world of *xocolata de disseny*: designer chocolate.'

He gave me an itinerary for a chocolate-based tour of the city. As I followed the list that afternoon, I found that, indeed, *cacao* in Barcelona was being put to some pretty fantastic uses. A chocolate boutique called Sampaka was sleek and beautiful inside, and sold chocolate in the form of truffles with balsamic vinegar, with olive oil, with anchovies and hazelnuts, and a chic little café at the back served such novelties as chocolate sandwiches and toast spread with tomato-and-chocolate jam. At Xokoa, I bought chocolate CDs in proper CD cases, and hot chocolate lollipops flavoured with chilli. And, at the headquarters of master *patisser* Oriol Balaguer, where you are admitted via entryphone through an industrial iron portcullis, the high-design creations had names like 'substance', 'intensity', 'pleasure', and 'paradigm'. They were displayed like jewellery, in exquisite black boxes on slabs of plate glass. They had no price tags, but I got the feeling Balaguer's place was a little like a fashion boutique in another sense – that, if you had to ask the price, you probably couldn't afford them.

Next day was another bright March morning, and I had more food-shopping to do. Crossing the Raval from south to north, I came out directly on to the Ramblas, dodging the living sculptures, the pampleteers, the British tourists in their shorts and sandals, and turned right towards a grand entrance set back from the street which excitingly presages the splendour that lies within.

First time visitors to Barcelona are often surprised to discover that, along with the Gaudí buildings and the Picasso Museum, the city also possesses a food market that is practically a work of art. Of the two greatest Spanish markets, Barcelona's Boqueria (properly known as the Mercat de Sant Josep) and the Mercat Central in Valencia, I would be hard pushed to say which I prefer. Perhaps I'd have both in joint first place, with Bilbao's Mercado de Abando or Madrid's Maravillas coming in second. Valencia scores highly for its glorious building, and for the brisk authenticity of its functioning, so genuinely valenciano. Barcelona is more exquisite, more expensive, and comes perilously close to a kind of super food hall, but wins out overall on sheer good taste and passion for food.

La Boqueria was a convent of Carmelite monks until the convent burned down in 1835 and a fine new market was set up in its place. In 1914, it was given a roof and a stained glass modernista entrance at the front, which, as in the Mercat Central of Valencia, gives the building a touch of ecclesiastical grandeur.

In an age of hypermarkets and convenience foods, there is something positively heroic about a food market where everything is of the finest imaginable quality, almost everything is locally produced, and the place is busy – and not just with tourists, though they do gawp with understandable awe at the spectacular displays. Equally, it's a cause for celebration that this huge and vibrant market – at 6,000 square metres the largest in Spain – is still alive and kicking at the heart of the city centre and hasn't been hauled out to the suburbs to make way for ritzy shops and apartments.

I plunged into the fray, starting at Marisc Genaro at stall number 743, where I took away a half-kilo of Palamós prawns. At Especialitats Salaons, round the corner at number 737, I bought a big slab of salt cod loin, pearly white and virtually boneless. The stallholder wrapped it up in wax paper and threw in a tin of anchovies into the bargain, thereby ensuring my continued patronage of Especialitats Salaons. From there, I worked back towards the vegetables, taking a detour through the fish section, where the merchandise was laid out theatrically on raised marble slabs, the fishwives standing behind the slabs like music-hall actresses about to start their number.

The sunlight flooded in through the glass roof, picking out the colours of the exotic fruit on Marisa's stall by the front entrance. Marisa brings in stuff that had never been seen in Spain until it appeared on her stall: durian, starfruit, jackfruit, kumquat. A gaggle of Spaniards from some other community stood jabbering and pointing before the display, amazed by such a kaleidoscopic collection of novelties. A few steps away was a tiny, nameless stall selling snails in various sizes – 'autèntics cargols de Lleida' (real Lérida snails) – hanging in slimy clusters in fat string bags. There were more wild things hanging from the roof at Salvador Capdevila, the Boqueria's great expert in game meats, where I fantasised about buying a whole hare and making *liebre a la royale* for dinner; and, at Llorenç Petràs, fungi king of Barcelona, who has his stall at the very back of the market beside the Plaça de la Gardunya. Petràs is one of Spain's great authorities on fungi of all kinds. He remembers that twenty years ago there was only one species the Catalans would touch: the *rovelló* or *níscalo* (*Lactarius deliciosus*), known in English as the saffron milk cap. Nowadays, there is no limit to their lust for any and every edible species: on the stall today Petràs had chanterelles, parasols, Saint George's Mushroom, not to mention a selection of local rarities in dried form, wrinkled and grey-brown, with unappetising names like *orelles de gat* (cat's ears), *potes de rata* (rat's legs), and *pets de llop* (wolf's farts). I noticed a tray of dried *moixernons*, the fabulously aromatic little mushroom that some Catalan cooks add to their beef *fricandó*. I picked up a handful of them and raised it to my nose, breathing in their essence of earth and wilderness. I bought a hundred grams and left them in a box in my kitchen at home, where they are still awaiting a moment of culinary glory that may never come.

It was now coming round to midday, and all this sensory stimulus had given me a powerful appetite. Fortunately, the market bars of the Boqueria would be there when I needed them. These bars are a vital element of the market's body politic, serving up hearty breakfasts of pigs feet and *fricandó* for market workers at a time of the morning when most of Spain is only beginning to contemplate a cup of coffee and a croissant. They are all good places to eat, but only one is really good: the Bar Pinotxo, just inside the market from the Ramblas side, and just at the point where the froth of passers-by gives way to the serious foodie action of the interior.

The Pinotxo belongs to the Bayen Asin family, who have run it for years. The bar's patriarch and visible head is Juanito, a Boqueria personality with his trademark bow tie and permanent smile. While Juanito chats with customers over the counter, preparing coffee or pouring drinks, the younger generation cooks up a storm at the back of the tiny galley kitchen. The steaming casseroles they dish up at midday are a natural reflection of their morning's adventures around the stalls. Never was 'market cooking' more precisely that.

I grabbed an aluminium barstool, leaving my bags of swag on the floor, savouring for a moment the return to one of my favourite places on earth. Here was Juanito, looking the same as ever in his waistcoat and red bow tie, smiling genially as he loomed up to tell me that today the chickpeas were very good, and that also there were langoustines *a la plancha*, new-season peas with *morcilla* and ham, breaded lamb chops . . . I ordered a plate of chickpeas – they were rich, oily, and perfectly tender – and a crisp bread *flauta* rubbed with tomato and dribbled with olive oil (*pa amb tomàquet*, the greatest of all Catalan contributions to human happiness). Then, as an afterthought, thinking this might not be enough, a piece of tortilla with wild asparagus. '*Y para beber?*' Juanito suggested a glass of cold sparking cava, and it did seem like a good idea. Barcelona is almost the only place in Spain one can drink champagne in a bar without it seeming like the height of pretension. So I sat on my barstool and flicked through the newspaper that the Pinotxo keeps bound on a pole, and lost myself in a bubble of quiet contentment while the noise and colour of the Boqueria swirled around me.

The cut and thrust of the market had taken the edge off my urge to shop. Besides, I had now embarked on the aperitif phase, the delicious downward slope towards lunch.

I would jump in a taxi and visit a few of my favourite bars, taking a drink and a tapa in each, before crash-landing at a certain '*restaurant de disseny*', where I had a table booked 2.30 p.m.

The car sped off down the Ramblas in the squinting sunshine, heading for a one-room bodega in Poble Sec, where the house speciality is a miniature feast of wild mushrooms in oil, tuna *escabeche*, pickled baby onions, and slices of *mojama*. Some of the best foods in Barcelona are the tangy and appetising snacks composed of cured and pickled goods, traditionally taken with a glass of vermouth. From there I moved on to Txampanyet, beside the Picasso Museum in the Carrer Montcada, for a plate of green olives and another of pickled garlic cloves, cool and crunchy and surprisingly mild.

What would Spanish food be without tapas? More to the point, where would it be without tapas? The idea of nibbling on something savoury along with your drink is as old as the hills. Because, as every drinker knows, a little something salty helps the booze go down, and also stops you getting tipsy quite so quickly. But the Spanish have made the custom part of the experience of Spanish life, at the central core of the brand.

In the meaning of the word ('cover') lies its secret history. The tapa was invented as a way of keeping the flies out of your glass of wine, in the days when drinks were taken in the dark and dank bodegas in which the same wine was stored. First a piece of bread would be placed over the glass; then it came with a slice of cheese or ham, or perhaps an olive or two on the side, and, before anyone knew it, the tapa was born.

If the tapa did not exist, however, it would be necessary to invent it. In a society where breakfast is so peremptory a meal that, for many people, it simply doesn't exist (a recent survey showed that almost half of all Spanish children had nothing to eat before school), and where the midday meal is often at three in the afternoon, the idea of snacking on something savoury and salty with some bread and a drink at the end of the morning is not so much a luxury as a life-saver.

Any decent bar in the Spanish state, from Cádiz to La Coruña, from Girona to Jerez, will be able to offer the drinker at the very least some potato crisps, some olives and/or almonds, if not a slice of cheese and a few rounds of chorizo, and a basket of bread to make the thing into something resembling a meal. Beyond these basics, over the years a standard, pan-Spanish tapas menu has developed, taking in the tortilla de patatas, the fresh anchovies in vinegar, the chicken or ham *croquetas*, the meatballs, the *patatas bravas* (brave potatoes!) in their spicy sauce, the prawns *al ajillo*, the 'little Russian salad' of cooked vegetables in mayonnaise . . .

Then comes the great divergence. Every Spanish region, every city, has its own take on tapas culture. Seville, historical heartland of the tapa, is strong on the fried side of things, and also on traditional *guisos* like chickpeas and spinach, bull's tail, and so on, but (and the same goes for other areas of sevillano life) has not made much of an effort to update its repertoire. Madrid, being the city where every Spanish region is represented, has an unrivalled variety of tapas as well as its very own *callos* (tripe) *a la madrileña*, and Madrid still respectfully observes the ritual of the midday aperitif. The *pintxo* of the Basque country is a sophisticated offshoot of tapas, forming a culinary genre of its own.

As for the tapas of Barcelona, the question of whether, and, if so, what, is vexed. There is no real tradition, as in the South, of whiling away the hours before lunch over endless glasses of beer or wine. This has a lot to do with the Catalan character, which places a high value on the work ethic and is not prone to wasting time. Unlike the andaluz or madrileño, the Catalan worker traditionally preferred to eat sitting down. He had his midday meal at home, and didn't dilly-dally on the way.

Of course, all this is changing fast. The Catalan aperitif tradition is still alive, though only just. But other Spanish regional traditions are making their mark: a rash of Basque bars has recently broken out all over town, with fascinating *pintxos* on trays on the bar top. Galicians were probably the first immigrant community to settle in Barcelona, and many of their bars offer regional tapas, like *pulpo a feira* or tuna-stuffed *empanada*. Meanwhile, the new-style *cervecerías* – beer halls with more than a touch of Madrid – cheerfully mix and match local traditions with whatever takes their fancy.

When I last looked, however, the newest wave of all in *Barcelona tapas* was the *tapa de autor*. The addition of *autor*, as in *cine de autor*, was significant. It made it sound as if this tapa had a creative genius behind it, not just a short-order cook doling out *patatas bravas* and *croquetas*. There were three or four hot spots in town for *tapas de autor*, but Comerç 24 was the headquarters of the genre. When it first opened in June 2001, this was a pioneer of the playful new Spanish cuisine that was at its apogee of fame. As the years have gone by, there have been imitators, but nothing has quite dislodged it from pole position as the coolest restaurant in a town that takes the notion of coolness with touching seriousness.

Comerç 24. The name is also the address. So that, when letters arrive at the restaurant, they put the same thing twice: Comerç 24, Comerç 24.

This was the place to be: a restaurant that summed up in a single experience the sunny optimism of modern Barcelona in food, interiors, and clientele. It was down in the Born district, the city's art and fashion neighbourhood. I walked the mile or so from the Picasso Museum, arriving a little short of breath and flushed from half a bottle of cava.

If you weren't in the mood for high design or were having a shy day, you might find Comerç 24 an intimidating sort of place in which to eat a solitary lunch. The dining room was sunk in a penumbra of moody gloom, lit up by spotlights on walls coloured deep-wine red and rich mushroom grey. Iron columns, leftover from some former industrial incarnation of the building, grimly stalked the room.

I sat at a high chair looking out over this broodingly minimalist landscape. To my left was a plate-glass window behind which lay the all-white world of the kitchen. Within a metre of my table, an Asian chef was hard at work with the raw fish, sniffing, slicing, and arranging on curvy white plates. Two giant vases in brightly coloured glass held a stook of massive calla lilies. The Germans at the next table were snapping away with their mobile phones. I heard English, Japanese, and French conversations. There was barely a Spaniard in the room.

'*Marchando un festival*,' someone called in the kitchen. The festival is the Comerç 24 term for the long, thin *menú degustación*, so in vogue in Spain. A series of small dishes, brought to the table in rapid succession, rather in the manner of El Bulli – where, to be sure, the chef at this Barcelona place earned his stripes in the 1990s. The menu at Comerç 24 included Kinder Surprise Eggs, asparagus with parmesan and mandarin, and 'our onion soup'.

Carles Abellan had thought deeply about the theory of tapas and its application to the modern restaurant. What was interesting to him was the custom of tapas, the atmosphere surrounding it, and its democratic character. He found it fascinating that, for example, by the mere fact of serving tapas, a restaurant became somehow more informal, more comfortable, more fun.

'You would never wear a jacket in a tapas bar. Anything goes. It's more like being at home,' said Carles. He was a dark-haired, strong-faced, handsome guy, with a dark countenance more andaluz than catalan. You could see how the Spanish got their reputation for devilish good looks.

An Indian waiter in a black suit was sashaying towards our table, bearing a tray laden with interesting objects.

'OK, now first I want you to try this,' said Carles.

On the tray was a selection of tins in the ovoid forms of old-fashioned sardine tins: you pulled back the ring to reveal the nuts, olives, caper buds, and potato crisps, that you might find at an aperitif bar like Txampanyet. A glass of sweetish, spicy vermouth, foamed up with soda from a canister.

'It's a classic. It's the essence. The idea of starting with vermouth and snacks. Vermouth, and aperitif. One goes with the other. It's a Barcelona thing', said Carles.

The chef sat down opposite me and watched my reactions as the festival progressed. His dishes were all small, but perfectly formed, and ingeniously presented on Japanese lacquer and slate slabs and white porcelain squares. There was a tiny sandwich of jamón serrano, mozzarella and black truffle – a little homage, perhaps, to the mutual admiration society that exists between Spaniards and Italians. And then two cold soups, cherry gazpacho and melon with grapefruit and mint.

Then came a strip of raw salt cod with two small puddles of sauce, *pil-pil* and *samfaina*, a witty mix-up of two regional traditions, poking fun a little at the po-faced culinary nationalists who say that never the twain shall meet. As if to add a little oriental spice to the mixture, I had seen it being prepared a little earlier by the Japanese chef behind the plate glass window.

'Of course we must vindicate the traditions from here and there, but they can live together perfectly and *no pasa nada*,' said Carles, with a carefree movement of his hand. 'Maybe it can't happen in politics, but in cooking it can. Everything mixes, everything enriches.'

Carles grew up in the working-class *barrio* of Gràcia, where his parents still live. One of five children, his mother's cooking was straight-down-the-line traditional Catalan cooking, of a kind that few Barcelona households are still familiar with. Proper stews with a base of *sofregit*: macaroni in the Catalan style with ground meat, onion, sausage, ham; *fricandó* of beef, rabbit with *samfaina*, chicken with prawns – and, every Sunday, the eternal *escudella* with its full complement of meats, vegetables, and of course the *pilota*. Salt cod with peas, or *a la llauna*. A lot of traditional casseroles, because a nice *guiso* was a good way of feeding a big family like his.

'*Per mullar pa*. It's a Catalan expression. Good enough to dunk your bread in. It means the dish is succulent and tasty.' I had a quick mental picture of the whole family around the dining table, mopping up the last of the rich sauce with hunks of crusty white bread. 'And this is what our food was like. *Per mullar pa*.'

It made me smile to think of this super-cool chef, in his super-modern *restaurant de disseny*, secretly lusting after the home-cooked dishes of his childhood. It reminded me that, though the energy and confidence of Spain's contemporary cooks has brought about a food revolution, it could never have happened without the psychological anchors of tradition, family, and regional identity. The glittering edifice of the new Spanish food is built on the solid foundations of the old.

'You know what's happened? We have changed very quickly', mused Carles. 'We have taken to creative cooking with tremendous speed. And now we're missing a different kind of food. Look at me. I'm an example. I still want to do modern things. But, more and more, I'm interested in things that just taste good. I do a black rice, with cuttlefish ink and garlic. And I've had customers who said, you can't have this rice on your menu. I say, why on earth not? And they say, because you can't have this dish next to a Kinder Surprise Egg. And I say, yes I can. Finding a rice like this, it's like putting your feet on the ground, you're on home turf. And anyway, if everything was modern, it would be boring. Don't you think?'

CHAPTER FIFTEEN

MADRID

On the Tuesday after Easter, when the Holy Week processions had all gone by, I took a train from my home to the mainline station of Atocha. The countryside was in full bloom; there were cherries in the gardens, and thickets of broad beans in the vegetable patches that lined the fringes of the railway tracks. The city itself, too, was caught up in the euphoria of spring. Even its grey-stoned tenements, so gloomy in the rain and snow, seemed to be making an effort to look picturesque.

Madrid is the centre. When Philip II made it the capital of a united Spain, wresting the title from Toledo, this dusty one-horse town had little to recommend it beyond its position at the geographical heart of the nation. And, ever since, what Madrid does best is to concentrate, bring to the centre, the cultural currents operating in the country at large, as well as adding a special flavour of its own.

Unlike Barcelona, which is sure it wants to be modern, Madrid has not quite made up its mind. But, when it does, Barcelona better watch out. For the energy of this city, once it gets an idea in its head, is irrepressible. Even more than Barcelona, Madrid has been the focus for an extraordinary process of social change. In just over fifty years, the city has gone from being the war-torn capital of one of Europe's poorest countries, where its inhabitants were dying of starvation, to the prosperous hub of a wealthy nation.

Ricardo Miranda and Amparo Camarero were born in the late 1920s (1928 and 1929 respectively) and witnessed at close quarters some of the most turbulent years of Spanish history. They were born at opposite ends of the great Castilian plateau: Ricardo in Valladolid, and Amparo in Alcubilla de Avellaneda, on the high plains of Soria. Even in those days, the metropolis exercised a powerful attraction over the rural population, and their families duly ended up in Madrid, where Amparo's father eventually found a job for life with Telefónica and Ricardo's father was a telegraph operator in the army.

I first met the couple in a bar in the Valdeacederas district, up at the northern end of the Paseo de la Castellana, where I'd been browsing in a bookstore on the Calle Tetuán. When the bookstore closed for the evening, I walked into the bar next door and ordered a café con leche (early evening being the only time other than the morning, by the way, that Spaniards will countenance the drinking of coffee with milk). Ricardo and Amparo were sitting at the next table, also drinking café con leche.

I think we started talking about the luxury of milk and how we all tended to take it for granted these days, and how the centre of

Madrid had proper dairies, with cows and all, right up until the 1960s. Where Ricardo first lived when they arrived from Castile, there were open fields, the houses stood on their own, and his mother had night frights at the emptiness around them.

'During the war, of course, there was no milk for breakfast,' said Ricardo. Then he paused, unsure of the direction the conversation ought now to take. There are subjects that are still not very much discussed, chief among them being the three-part Spanish tragedy of the democratically engendered Second Republic, which briefly offered hope for a brave modern Spain; the civil war which snuffed out that hope; and the thirty-six long years of joyless dictatorship that followed the war.

'During the war, of course, there was a great deal of hunger . . .' Ricardo ventured to add. 'One really would eat almost anything. There was money, but there was very little supply. You exchanged things, clothes, shoes, whatever you had that anyone else might want, for sugar, rice, lentils, coffee. We ate things we hadn't seen before.'

'You got used to making the most of everything,' spoke up Amparo, a bright-eyed woman with a timid smile and a piping grandmotherly voice.

'It lasted for three years,' said Ricardo.

'We slept fully clothed, in case there was a bombing raid and we had to get down to the basement,' said his wife.

The Spanish Civil War broke out in July 1936, when an uprising began among Spanish troops in North Africa and quickly spread to the area around Cádiz. Almost from the beginning, the majority of Spain's arable, cereal-producing lands were in the hands of the so-called 'nationalist' side, while the cities remained under the control of the Republic. During the three years of the war, the 'nationalist zone' never suffered any serious problems of food supply. Meanwhile, in 'loyal Spain', especially in the cities and, above all, in Madrid, famine and malnutrition reached unspeakable and, from the contemporary perspective, quite unthinkable levels.

In August 1936, when Madrid was not yet even on the front line, the city began to see the first signs of trouble. By September, there were shortages of eggs, potatoes, and sugar. There were queues in the street for even the most basic foodstuffs. By the autumn, rationing cards were being issued, whereby each citizen was allowed, per day, a total of one hundred grams of lentils or beans, a quarter of a litre of milk, half a kilo of bread, one hundred grams of meat, twenty-five grams of *tocino*, half a kilo of fruit, fifty grams of soup, and a quarter of a kilo of potatoes.

The problem was as much one of poor organisation and lack of planning as of scarcity per se. Those parts of the country that were Madrid's principal sources of supply, namely Galicia and the two Castiles, had fallen into fascist hands before the siege began. But the city authorities did not foresee a protracted and difficult war, and there was little attempt at a rational distribution of what limited resources were still available. In the Sierra de Madrid, which became a lifeline, as far as food was concerned, huge numbers of cattle were slaughtered during the first few months of the war. At a time when railway links with the outside world were still open, large amounts of food and coal could have been brought in for stockpiling. Yet this was not done, and, by the following winter, the city was shivering with cold and hunger.

On 23 January 1937, the governing Junta of Madrid announced in one of its periodic briefings: 'Today, we can be sure that the population has almost nothing to eat. It will be of no use to have weapons if Madrid dies of hunger.'

Madrid did not die of hunger, though many of its people came agonisingly close, and, according to a, perhaps partisan, report in the London *Times* in February 1939, between 400 and 500 people were perishing every week. How did the survivors survive? By a combination of resourcefulness and ingenuity. Rice and oranges came in by train from Republican Valencia, at least until the battle of Jarama, when the supply lines from that city were broken. There was very little meat, at least not of the commonly available sort. In the Calle Lista was a private house where horsemeat was sometimes sold. Whenever a horse broke its leg at the old Hippodrome by the La Coruña road, and had to be put down, the carcass was shared out between the employees. The Spanish phrase *vender gato por liebre* – 'to sell cat as hare', meaning to cheat or fake – has its likely origins in the Civil War. Survivors of the siege of Madrid remember that the city was virtually emptied of cats, most of which undoubtedly found their way on to the table.

Necessity was the mother of invention. Some families kept a chicken or two in the attic. If there was not much in the way of vegetables to be found in the markets of the city, there was always plenty of purslane for salads – it grew on the rooftops, and was harvested and sold in bunches. When the lentils ran out, a substitute was found in the seeds of the carob pod, which resembled them in everything except taste. Above all, one learned to be flexible.

Amparo had finished her coffee and was fiddling with the unopened sugar sachet, laying it like a tiny pillow on the tabletop in front of her. 'My mother used to save potato peelings and fry them,' she told me. Her voice had taken on a wistful, faraway sound. 'We made *croquetas* with plain white rice. The pods of broad beans . . . they tasted of green peppers. My father smoked a lot. So, when there was no tobacco, he used to dry orange peels, and smoked that instead.'

Generally speaking, wars are bad for the art of cookery. They tend to concentrate the mind on the basic facts of existence, such as whether or not one has enough to eat, while the subtleties of taste and aroma suddenly seem like ridiculous frivolities. During the three years of the Civil War, almost nothing was published in Spain in the way of a cookbook, but a slim volume of hard-times recipes entitled *Cocina de Recursos: Deseo mi Comida* (it translates roughly as 'Resourceful Cooking: I Want my Food') was written in Barcelona and published after the end of the war. The book's author was Ignasi Domènech, a Catalan who had worked as a cook in the houses of the Spanish nobility and in various embassies, and who was well known before the war for his *Nueva*

Cocina Elegante Española, a recipe book cleverly interweaving the Spanish culinary tradition with the famous dishes of French and Italian cuisine.

In the winter of 1938, as the war entered its desperate final year, there was little room for elegance in the eating habits of the divided nation. The list of recipes in Domènech's book says much about the reality of wartime Spanish cuisine: we find such curious paradoxes as 'egg-less tortilla', 'fried calamares without calamares' and 'bouillabaisse without fish', not to mention cunning ways with stinging nettles, chrysanthemums, and the leaves of wild thistles.

If the Civil War brought hunger back into Spanish life, the post-war made it common currency. Even today, the word *posguerra* carries a charge of misery and despair. The post-war brought a new set of hardships, subtly different from the old. The daily bread ration of 150 grams was supposed to last all day. Lentils came to form the central plank of the national diet – but they were often contaminated with insects, and it was common to see black weevils floating on the surface of a bubbling pot of *lentejas*. Those who had no fuel for cooking ate their potatoes raw. According to a popular urban myth of the time, there existed a figure called *el sustanciero*, a man who went from house to house with a ham bone which, at a small price, was left for a while in each pot of chickpeas or lentils, to add *sustancia* (substance) to what would otherwise have been a weakly flavoured stew.

This was the era of *estraperlo*, the black market, and the *estraperlista*, a Dickensian character who made a fortune from the misery of others. Almost anything could be bought from the *estraperlistas*, if you had the money (but not Republican money, which was now invalid), and the authorities mostly turned a blind eye to their activities. The most visible signs of this immensely lucrative and widespread business were the women who hung around the markets, offering loaves of bread, bags of flour, and litres of olive oil, either for cash or barter.

The low point came in 1941, known ever after as 'the year of hunger'. Rationing was harsher than ever, and a series of savage droughts had reduced the country's ability to feed itself.

'We were left with nothing more than the day and the night,' said Amparo.

'You had to find ways round the problem. In our family we had sixty kilos of chickpeas for the whole year, at five pesetas the kilo. On the black market, you understand. If you went to have a glass of wine, there were no *aperitivos*. I used to carry a lump of salt cod in my pocket, and I would gnaw on that,' said Ricardo.

'I remember a product called *huevina*, a substitute for eggs, a kind of powder.'

'And the meat that came in from Russia, in big tins. How delicious that was, *madre mia!*'

If anything kept Spain alive during the dreadful 1940s, however, it was probably *gachas*. In the years following the Civil War, when its calorific and stomach-filling qualities were needed more than ever, this savoury slurry became once more a staple of the national diet – along with other 'prehistoric' foods, like *migas*, chestnut stews, milled acorns, and *altramuces*.

As though to dignify an embarrassing fact, this greasy porridge was now known by the euphemistic name of *puré de San Antón*. *Gachas* were most often prepared with the flour of the *almorta*, *Lathyrus sativus*, a relative of the lupin. *Almortas* are squarish little beans which are still cultivated in some rural areas of Spain; in the Balearic Islands country people know them as *guixes*, and prepare them with wild greens for the Lenten dish *cuinat*. The problem with the *almorta* is that it actually constitutes a health hazard. It contains a toxin which, if consumed excessively over long periods, can lead to muscle weakness, trembling, and paralysis of the limbs. The pathology known as *latirismo* had been described by Roman medical authors, but had been a rare phenomenon in succeeding centuries. Until the year 1943, when it reappeared. Apart from the big cities, which were rife along with dysentery, typhus and tuberculosis, the epidemic was especially severe in the provinces of Ciudad Real, Cuenca, and Toledo, where the post-war diet frequently consisted of little more than *gachas de almorta*, day in, week out.

'There were so many of us in my family . . . Seven children, nine including my parents, and my grandmother made ten,' continued Ricardo. 'We lived in the Calle Santa Isabel, down towards Atocha Station. Before the war, my mother made *cocido* almost every day of the week, with chickpeas. And, on Sunday, paella. But my favourite was always *gachas*. In winter, we ate them a lot. As a child, I thought they were delicious.'

'*A mi me hacen gracia las gachas*. I'm fond of gachas. Ricardo's mother made them very well,' said Amparo, smiling at a memory that had bubbled up from nowhere.

Clearly the technique, or the aptitude, or something, had been handed down from mother to son, because Ricardo was also quite a specialist in the making of this prehistoric porridge. It was his party piece, the dish he made when he wanted to cause an impression. His current version, it seemed to me, was a good deal more sophisticated than the oily gruel that sustained the nation during the grin-and-bear-it years of the *posguerra*.

'You make them in a frying pan like the ones you used to see in the old days, with high sides,' he explained enthusiastically. 'You fry pieces of *tocino*, and chorizo, and liver, and slices of sausage, and, with the fat leftover from the *tocino*, you add the *almorta* flour, you toast the flour a little, and you add water, little by little. And you see how it begins to get thicker and thicker, and you keep on stirring, and you know when it's almost done when it starts to bubble, plup, plup, like the lava in a volcano. It's at this moment that you add the fried things, the chorizo, the liver, the sausage, and *tocino*, whatever you like. You can also add some caraway, some cumin, some parsley, ground up in a pestle and mortar with a little water. A little salt. *Y ya está*. It's winter food, plenty of calories. A bowl of *gachas* on a cold morning, and you'll be set up for the rest of the day.'

'More like the rest of the week,' quipped Amparo. She shot me a mischievous glance across the table.

*   *   *

As a food city, Madrid has a double personality. The capital of Spain, like the nation as a whole, in a way, seems caught between the rush for modernity and the comforting slow undertow of tradition. On the one hand, it harbours a secret passion for the old-fashioned life and food of its forefathers: the vermouth at midday, the tapas of tripe and tortilla in the creaking taverns of the old town, the *cocido madrileño* in its interminable chapters of soup, meat, vegetables, and chickpeas. On the other hand, it likes to show the world that it, too, can be avant-garde and avant-la-lettre, and that, anything New York and London can do, it can do just as well.

I took the Metro to the Puerta del Sol, climbing the staircase into the dazzle of a Spanish spring morning. The semi-circle of the square was a cauldron of dust, noise, and humanity. Pile-drivers thundered behind a labyrinth of barriers; frustrated drivers leaned on their horns.

I took off down the Carrera de San Jerónimo, my senses attuned to the uneasy co-existence, in this schizoid city, of the obstinately old-fashioned with the racingly, bracingly new. Here was the grand doorway of Lhardy, founded by a Swiss in 1839, where you could still take your cup of consommé from the silver samovar at the back of the shop, and the upstairs dining-room served up a *cocido madrileño* that would shut down your digestive system for the rest of the afternoon. A little further on was the Casa Mira, renowned since 1855 for its luxurious and expensive *turrón*. Doubling back to Sol, I worked my way along the Calle Mayor towards the old market of San Miguel, housed in a delicate construction of ironwork and glass dating from 1914, and somehow clinging to life in the twenty-first-century jungle of supermarkets and hypermarkets, their clientele now reduced to a dwindling congregation of old town residents. Down a narrow street that juts off Mayor, I recognised the church of San Ginés with the famous Chocolatería San Ginés right next door, where I remembered going on a Sunday morning in the late 1980s, straight from the *discoteca*, stumbling in there with a gang of friends for a restorative breakfast of crisp fried churros dunked in cups of hot chocolate as thick as custard.

On a street corner someone handed me a free newspaper, and I ducked into a quiet cafetería to read it. Among the restaurant pages was a review of a place I had never heard of before, a curious-sounding hybrid of tapas bar, fast food joint, and designer eaterie. Fast Good, as it was called, was the brainchild of that grand master of modernity in Spanish food, Ferran Adrià. It was up in the Salamanca district, Madrid's own version of the Upper East Side.

When morning rolled round to midday, I climbed on the Metro again, getting out at Goya. Life in the scuzzy old town had ill prepared me for the elegance of an uptown neighbour-hood with tree-lined avenues and tall houses. The air in this *barrio* smelt of money and clean pavements. The people up here looked thinner, blonder, whiter, than the folk downtown; their skin was clearer, their hair more lustrous. On this weekday lunchtime, the men were in suits and ties, the women brand-ished designer handbags and wore big sunglasses pushed up over their hair.

Fast Good had a retro, pop-art, nostalgia-for-the-future feel. I sat at a window where three giant plastic lamps coloured bright blue, purple, and emerald green, cast the light from the street on the floor like stained glass. Well-groomed young mums sat in white leather armchairs, while their friends and husbands queued at the cash-desk, taking sips from big glasses of mineral water as they chatted idly into mobile phones. White vinyl arches divided the space, with white vinyl baubles suspended in curtains beneath them. You might easily have been in some groovy nightclub in 1960s London at its swingingest.

The idea of the working lunch, American-style, has finally been subsumed into Spanish life, but has lost something of its Protestant urgency in the process. Here in Madrid, it seemed less about being in a genuine hurry to get back to the office, and more about the need to demonstrate to the rest of the world that, as a modern person, you were fashionably short on those faintly embarrassing traditional commodities: appetite and time.

I looked around the various counters, where you could choose from a range of tiny goodies in space-age portions tightly wrapped in cellophane. Miniature sandwiches of chicken, lemon, and rocket, or black olive and mushroom, or soy-marinated tuna with sesame paste; a tapa of roasted vegetables with hazelnut dressing. A separate section held kits for making modern food at home. A cutely packaged box included two organic eggs, a block of parmesan, a packet of saffron, and some hazelnuts, together with recipe instructions for a kind of savoury flan. There were good wines by the bottle (the new Spanish working lunch by no means precludes a glass of wine) and cold beers, and the kind of teas and tisanes that never had much of a presence here, until health and hippies brought them into circulation. Everything was clean and small and neat and bright. By two o'clock, zero hour for the Spanish lunchtime, a queue of neat, clean people was snaking across the floor. Balearic chillout music murmured in the background. It was a vision of a contemporary urban lifestyle that would have astonished anyone who had known Spain in its 'black' version, grim and dark and primitive.

But Fast Good was merely an aperitif before the day's main meal of modern gastronomy: the restaurant La Broche, personified by Catalan chef Sergi Arola. Both Fast Good and La Broche bear the imprint of Ferran Adrià: one, because the idea of a designer snack bar was his; and the other, because chef Sergi Arola is, of all the various alumni and followers of the master, the one to have brought his philosophy to the widest public.

I walked the few blocks across the Barrio de Salamanca to where the hotel Miguel Angel sits beside the squalling Paseo de la Castellana.

One can understand the appeal of minimalism as a reaction to the dark, cluttered Spanish interiors of the past, but La Broche was a cool-box in which colour had been banished from everything, except the bright assemblies on the big white dining plates.

Sergi Arola was the very model of a media chef, a phenomenon which, in the early years of the twenty-first century, was still a novelty in Spain. Handsome and fashion-conscious, he was known among magazine editors as a good sport who would happily pose undressed in the kitchen for a feature on naked celebrities, or reminisce about the alternative rock band Los Canguros (The Kangaroos) with which he played guitar in the Barcelona of the early 1980s. It was TV, however, which cemented the foundations of his fame. I had seen him recently on two occasions: as guest chef on a game show in which two teams of cooks compete with each other to produce a meal in the shortest time, and as the star of an advert for a kind of crispbread. Arola was shown in a domestic situation with his two little daughters, offering one of them a dish of 'ciabatta crisp with fillet of beef', to which she appeared to consent in the manner of a haughty client. 'Crispbread Espiga de Oro: so that my best little customers are satisfied', came the tagline, followed by a kiss from daddy and a gruesome forced laugh, to camera, from the debonair chef.

Since its opening in February 2000, La Broche had soared into the heights of fashion, galvanising a Madrid food scene that had hitherto lacked a little sparkle. When the Reina Sofía art museum opened a gleaming new wing designed by Jean Nouvel, it went without saying that the new building would include a fabulous café/restaurant to match, and there can have been few doubts in anyone's mind about who would be hired to create the menu.

Today I was lucky enough to catch him at home in the kitchen of La Broche, from where he served me a *menú degustación* that fairly took my breath away, what with a deconstructed *escudella* of beans and meatballs with foie gras, confit of cocks combs, and a surrealist combination of sea and land snails roasted in lard with a mad salad of tiny violet potatoes, capers, marinated onions, and chanterelle mushrooms, all arranged on a square of fine filo pastry. I wished I could have tried the loin of horse with tomato bon-bons, if only because seeing it there on the menu reminded me forcefully of the Civil War and post-war in Madrid, when the eating of horse was more a matter of desperate obligation than of scaling the summits of exquisiteness in food.

When I first lived in Spain, there were no restaurants like Broche. There was little general awareness that anything else existed beside *la cocina de siempre*: the cooking we've always known. Book-shops, if they had a food section at all, would carry only a feeble selection of the large-format glossy cookbooks that fill the shelves today. Most Spanish newspapers had no restaurant critic, and chefs were rarely in the news. Gastro-writing was a furrow-browed genre dominated by male writers (in the Anglo-Saxon context, interestingly, it is women who have flown the flag) who solemnly pontificated about the correct recipe for suckling pig or the origins of mayonnaise.

Every revolution needs a person with the clarity of vision and expression to convey its message to the wider world. For the new Spanish cooking it's José Carlos Capel. Capel writes a column in the newspaper *El País*, which has, for ten years, acted as a register for everything new, appetising, and not-so-appetising, in the national gastronomic life. Today he had found me a half hour in a schedule even more hectic than usual, since he was organising a three-day food fair in Madrid, to be inaugurated the following day, at which most of the leading Spanish chefs would be present, as well as a healthy showing of the world's gastronomic media.

'I've been writing about gastronomy for, what, twenty-four or twenty-five years, so, really, you could say I've been a witness to the evolution of what's been going on in Spain since at least, oh, 1976,' said this elegantly spare gentleman with a shock of crimpled grey hair.

While he took a phone call, I browsed through a book of his that lay on the table before me, a breviary of the *tortilla de patata*, in which a galaxy of modern chefs, from Sergi Arola to Joan Roca and Pedro Subijana and Manuel de la Osa, provide artful reinter-pretations of the plainest and most universally loved of all Spanish national dishes. I was especially taken with Andoni's egg poached at 70°C in a consommé of onion, potato, and green peppers – in essence a deconstruction of the Basque tortilla of his youth.

'The movement begins in 1977,' he said, as he put down the phone. 'Well, the eighties were a tremendous time. We had no idea where we were going; there was a sense of perpetual change in the air. Zalacaín opens in 1973, and three or four years later gets its third Michelin star. Subijana, Martín Berasategui, have their moments of greatness. Then, in the early nineties, there is a pause. After the Olympic games in Barcelona and the Expo in Seville, there is a crisis. Many restaurants are forced to close; those that stay open must lower their prices. Zalacaín is sold.

'Until that moment, of course, what had been happening was a bringing-up-to-date of traditional cooking. What there had never been were entirely new techniques. What happens in 1993, or 1994, is that we begin to hear about a new figure on the scene, a Catalan chef who is astonishingly innovative. He is creating a new cuisine with concepts and techniques that no one has ever thought of before. How should we cook shellfish? Should we cook them at all? In the old days, to make a French-style mousse, you needed some kind of fat, or whipped cream. He discovered that you could create a foam with CO_2, and it would have a delicacy that no mousse had ever had. Health, and lightness. Both were fundamental. And it's at this point that the seed is sown. The seed of creativity and change. The techniques of this new man are the ones to be copied. Which all the major chefs in Spain are naturally inclined to do. There is no doubt that he is the revolutionary figure. He is the Robespierre. And he is proclaimed a genius.

'There had always been fashions in restaurant food. The 1980s was the era of salmon, and lobster, and *piquillo* peppers stuffed with everything under the sun. But nothing like this. Now everyone was creating foams, deconstructing every dish that crossed their minds. When the fad for liquid nitrogen came along, everyone started making dishes with nitrogen.'

José Carlos has seen it all. The chefs he still rates highest are those of the first wave: Adrià, Arzak, Roca, de la Osa. But there's a new generation coming through. He mentions Quique Dacosta, Dani García, Nacho Manzano. 'And a young man who has a restaurant in a farmhouse outside San Sebastián, fantastically talented. He'll be one of the greats, no doubt.'

Not Andoni Luis Aduriz? Yes indeed, the very same. José Carlos was there at the Barcelona Ritz when Andoni Luis served his famous alcohol-free banquet. How wonderful that was, we agree. But how very surprising, and how very strange.

'It's madness,' he said mildly, seeming to refer not so much to Andoni's experimental cooking as to the restaurant world in general, the chefs, the fads, and the sheer amount of work it puts him to. 'Madness,' he said again. His gaze became momentarily vacant, losing itself for a second in mid-air.

He glanced at his watch: my time was up. Half an hour of this man's time on a day like this was already a major favour. But José Carlos had another one to offer, as we wound up the conversation: a VIP pass to the big show tomorrow.

A phone call to his assistant, and I was set up with a plasticated security tag to hang around my neck or clip to my shirt pocket. The event had sold out long ago, and José Carlos's secretary was busy fending off calls from frustrated food folk all over the world who had left it too late. I tucked it in an inside pocket of my briefcase, feeling like a lucky man. There would be people outside the conference centre begging for returns. The show was in all the papers, on the national TV news. Madrid Fusion: the name had resonances of 'fusion food' and 'fashion', but also of a coming together of heterogeneous elements, a blending into a whole. It sounded modern and optimistic and somehow inclusive: you too could be fused, if you could afford the asking price. I felt it to be the culmination, in a peculiar way, not merely of my own life experiences in the world of Spanish food, but of the history of Spanish food itself.

On a clear day, Madrid is a mountain town. The sky is piercingly bright. The air is refreshingly cold, and so dry it cracks and chafes the lips. The horizon ringed with sierras where patches of late snow still cling to the shadier slopes. *De Madrid al cielo*, runs the saying: from Madrid to heaven.

The next morning I'm sitting in a big white taxi on the way to a conference centre on the outskirts of town, a strange outpost of society in a landscape of plate-glass glitter, a suburb open only in office hours.

Women in neat short skirts and high heels, men in dark suits, filing in fast through the big chrome doors. Legions of attendants, checking passes, talking into walkie-talkies, handing out programmes. The echoing whiteness of the foyer, filled with the noises of expectation and organisation, like the forecourt of some gleaming new railway station. From the ground floor, a white marble staircase ascends to the upper level, where a theatre stands on a central island, under a high glass roof. Bridges radiate out to other zones, other departments of the show. There is a product fair, a room for tastings, coffee bars and beer bars and sherry bars. Some of the bars have serranos hams on stands at the front, with a professional slicer furiously carving away.

Food in Spain is production and consumption, and tradition and the humdrum business of cooking and eating. Over and above all that, it's an industry that moves millions of euros and gives employment to millions of workers. Anyone who had been used to thinking of Spanish food merely as a pleasurable adjunct to the good life on the Costas, a plate of tortilla and some olives to go with your glass of wine, would be amazed at the power and influence of the industry that exists to present such food to the world. A full 22 per cent of Spain's Gross National Product is made up by the food industry in its various forms, compared to the 10 per cent accounted for by tourism. From the obvious fact of the restaurants themselves, the human resources necessary to staff them, the tourist industry which provides a large percentage of their clients, and the suppliers of the necessary raw materials, its sphere of influences radiates outwards into a constellation of ancillary industries. Here they all are. The suppliers of glassware, crockery, cooking equipment, uniforms, cookbooks . . . A number of the autonomous regions have their own stands at the fair, and well-presented girls are smilingly handing out handsomely produced literature – books and recipe leaflets and CD-ROMs. The most forward-looking Spanish regions are belatedly realising that visitors not only want to eat the specialities of the province in question, but are able to make a close association between food and sense of place. Sell them the gastronomy of Tenerife, therefore, and you're selling them Tenerife. Build the food into the core brand: it's basic marketing.

There is plenty of fun to be had. Food as entertainment, food as pastime. If you had the stamina and time, you could spend three days doing the rounds of the seminars, tastings, round tables, demonstrations. There are workshops on tapas, the art of the grill, cocktails, desserts. On the properties of dried fish scales and eyes and bones. On the uses of aloe vera in haute cuisine. Tomorrow, there will be cookery demos by Sergi Arola, and Joan and Jordi Roca, and a legion of Basque chefs with unreproducible names.

For now, the fair-goers have ahead of them an appetising morning. Now, ten o'clock sharp, and the whole place shuts up to listen to the Mayor of Madrid, who gives a short speech to open the show. He talks about the value of 'interculturality', the breaking down of barriers, the opening of frontiers, the sharing of experience, and the importance of his city on the international restaurant scene. What he doesn't say is what I'm thinking: that a city which now prizes itself as a producer of audacious avant-garde cuisine, was, just sixty years before, a city where people were reduced to eating dogs and cats.

First off on the cookery stage is Martín Berasategui: three-star general of the new Spanish cuisine. San Sebastián born and bred, Martin grew up in his parents' wine-cellar in the old town. He walks on to a set that gleams with stainless steel, bristles with gadgets. Behind him on the kitchen wall, the names of the sponsors, never out of sight: Maggi, BMW, El Corte Inglés, the Madrid Olympic bid, Mahou – the beer of Madrid. Martín is a solid professional, and a businessman, but a man of great taste.

His raw-pea purée is a classic of contemporary cuisine: I have eaten it myself, at Martín's restaurant in Lasarte. 'My cooking begins with the product. My first loyalty will always be to the farmers, the fishermen, the winemakers of our land.' The pony-tailed figure of Floren Damenzain, king of the vegetables, flashes up in my head; I remember Martín's tribute in Floren's catalogue. He prepares a dish of soy-bean sprouts and oysters with coffee, pepper, and curry, and tells us the importance of cooking vege-tables without water. 'I'm not the kind of chef who throws much of a shadow,' he says modestly, almost to himself, leaning over the worktop to slice a beetroot into paper-thin sheets. 'I'm more the older brother who's here to help.'

Then Juan Mari Arzak takes the stage. We applaud like mad as he bumbles onstage, genial and beaming.

'People talk about cooking as technology, as art, as raw materi-al. Well, today I want to talk about cooking as diversion,' he announces.

'Cooking is a game; a serious game, but still a game. I have never in my life cooked anything without enjoying myself. It's so im-portant to think like a child, to develop the capacity to amaze and delight. You need to get out and about. Into the street. Discover the world.

'Look at this dish,' he says, showing us blown-up digital images on a screen behind him. It's the poached egg with the parsley and squid-ink sprays; I ate it last year at his restaurant. The roots of the dish are in Basque home cooking: when there were leftovers from the squid-in-its-own-ink, they'd be eaten the next day with fried eggs and parsley. But then came the twist. Arzak was inspired, he says, by a graffiti artist he saw working on a wall one day: those sprayed starbursts of colour. He's a man of nearly seventy, but as open-minded as a twenty-year-old. The old rocker, he calls himself. He shows us the making of his *cordero con café cortado*, the process of rolling a tender piece of lamb in a sheet of coffee as thin as cellophane, peeled from the base of a frying pan, so that, when the sauce is poured into the tube, it gently disintegrates. 'Wow, I love this, it's a fantasy, it's like a game,' he chuckles, as the sauce goes in and the translucent brown tube falls in on itself like a fairytale tower. It is difficult to understand, but wonderful to see, how anyone at this moment of the world can be so brimful of optimism.

'The young generation is so much better prepared than we ever were,' says Juan Mari, from the edge of the stage. 'Which is why I can't see that there's a problem with Spanish cooking. On the contrary: things are getting better and better.'

At the end of the morning, I leave a jumper on my front row seat, hoping this will be enough to dissuade fellow food fans from stealing my place, and roam the stalls in search of something to eat. My programme says there's to be a tasting of regional tapas, with local wines to match.

From my place at the bar, I watch a parade of waiters emerge from their field kitchen. 'Let's see what they think of this fancy shit,' mutters one as he balances a tray on one hand and strides out into the fray.

The canapés are creations distantly inspired by the cooking of Navarra. Which means that there is *chistorra* in a crisp pastry case, and *menestra* served in tiny pots, and Swiss chard stalks fried with béchamel and Roncal cheese.

As the Navarrese wine begins to flow, however, culinary considerations begin to take second place to the need to eat. The waiters' route takes them from the kitchen door and across the bridge separating the stage area from the rest of the hall. The cleverest and hungriest of the fair-goers, I see, have quickly learned to position themselves at the end of the bridge, in order to pick off the best morsels before they reach the desperate masses on the far side. Now the battle is on to seize as many canapés as will fit in a hand, on top of a programme, or wherever else the booty can be conveyed. As tempers fray, the scene degenerates into a free-for-all. Raiding parties can be seen looting entire trays of tapas from the agitated waiters. One woman, a smart executive in Blahnik heels, holds aloft a paper carrier bag, shovelling half a dozen *pinchos* into it from on high, calling to her friends behind her: 'OK, guys, I've got something. Now we can eat.'

I stay at the bar to watch this comic scene and settle for a plate of acorn-fed ham, some green olives, and a free glass of Mahou beer.

Now a voice comes over the tannoy: the next master class will begin in five minutes, FIVE MINUTES.

A shiver of excitement runs through the conference centre, from the ground floor all the way up to the back row seats of the theatre.

The atmosphere is suddenly akin to a busy foyer in some concert hall where some charismatic pop-star is about to perform, with people hurriedly grabbing their hotdogs and Cokes and checking their tickets and chattering. The last of the wine is swigged, glasses are dumped on tables strewn with abandoned leaflets, and the throng can be felt to move, gradually but inexorably, towards the theatre.

The stage now resembles a TV set, blazing with lights, buzzing with cameras. The foot of the stage seethes with punters, some trying to get to their seats in the stalls, others peering at the set-up onstage, which includes a giant industrial gas bottle that looks like an unexploded bomb, but is actually some kind of siphon, others simply milling about, perhaps hoping for a glimpse of the man who is himself a living incarnation of the transformation their country has recently undergone. From my seat, he is just a few yards away, adrift in the crowd in his white chef's jacket, fending off questions to right and left. A group of Japanese journalists surrounds and traps him, making little nods and bows, assembling themselves around the man while one of them backs away with a camera. The journalists pose for the photo-op with delighted grins – if their friends could see them now! – while the star's smile is merely friendly and a little distracted.

At the seaside on that evening last summer, I found him affable, sure of himself, but in a self-effacing kind of way. Here in Madrid, he looks different: a bigger, widescreen version of himself. Not a trace of nerves. He seems energised, enthused. I would never have suspected it, knowing what I know about his mistrust and rejection of celebrity. But, up here in front of the world's media and his peers, he is in his element. Caught up in the atmosphere I sense affection, admiration, perhaps a dose of gratitude towards a man who has done at least as much for the power of Spain as a brand as anyone else alive. At least as much as Placido Domingo, Montserrat Caballé, Pedro Almodóvar, King Juan Carlos II, Antonio Banderas, or Penélope Cruz. Though not quite as much, heaven knows, as Julio Iglesias.

A man in an olive-green sports jacket bounds on to the stage. It is José Carlos Capel, the Summit's master of ceremonies. José Carlos begins saying something inaudibly into a microphone. The crowd disperses: the hubbub fades into a murmur. It's time.

'*Por favor*, ladies and gentlemen, *por favor* . . .' he says three times, until the noise has subsided and he can just be heard.

The *mise-en-scène* is impeccable. It feels like an apotheosis, a consecration. I can see down below, there he is, the man is waiting to go on, smoothing down his jacket, checking his mike. What is he going to do? We don't much care. It'll be enough just to see him up there, strolling about onstage, chatting to us about food and life and the restaurant and his inspirations. It might not even be a demonstration by any conventional definition, more of a rambling disquisition on originality in art and the meaning of electric milk. But that's fine by us. We just want to see him.

Thousands of watts of spring sunlight pour through the roof. The stage is a white-out.

José Carlos is speaking in measured tones, conscious of the charged nature of this moment. But he's smiling, too. There's a sweetness in the moment, a sense of triumph.

We know what is coming; he can't shut us up any more. Some of us are already on our feet, cheering, hands clapping, loose papers fluttering from files over the heads of the rows in front.

Now the decibel level is rising again. It flashes across my mind that this is the noisiest country in the world; they've done surveys, measured the midnight shouting in the streets and the motorbikes that roar by in the squares. Our massed voices echo off the glass roof, booming around the lower floors. It looks like José Carlos was going to say something more. If he was, he now gives up, letting his hands fall to his sides in mock-exasperation. The only thing left for him to say now is the inevitable, showbusiness formula. The words that raise the curtain.

'*Señoras y señores*, Ferran Adrià.'

EPILOGUE

Sitting in a small stone house with the generator humming. A gentle mist flooding the valley, muffling the sounds of dogs barking further up the hill. Then comes the rain: at first a soft pattering, now a furious downpour, drumming on the roof tiles, picking off the moss from the stones. A black cloud has squatted like a giant sulky toad at the head of the valley. On an afternoon like this there is nothing to do but read, think, write, cook, and eat.

After the cities, it was good to slip back into home and routine. The farm and its produce resumed their rightful place at the centre of my life. In springtime, there were peas and beans, the first spring onions, and lettuces of all shapes and colours. When the hens started laying again, I made little omelettes with fresh peas and garlic, and *habas con jamón* with shreds of our own home-cured ham. In May, I planted potatoes, French beans, cucumbers, corn, and the rest of the hot-weather stuff. On 15 June, a hailstorm pulverised it all, and, the following week, I planted it all out again.

I spent the summer quietly, my routine a slow round of mornings up at the farm, afternoons by the river with friends and books, and late nights in the kitchen. Spanish summer eating is about measure and modesty: we want energy and refreshment in easily manageable forms. I made litres of gazpacho and kept them in a flat glass jug in the fridge door, for those dog days when I want nothing more for lunch than a glass or two of cold gazpacho along with a piece of goat's cheese or an anchovy fillet, some bread with olive oil, and a ripe peach for *postre*. Towards the end of the summer, when the aubergines and peppers kicked in, I made huge quantities of *pisto*, Spain's answer to ratatouille. My summer nights were spent processing boxes of fruit and vegetables before the heat turned them rotten. Luckily, there are always people glad to take a box of courgettes off your hands in return for a cheese, a loaf of home-made bread, a bag of lemons.

After the autumn rains come the last tomatoes of the season, as precious and special as the first. While they were coming in bucketfuls, all through the hot summer, I held them almost in contempt. Now I realise that a long winter beckons without their familiar acid-tinged sweetness and musky aroma, and I decide to treat these late specimens with a little more respect. I bring them out, these October tomatoes, which have been slowly ripening on newspaper on the kitchen table, in careful slices on white plates, with an announcement around the table that this just may be one of the last two or three tomato salads of the year.

It has been a good year for quince, and my trees are still laden with big knobbly fruits that, once you wash off their grubby felt, become bright, shiny yellow boulders, hefty in the hands. Now is the time to make *dulce de membrillo*, the favourite Spanish sweetmeat par excellence, essentially a fruit jam poured into moulds and allowed to set until firm enough to be cut into slices. I have made ten kilos this year, and there is more to come.

Nacho returned from Palestine last week, full of stories of orchards in Jericho with all-year-round vegetable patches and wondrous fruit. While it is still raining, there is a lull in our agricultural routine. But soon there will be important tasks to consider: winter tasks. The pig must be killed. The olives must be picked and taken to the mill, the wine racked off into clean glass demijohns. On a bright, short, cold day, when there is nothing else to do, we might spend the afternoon making the *aguardiente* – literally 'burning water', the Spanish equivalent of *grappa* – in a copper still set up in the open air, distilling it from the skins and stalks leftover from the grape harvest. When the oranges are at their best, in the month of January, I make a dark, bitter marmalade without which breakfast at my house could never be the same.

It is no exaggeration to say that most of what I know about food has been taught me by the people and landscapes of Spain. But the rest I have discovered myself, through an apprenticeship as a small-time farmer who doesn't mind getting dirt under his fingernails. When food production is taken out of our hands by industrial processes and global economies, we lose out in understanding, in the effects on our health, and in the loss of true flavour. Taking back control of the process, however, can be empowering. Until I made butter from the cream of my own cow, I never understood that butter could be a rich oily paste, almost as yellow as saffron, smelling of pasture and flowers. Until I ate slices of sirloin from my own home-slaughtered pig, I never realised that, if the animal has eaten figs and apples all summer and foraged for acorns all winter, the meat will be incomparably tender and fine-textured as a result. Life in the country gives me daily lessons in the way things ought to taste.

She came up again this afternoon, bringing food and conversation. Everybody should have neighbours as good as her.

My friendship with Petra sums up most of what I have learned from these years in Spain. The particular rhythm of passing time, the texture of life, and how that which is of value is celebrated.

As a cook and as a farmer, I model myself on her, because she understands better than anyone I know that growing things and cooking things are two sides of the same coin. She does all the country things I try to do, but does them very much better, with an unassuming brilliance born out of natural aptitude, and after years and years of hard experience. From the milk of her husband's goats, she makes a cheese so true-flavoured that, if it were available on the open market, it would win prizes at every cheese fair in the country.

This afternoon we stood among the cabbages, talking about what can be done with them. She had brought me a clutch of oranges she had picked on the way up.

Before lunch, she tells me what she intends to cook; in the afternoon, what she and her family have eaten at midday. There might have been a nice hot *caldo*, a Spanish consommé, to which people here attribute miraculous powers of defence against the demons of cold and damp. A big pot of *costilla con patata*, the savoury winter stew of pork spare ribs and potato with garlic, onion, olive oil, and pimentón. Or, on Sunday, a proper *cocido* of beans and meats, to send her husband stumbling to the armchair while the rain falls harder and the afternoon darkens into evening.

My talks with Petra are proof that the rustic cooking of the region, though suffering under the onslaught of Convenience, still has plenty of life left in it. Sometimes, when I am walking down from the farm at lunchtime, through narrow streets of modest stone houses, I can hear the sound of pots and pans, smell the fine smells of frying and simmering on either side of the street, and it makes me happy to think that there is a corner of old Europe that still cares about proper home cooking and regional dishes, and that hasn't sold its soul to bottled sauces and just-add-water noodles.

Where I live, the supermarkets have a special shelf for sacks of salt, sausage casings, kilo bags of pimentón, and the paraphernalia of the *matanza*. Street markets sell not just the fruits and vegetables themselves, but trays of seedlings and fruit-tree saplings for people to grow their own. I take these to be signs that the traditional rural idea of food – which is to say, that it is entirely normal for the consumer to produce at least some of it himself – is here, alive and well, if losing a little currency with every passing year.

Night has fallen, the stream is rushing in the darkness. Inside the house the fire is lit; Nacho is asleep in front of it.

The church clock rings the hour: it is just ten o'clock. A good time to eat a simple Spanish dinner. I list in my mind the available ingredients: half a pumpkin (the other half we ate yesterday, in a rice with saffron), a head of purple garlic, half a dozen eggs. I will venture out with a torch, if need be, for some parsley, an onion, a head of lettuce. A pair of precious late tomatoes, to be rubbed on toasted rye bread, and a bottle of our own olive oil. Salt and pepper and pimentón. I lay it all out on the kitchen table, an Old Master still-life of rich and appetising colour. Just at this moment, the soul of Spanish food is all around me, out in the fields, in the olive groves and orchards, and right here on the table in front of me.

I ponder the possibilities as I put another log on the fire. And, in half an hour, we are sitting down to a *revuelto de calabaza*, the yolks with their warm maize yellow tinged a deeper shade by the pumpkin pieces, which have softened and melted a little round the edges. Somewhere in there is a garlic clove, bashed and roughly chopped, to be sizzled in the heating olive oil. And parsley, the greenest thing I've ever seen, torn with the fingers over the top. There is bread rubbed with tomato and our own aromatic, smoky white wine. And, for dessert, Petra's gift of oranges. They are the first of the season's very first crop: a harbinger of winter. Yet they have a taste, not of hard times and leafless landscapes, but of holidays and sunshine, the bright sweet taste of being alive.

ENTREMESES[1]

Dichos Culinarios
(food-related Spanish sayings)

Most languages have a number of sayings relating to food. English has, just to quote the first five or six that come into my head, 'to be worth its salt', 'our daily bread', 'bringing home the bacon', 'to sit there like a lemon', 'salad days' (well, this is from Shakespeare, so it may not count). Spanish is no exception, but there is something about the sheer quantity of food-related *dichos* (sayings) and *refranes* (proverbs) in the language that gives one pause for thought. Whole anthologies have been published of Spanish culinary proverbs. Most of them have fallen out of use, but a host remains. They are the product of a society that, until the 1970s, was overwhelmingly rural, and for which the rural world was still the major source of simile and metaphor. The rich legacy of Spanish sayings allows us to glimpse a society that is still able to see human life as a manifestation of nature. *De higos a brevas* – from figs to early figs – refers to the fact that figs are in season during late summer and autumn, whereas early figs appear in June, and so means, in English, 'very occasionally'. When you don't care a fig for something, the Spanish don't care a cucumber. *Estar en un*

---

1 *Entremés* (cul.): hors d'oeuvre. The term 'Entremeses' was also used by Miguel de Cervantes to describe the short plays he wrote in the last year of his life. These 'interludes' are light-hearted pieces which Cervantes is said to have 'chuckled as he wrote'.

berenjenal, literally 'to be in an aubergine field', means to be beset with intractable problems. Why the aubergine should have been chosen to represent hardship and complexity may seem at first like a mystery; except that, as anyone who has ever grown aubergines will know, the plant often has terrible spines around the base of the fruit, so that walking in a field of them might become a prickly and difficult business.

Spanish proverbs relating to cookery mine a rich vein of comedy and colour. Someone who is putting their best foot forward, or making an all-or-nothing effort, is said to be 'putting all the meat in the roaster'. When it comes to cooking utensils, we have *coger la sartén por el mango* – to 'grasp the frying pan by the handle', i.e. to get serious about something, or to take the bull by the horns. *Se le va la olla* – literally, something like 'he's overcooked the pot' – really means 'he's lost it' or 'he's gone crazy'. And *se me pasa el arroz* – 'I've overcooked the rice' – is the comically rueful phrase a Spanish girl might utter when she thinks she's now too old to get pregnant by traditional means.

But my favourite sayings are the ones that yoke together metaphorically sexual desire, or passionate love, with the act of eating. There is an earthiness about these expressions that, to English ears, sounds faintly embarrassing and possibly in bad taste. You might say of a particularly sexually appealing person *está como un queso*: 's/he's like a cheese'. (It would have to be a ripe, oozingly delicious cheese, possibly a Torta del Casar, into which you dip crisp slices of toast or sticks of raw vegetables in the manner of a fondue.)

If, to the Spanish imagination, cheese represents lust, bread stands for everything that is reliable, virtuous, and genuine. You often hear it said of people or things that they are *más bueno que el pan* ('better than bread'). And, if you want to describe a thoroughly good, thoroughly well-behaved person, you might well describe them admiringly as *un pedazo de pan* – 'a hunk of bread'.

I remember clearly the first time I heard an adult man say to his daughter that he found her so 'delicious' that he could 'eat her up whole'. *Estás más rica . . . ¡te voy a comer entera!* It was said with a lip-smacking sensuality that my latent Protestantism found shocking, and it was only when I thought about it carefully that I began to see the equation of hunger and love, the two great overriding human needs, as something not only poetically appropriate, but also hiding an important psychological truth. It may be a Latin thing, but there is sometimes a fierce intensity about a parent's love for his or her children that, in actual fact, is very well expressed by the metaphor of hunger for a home-made morsel of juicy, meaty, substantial, delicious food.

La Cocina Española
(the Spanish kitchen)

The Spanish kitchen – in other words, the place where Spanish cooking goes on – sometimes has a rather Spartan look about it: decoration and clutter are normally at a minimum, this being essentially a place for work, not leisure. It might be thought under-equipped by Anglo-Saxon standards; in reality, of course, it corresponds perfectly to the kinds of dishes to be prepared in it. Especially in rural areas, Spanish kitchens aren't big on electric toasters, sandwich makers, ice-crushers, and the dozens of other gizmos that increasingly clutter our Western urban lives – with the exception of the pressure cooker and the hand-held mixer, which is much used for soups and purées. English visitors are often surprised by the total absence of electric kettles, which play such a pivotal role in the making of our national life-blood, tea. There is still no proper word in Spanish to describe this device (*la tetera* is sometimes used, though it really means 'teapot'); when tea is made in a Spanish kitchen, the water is boiled, and the tea often made, in a small metal saucepan called *el cazo*.

Pre-modern societies have an inbuilt sense of measure, of economy, which, as postmoderns, we vainly struggle to recapture. The need to reuse oil for frying gave rise to a special pot into which the hot oil was poured, straining out the bits at the same time. The phenomenon of the giant fridge obscenely groaning with food, for example, has only recently made its appearance among the landscape of the Spanish kitchen – for obvious reasons, since Spanish cooks never relied very much on perishable items that needed to be kept in fridges: they shopped in the market on a daily basis, and many of their ingredients were preserved by other means than chilling, whether dried, smoked, salted, put up in brine, or canned.

If there are things they lack, by the same token, there are kitchen things in Spain which we might regard as oddities. Cooking Spanish dishes in English kitchens, for instance, can be a frustrating business, because the implements you are accustomed to using aren't there, and you are therefore forced to improvise. Most of all I miss the stacks of terracotta dishes without which many Spanish dishes simply don't taste the same. The pestle and mortar, whether made of wood or ceramic, is an essential element of any kitchen batterie, however basic, and especially prominent in Catalunya, where pounded mixtures of nuts and herbs (the *picada*) are used in all manner of ways. Equally, the perforated metal skimmer, or *espumadera*, present even in the humblest Spanish kitchen, is the perfect tool for a nation that loves to fry, and can be applied to all aspects of the task, from basting and stirring to straining off the hot oil. After fifteen years of using it almost daily, I can't imagine frying with anything else.

Globalisation and the powerful influence of American habits are rapidly smoothing away the rough edges of our differences – more's the pity. But there is, still, no accounting for taste. Generally speaking, and it's an odd fact considering their centuries of cohabitation with the culinary cultures of the Middle East, the Spanish are no great lovers of spice and heat in food. It follows that you won't find mustard in most Spanish larders, or bottled hot sauces, or anything pronouncedly piquant, with the exception of those long green Basque chillies in jars, and perhaps a string of little dried red peppers to be added, cautiously, one at a time, in such dishes as prawns *al ajillo* and salt cod *al pil-pil*. Even black peppercorns are not common, and the pepper mill, such a staple of life in Italy and France, is still a comparative rarity. (Grind too much into a dish, and you will hearing protesting voices: *¡cómo pica!*, 'it's so hot!') The spices these people love are not so much piquant-hot, as generous and warming. Near to the stove, where it can be easily reached, you're bound to find a tin of pimentón, the smoked dried powdered pepper that is the Spanish spice *por excelencia*. In a rack on the wall, there may be pungent saffron, or else its inadmissible, frankly unbearable substitute, orange food colouring. There will almost certainly be cumin seed and aniseed. And cinnamon – for a good *arroz con leche*, a *leche merengada* – a nice wobbly flan, or a creamy *natillas*, are all unthinkable without the warm glow of cinnamon.

Almuerzo

Almuerzo is actually the correct Spanish word for 'lunch'. In the population at large it has been almost entirely superseded by the catch-all term *comida* – food. It still lingers on in a couple of particular senses, or maybe three. *El almuerzo* is a business lunch, a no-messing-about, hard-talking sort of lunch where to talk about the food on the table, for example, would be to betray a certain feebleness of mind. The only other regular use of the word happens at the opposite end of the social scale, when workers who get up at the crack of dawn, such as labourers or builders, stop work mid-morning and have something to eat. They can often be seen, at ten or eleven in the morning, sitting in the cab of the tractor with the engine off, or squatting in a line on a concrete beam, unwrapping their *bocadillos* out of aluminium foil, washing down their *almuerzo* with a can of beer. As Spanish lunchtimes seem to slide inexorably towards the trough of the afternoon, there are times when I rather envy the early lunchtime of the working class, and wouldn't mind at all replacing the plodding, ineluctable *comida* with a quick *bocadillo* and a beer before getting back to work.

Merienda

Merienda is a gerund, a something fit to be somethinged. Objectively, it falls somewhere between 'snack', 'picnic', and 'tea', as in the English meal-time, rather than the drink. Yet, as is often the case with Spanish eating habits, the word takes its true meaning rather more from an attitude, an understanding of the circumstances involved, than from a rigorous set of conventions. The custom of *la merienda* is most commonly observed by children when they get out of school in the early afternoon. In the past, Spanish mothers, waiting at the gates, might hand their offspring a hunk of bread with a slab of chocolate (like the French *pain au chocolat*), or a *bocadillo* of jamón York, cheese, or both, wrapped in tinfoil. Alternatively, the *merienda* might be served at home, especially on a cold day, with hot chocolate or Cola Cao (*the* Spanish childhood drink, bar none) and biscuits, or toast sprinkled with olive oil and sugar.

But there is another sense to *merienda*: it is the kind of impromptu meal you might take with you on a country walk, with a juicy tortilla de patatas, a length of chorizo, and perhaps a Galician *empanada* stuffed with tuna and red peppers. It therefore becomes a moveable feast, something nourishing and robust that will boost your blood sugar levels just at the moment when they most need boosting. To me, it suggests not just a stop-gap measure, a bite of something to keep you going till dinner, but also something special that falls somehow outside the general scheme of things: a treat.

Comilona

'Big meal' doesn't quite get it. Neither do '*grande bouffe*' or 'pig-out'. To my mind, what the word implies is a get-together of family and/or friends around a table on a Saturday or Sunday lunchtime, or at Christmas or Easter, a long celebration based around some festive food – it could be a rice dish such as paella, a roast lamb or piglet, a whole baked fish, or a proper *cocido* with all the trimmings, the soup with the *fideos* followed by the chickpeas and meats on one big platter and the endless vegetables heaped up on another. *Postres* (desserts) are a matter of course, as are cheese, fruit, and copious wine. If the meal is held at Christmas, it will necessarily wind up with sweetmeats, chocolate truffles, almond *turrón*, and powdery *polvorones* that stick to the roof of your palate. The meal may begin decorously enough, but may well end in shouting and laughter, with children running riot around the table and their elders supping shots of ice-cold *aguardiente* and home-made *pacharán*.

Hoy me toca la comilona con la familia. 'Today I've got the big meal with the family.' I sometimes fancy I hear a bat's squeak of resentment in the word, as if to imply an obligation that, though enjoyable enough, a part of you would rather like to wriggle out of.

Sobremesa

Portuguese speakers are often confused by the term *sobremesa*, because, in their language, it means simply 'dessert'. The literal meaning is 'over table'. In Spanish, however, it refers to what happens after a meal, or more precisely, after the main part of the meal, when the dishes have been cleared away and it's time to relax, to digest, and most importantly, to talk. More than anything, the *sobremesa* is an opportunity to indulge in freewheeling, lighthearted, pleasurable conversation. The smell of coffee drifts in from the kitchen. There may be *digestivos*: icy-cold shot glasses of *aguardiente*, or balloon glasses of brandy, anis, or whisky. Those Spaniards still smoking – as I write, just under a quarter of Spanish adults – will find this the moment to bring out their cigarettes, their rolling tobacco, or a nice little cheroot from a tin.

La sobremesa encapsulates what for many people is the defining characteristic of the Spanish lifestyle, namely the emphasis on informality, lack of stress, and unhurried enjoyment of the moment. Tamara Rojo, the ballerina who has become a star of the Royal Ballet in London, was once interviewed by a Spanish newspaper about her life in Britain. She told the journalist: '*Aquí no hay sobremesas.*' 'There are no *sobremesas* here.' It was a neat way of implying, in a few words, that in London people lived a hurried, purposeful life which didn't allow for the casual Spanish attitude to passing time. Rojo seems to have meant no disapproval by her remark: for her, it was just a fact.

The *sobremesa* varies in length depending on the meal in question. At lunch on a work day, it might last just a few minutes, half an hour, or more. Whereas, on high days and holidays, it might stretch out languidly long into the afternoon, with the dishwasher going in the background and the coffee pot empty on the hob, until the guests drift away from the table and the *sobremesa* eventually gives way to another fine traditional custom: the siesta.

Siesta

The custom of an after-lunch sleep exists in all Mediterranean countries, though nowhere is it such an institution, such a pastime, such an art-form, as in Spain.

The word comes from the latin *sexta*, meaning the hours from noon to three in the afternoon. Quite how it began, as a custom, no one really knows; it seems likely to have been around for ever. It is certainly on the decline, and most Spaniards say they don't take the traditional nap after lunch, at least not for most of the year. The custom has largely retreated into particular times of year, especially hot summer days, when there is nothing else for it, and on holidays, when there's nothing to stop you.

The interesting thing about the siesta is the variety of forms it can take. For some people, it's a ten minute shut-eye in a chair. Others, like me, actually get into bed, under the covers, and go into REM sleep for as long as the body requires. Some might lie down with a book, others slump on the sofa with the afternoon movie (cinema on Spanish TV in the afternoon being generally unchallenging, fluffy stuff, third-rate Hollywood or 1960s Spanish films that won't interfere too much with a good snooze and might, indeed, provoke one).

Traditionally, the Spanish had a cheerfully functional and uncomplicated view of the business of sleep. My impression is that, generally speaking, people in this country have tended to sleep soundly, without much insomniac tossing and turning or recourse to sleeping pills and herbal tisanes.

With Spain's arrival in the club of the rich and worried, everything has changed. But still, it seems to me, Spanish culture does not fetishise sleep in the way that other cultures do. The act of sleeping is not surrounded with the universe of products and practices, the pyjamas and bathrobes and buckwheat pillows and breakfast in bed (the idea of *eating* in bed doesn't sound to the Spanish mind like much of a pleasure) that the Anglo-Saxon world enjoys. Sleep is a commodity the body needs more or less of, like water or Vitamin C, which is not to say it can't be cheerfully forgone if an all-night fiesta, a mammoth philosophical discussion, or a moonlit walk in the park with the kids, should happen to present itself. Lorca wrote somewhere that there's a moment just before dawn, when the first light is nothing but a dull glow on the horizon – this was the best moment, he believed, for human beings to go to sleep.

A friend's grandmother, a great purveyor of ancestral wisdom, had a favourite saying: '*la comida reposada y la cena paseada*'. It means something like 'rest after lunch and walk off your dinner'. The phrase reflects, in part, the widespread conviction among Spaniards that one should not go to bed on a full stomach. This lady's grandchildren, who included my friend, were at the age when Spaniards believe they must go out every night, all night. They believed the saying too. But only because it gave them ammunition when the time came to plead with their mother to let them out of the house for some night-time adventures.

When I worked in offices, I could never understand how, at two o'clock sharp, after the universal hour-long lunch break, one was expected to continue work in the same alert and intellectually cogent manner as before. For an hour at least after eating, I would often feel faint and woozy, and my colleagues got used to the sight of me snoozing at my desk, head resting on folded arms.

So I took to the siesta like a duck to water.

*   *   *

Think back, think back. It was the start of the summer holidays, early August. A lunch of home-grown suckling pig, roasted on a rack of bay twigs. We sat, a gang of adults and children, in a hot kitchen with the summer sun pouring through the open window, sweating slightly as we gorged on the sweet oily meat with its heavenly fragrance of bay leaf and garlic, swigging down the red wine from glasses smeared with greasy finger-marks. But the conversation, oddly, was not so much about the excellences of the food, as about the monumental siesta we were all going to have afterwards.

There were peaches, a little cheese, coffee, cigarettes. The kids disappeared, clattering their chairs, to play with dolls and dump-trucks. A little glass of *pacharán*, brandy, or *aguardiente*? Why not? We're on holiday. There was a little more torpid chat while the dishes were removed, the congealing pork fat scraped from the pan. And then, one by one, we did that Spanish thing: we sloped off to our beds, our sofas, our hammocks and easy chairs, like animals after a feed, sloping off to their caves. I've known Spanish people check out the siesta possibilities of a given situation – a nice shady spot under a fig tree, a mattress on the floor of the bodega – well before the big meal begins.

'What a hell of a siesta I'm about to have,' muttered Enrique, groping his way towards his chosen site – a sofa just under a window where a faint breeze came in from the sea.

Then came the *siestón*: the big siesta. This time it was a two-or-three-hour one, an excessive, Baroque, holiday siesta. After a siesta like this, you wake not quite knowing where you are, who you are, or what day of the week it is. There are pillow marks on your cheeks. The street outside is slowly coming back to life. There's a disconcerting kind of morning feeling. You sit around the kitchen table dazedly, coming to your senses, drinking black coffee, as if it were breakfast all over again. Which, in a way, it is. The second part of the day is grinding into gear – to be lived, if at all possible, as maximally as the first.

RESTAURANTS:
A PERSONAL SELECTION

Andalucía

Café de Paris
C/Vélez-Málaga 8, Málaga (La Malagueta), tel: 952 225 043,
www.rcafedeparis.com

Calima
Hotel Gran Meliá Don Pepe, C/José Meliá s/n, Marbella, tel: 952
764 252, www.restaurantecalima.com

El Faro del Puerto
Crta Rota km 0,500, El Puerto de Santa María (Cádiz), tel: 956
870 952, www.elfarodelpuerto.com

El Campero
Avenida de la Constitución 5C, Barbate (Cádiz), tel: 956 432 300

Asturias

Casa Marcelo
La Salgar 10, Arriondas, tel: 985 840 991, www.casamarcelo.com

Casa Gerardo
Crta AF19, km9, Prendes, tel: 985 887 797, www.casagerardo-prendes.com

Basque Country

Akelarre
Paseo Padre Orcolaga 56 (Barrio Igueldo), San Sebastián (Guipúzcoa), tel: 943 311 209, www.akelarre.net

Arzak
Avenida José Elosegui 273, San Sebastiàn (Guipúzcoa), tel: 943 285 593, www.arzak.es

Mugaritz
Caserío Otzazulueta, Aldura Aldea 20, Errenteria-Renteria (Guipúzcoa), tel: 943 522 455, www.mugaritz.com

Arbola-Gaña
Museo de Bellas Artes, Alameda Conde Arreche s/n, esq. Plaza Eduardo Chillida, Bilbao (Vizcaya), tel: 944 424 657

Gaminiz
Parque Tecnológico Ibaizábal 212, Zamudio (Vizcaya), tel: 944 317 025, www.gaminiz.com

Guggenheim Bilbao
Abandoibarra Etorbidea 2, Bilbao (Vizcaya), tel: 944 239 333, www.restauranteguggenheim.com

Martín Berasategui
C/Loidi 4, Lasarte-Oria (Guipúzcoa), tel: 943 366 471, www.martinberasategui.com

Castilla-La Mancha

Las Rejas
C/Borreros 49, Las Pedroñeras (Cuenca), tel: 967 161 089,
www.lasrejas.net

El Bohío
Avenida Castilla-La Mancha 81, Illescas (Toledo), tel: 925 511
126, www.elbohio.com

Catalunya

Can Jubany
Crta Sant Hilari s/n, Calldetenes (Barcelona), tel: 938 891 023,
www.canjubany.com

Sant Pau
Carrer Nou 10, Sant Pol de Mar (Barcelona), tel: 937 600 662,
www.ruscalleda.com

El Celler de Can Roca
Crta Taiala 40, Girona, tel: 972 222 157,
www.cellercanroca.com

El Bulli
Cala Montjoi, Roses (Girona), tel: 972 150 457,
www.elbulli.com

Les Cols
Mas Les Cols, Crta de la Canya s/n, Olot (Girona), tel: 972 269 209,
www.lescols.com

La Xicra
Carrer Estret 17, Palafrugell (Girona), tel: 972 305 630

Bonay
Plaça de les Voltes 13, Peratallada (Girona), tel: 972 634 034,
www.bonay.com

Cal Campaner
C/Mossen Carles Feliu 23, Roses (Girona), tel: 972 256 954

Àbac
C/Rec 79–89, Barcelona, tel: 933 196 600,
www.restaurantabac.com

Ot
C/Córcega 537, Barcelona, tel: 934 358 048,
www.otrestaurant.net

Comerç 24
C/Comerç 24, Barcelona, tel: 933 192 102, www.comerc24.com

Ca l'Isidre
C/Les Flors 12, Barcelona, tel: 93 441 1139, www.calisidre.com

Comunidad Valenciana

Casa Salvador
Estany de Cullera s/n, Cullera (Valencia), tel: 961 720 136

Ca' Sento
C/Méndez Núñez 17, Valencia, tel: 963 301 775

Casa Carmina
C/Embarcadero 4, El Saler (Valencia), tel: 961 830 254

Casa Pepa
C/Partida Pamis 7–30, Ondara (Alicante), tel: 965 766 606

La Rosa
Paseo Neptuno 70, Playa de las Arenas (Valencia), tel: 963 712 076

El Poblet
Las Marinas km3, Dénia (Alicante), tel: 965 784 179
www.elpoblet.com

Paco
C/San Francisco 2, Pinoso (Alicante), tel: 965 478 023

Extremadura

Atrio
Avenida de España 30, Cáceres, tel: 927 242 928,
www.restauranteatrio.com

Il Cigno
Avenida de Extremadura 4, Hoyos (Cáceres), tel: 927 514 413

Galicia

Toñi Vicente
C/Rosalía de Castro 24, Santiago de Compostela (A Coruña), tel: 981 594 100, www.tonivicente.com

Casa Marcelo
Rúa das Hortas 1, Santiago de Compostela (A Coruña), tel: 981 558 580, www.casamarcelo.net

Dorna
Rúa Castelao 150, O Grove (Pontevedra), tel: 986 731 842

La Rioja

El Portal de Echaurren
C/Héroes de Alcázar 2, Ezcaray, tel: 941 354 047,
www.echaurren.com

Madrid

Santceloni
Hotel Hesperia, Paseo de la Castellana 57, tel: 912 108 840,
www.hesperia-madrid.com

La Broche
Hotel Miguel Angel, C/Miguel Angel 29, Madrid, tel: 913 993
437, www.labroche.com

Principe de Viana
C/Manuel de Falla 5, Madrid, tel: 914 571 549

La Terraza del Casino
Casino de Madrid, C/Alcalá 15, Madrid, tel: 915 218 700,
www.casinodemadrid.es

El Chaflan
Avenida Pío XII 34, Madrid, tel: 913 450 450,
www.elchaflan.com

Navarra

Maher
C/Ribera 19, Cintruénigo, tel: 948 811 150,
www.hotelmaher.com

GLOSSARY

Cat. = Catalan
Basq. = Basque
Gal. = Gallego

A

a la plancha: cooked on metal hot plate
a la romana: battered and deep-fried, most usually squid rings, hake
aceite: oil
aceituna: olive
acelga: Swiss chard
adafina: Sephardic dish from which *cocido* derives
adobo: 'marinade'; *cazón en adobo*: chunks of fish (*cazón* belongs to the
    shark family) marinated in vinegar and spices, and then deep-fried.
    Popular dish in Andalucía
aguardiente: firewater, alcohol
ajoarriero: cf. *bacalao al ajoarriero*, Navarrese dish of salt cod with garlic
ajoblanco: cold almond soup from Andalucía, often served with grapes
albóndigas: meatballs
alboronía: Andalusian summer-vegetable dish similar to *pisto*
aliño: dressing
allioli (Cat.): i.e. '*all i oli*', 'garlic and oil', powerful emulsion sauce made in
    the mortar and pestle, common accompaniment on the Spanish Medi-
    terranean coast to fish, meat, and rice dishes
almazara: olive oil mill
almorta: pulse similar to the lupin seed
alta cocina: haute cuisine
altramuz (pl. *altramuces*): lupin seeds, boiled with salt and eaten cold, a
    popular snack in summer and on festive occasions
alubias: beans grown for drying, can be white, red, or black
aperitivo: aperitif, snacks served with pre-prandial drinks
aplec (Cat.): celebration, festival
arros a banda (Cat.): rice 'on the side', cooked in a strong fish stock in the
    paella
arroz a la cubana: plain rice served with fried egg, fried banana, and tomato
    sauce

artesa: flat-based, long wooden container for kneading bread, mixing sausage meat, etc
asador: 'roaster', grill restaurant
azafrán: saffron

B
bacalao, bacallà (Cat.): salt cod
barra (de pan): long, flattish white loaf (of bread)
barrio: district, neighbourhood
berenjena: aubergine
bocadillo: Spanish sandwich, usually made from length of *barra* (see above)
borraja: borage
broa: maize bread
bullit de peix (Cat.): mixed fish soup-stew (Ibiza)

C
café con leche: coffee with milk
café cortado: black coffee with a dash of milk
café solo: strong black coffee
cala: rocky bay, cove
calabacín: courgette
calabaza: pumpkin, squash
calamares: squid
calçot/calçotada (Cat.): spring onion (scallion) and its related food-event
caldereta: casserole, most often based on lamb or kid (Extremadura) and lobster (Menorca)
caldero: heavy iron pot, and, by association, fish and rice dish made in this pot (*caldero murciano*)
caldo: stock, consommé
canelones: 'cannelloni', pasta tubes stuffed with minced meats, béchamel sauce
caña: small serving of (draught) beer
caracol: snail
cardo: *Cynara cardunculus*, in English, cardoon. Vegetable of the artichoke family, with the difference that it's the stalk that's eaten, not the flower
casa de comida: eating house
casquería: variety meats, offal
cecina: dry-cured beef, served in thin slices, a speciality of León
cerdo ibérico: traditional breed of black pig
cervecería: beer bar
chilindrón: sauce of tomato, pepper, onion and ham, most commonly applied to chicken and lamb, typical of Aragon
chipirones: baby squid; *c. en su tinta*: cooked in their own ink
chiringuito: beach bar/shack
chorizo: cured Spanish slicing sausage made with lean meat, garlic, and pimentón
churro: deep-fried tube of batter, often eaten with thick drinking chocolate

coca: bread-based tart, related to pizza

cochinillo: suckling pig

cocido: long-simmered stew based on chickpeas or other pulses, also including vegetables, meats and *embutidos*, e.g. *c. madrileño*

cogollo: lettuce heart, also dwarf lettuce

comedor: dining room

compangu: refers to meats and *embutidos*, used in *fabada asturiana*

cordero: lamb

cortijo: country house, farmhouse, esp. in Andalucía

costilla: spare rib

crema catalana: custard with a caramel crust, similar to crème brûlée, regional dessert of Catalunya

croquetas: breaded croquettes filled with a thick béchamel incorporating chopped ham, boiled egg, chicken, etc. Traditionally made with leftover meats from the *cocido*

D

de autor: 'authorial', implies a style of cooking based around the creativity of a particular chef

denominación de origen (DO): 'denomination of origin', official system controlling and protecting various speciality products and wines

dorada: gilt-head bream

dulce (n. and adj.): sweet

E

embutidos: generic term for sausages, from the verb *embutir*, to stuff

empanada: a flat, thin pie with a variety of possible fillings, most commonly tuna with pepper and tomato. Originally from Galicia

empanadilla: small turnover stuffed with tuna, minced meat, spinach and raisins, etc

encebollado: cooked with fried onion, especially liver or tuna

encina: holm oak

escabeche: mild pickle of vinegar, herbs and garlic, most commonly applied to rabbit or other small game, or sardines. The ingredient to be prepared *en escabeche* is previously roasted or fried

escalivada (Cat.): salad of chargrilled vegetables

escanciar: method of serving cider, pouring it from a height into a flat-bottomed glass in order to oxygenate the cider

escudella: Catalan *cocido* of pulses, meats, vegetables

estofado: meat stew, usually of beef

F

faba (pl. *fabes*): large dried bean used in *fabada asturiana*

fideo: thin macaroni-like pasta

fideuà (Cat.): pasta-based dish made in the paella, originated in the town of Gandía (Alicante) *fino*: abbr. form of 'Jerez fino', pale crisp white sherry of around 15 per cent alcohol, the traditional andaluz accompaniment to aperitifs, tapas, and seafood

flauta: thin, crisp, baguette-style loaf

fonda: lodging house, from the Arabic *fonduk*. In Catalunya, also implies restaurant.

freiduría: fried fish shop

fricandó: traditional Catalan beef stew

G

gachas: savoury porridge with fried *tocino*, *panceta*, etc

gallego (n. and adj.): native of Galicia, language spoken there, etc

gallina: hen; *g. en pepitoria*, traditional dish of hen with almonds and saffron

gamba: prawn, shrimp

garbanzo: chickpea

garrofó (Cat.): large flat white bean, used in paella

gazpacho: 1) raw vegetable soup, served cold 2) *g. manchego*, rich game-based stew cooked with crushed dry flatbread

granizado: water ice

guiso (n.), *guisado* (adj.): terms used to describe any dish made by boiling or simmering ingredients (as opposed to roasting, frying)

H

habas: broad beans

herboristería: shop specialising in herbs, natural remedies, etc

horchata: sweet milky drink made from ground earth nuts (*chufas*), common in Valencia

hórreo: stone drying shed for maize (Asturias and Galicia)

huerto/huerta: vegetable garden. Also collective term, e.g. La Huerta de Murcia, vegetable producing area close to the city

hueva: cured and pressed roe, normally tuna or grey mullet

huevos estrellados: fried egg and potato hash, as served at Casa Lucio in Madrid

I

ijar, atún de: tuna preserved in oil

J

jamón serrano: air-cured 'mountain' ham

K

kokotxa (Basq.): gelatinous 'cheeks' of hake, cod, etc

L

lacón: salt-cured sweet ham, common in Galicia and Asturias
lampuga: common dolphin fish
latifundio: large country estate
lentejas: lentils
lomo: loin; *l. embuchado*: whole cured pork loin
longaniza/llonganissa (Cat.): a variety of thin *embutido*

M

majado, majao: pounded mixture of spices, herbs, etc, often added to a dish in its final stages of cooking
manchego: of La Mancha, as in sheep's cheese *queso manchego*
manteca: pork fat
mantecado: sweet biscuit made with ground almonds and pork fat. Also called *polvorón*
manzanilla: 1) type of Jerez fino produced in Sanlúcar de Barrameda, 2) camomile for infusions, 3) variety of olive
mar i muntanya (Cat.): 'sea and mountain', any dish combining seafood and meat
marinera: general term for seafood cookery, as in *cocina marinera*
marisco: shellfish
marmitako (Basq.): tuna and potato casserole
matancera: female expert in the art of the *matanza*
matanza: traditional pig slaughter and processing
mazapán: marzipan
mejillón: mussel
membrillo: quince; *dulce de m.*: quince paste, typically served with cheese
menestra: vegetable dish made mostly in the spring, originally from Navarra. The *menestra* may also contain lamb or chicken.
menú degustación: tasting menu
merendero: picnic site, snack bar (see appendix one, '*Merienda*')
merluza: hake; *m. en salsa verde*: in a sauce with clams, parsley, garlic
michirones: murciano dish made from dried broad beans
miel: honey; *m. de caña*: sugar cane syrup
migas: fried breadcrumbs with garlic, chopped *panceta, tocino*, red pepper, etc
milhojas: millefeuille pastry. Also called *hojaldre*
mojama: salted cured fish, esp. tuna
mojo: sauce, esp. in Canary Islands, e.g. *mojo picón* (spicy), *mojo verde* (with coriander)
mona: Easter speciality in Catalunya. Originally a rich brioche, now more often a chocolate cake or figure
mongetes (Cat.): white beans; *m. amb butifarra* (with grilled sausage, popular dish in Catalunya)
morcilla: blood sausage
morros: snout, 'face' meat, usually of pork or beef
mortadela: similar to Italian *mortadella*, fine-ground pork slicing sausage used in sandwiches, in Spain stuffing often includes olives

N

níscalo (Cast.)/*rovelló* (Cat.): wild mushroom *Lactarius deliciosus* (Saffron Milk Cap)

Ñ

ñora: round dried pepper, mildly spicy, used in cooking of south-eastern Spain

O

olla podrida: substantial *cocido*-type stew typical of Burgos

P

pa amb tomàquet: Catalan snack, bread or toast rubbed with olive oil and tomato paella; shallow iron pan with handles; rice dish cooked in this pan, originally from Valencia
panceta: cured pork belly
panellets (Cat.): almond macaroons, often encrusted with pine nuts or other nuts, made in Catalunya for the feast of Epiphany
pargo: porgy fish, common sea bream
pastelería/pastisseria (Cat.): pastry shop
pata negra: 'black foot'. The term refers to the Iberian pig, to the hams produced from it, and, by association, to anything of superlative quality
patatas bravas: fried potato pieces with spicy sauce
percebes: goose barnacles
perdiz: partridge
perrunilla: sugary biscuit, made with pork fat
pescaíto frito: an andaluz favourite, small fish, and/or fish chunks, dredged with special flour and deep-fried
picada: pounded mixture of herbs, spices, garlic, bread, biscuits, etc, characteristic of Catalan cooking
picante: piquant, 'hot'
pil-pil: rich olive oil and garlic emulsion sauce, most often applied to salt cod for one of Basque cuisine's most famous dishes, *bacalao al pil-pil*
pimentón: finely ground dried red pepper, used as condiment
pimiento de Padrón: baby green pepper from Galicia, served fried, whose heat is notoriously unpredictable
pimiento de piquillo: variety of small, red, pointy-ended peppers, often stuffed with fish or meat
pintxo (Basq.): variant of tapas, find their highest expression in Bilbao and San Sebastián
piperrada: Basque dish of peppers, tomato, onion, etc
pisto: Spanish summer dish of aubergine, tomato, pepper, onion, etc, originally from La Mancha
pitu de caleya: free range cockerel (Asturias)
plato típico: 'typical dish', regional speciality
pocha: white bean, picked between fresh and dry

porra: 1) thick *churro*, 2) *porra antequerana*, smooth gazpacho from the town of Antequera

porrusalda: leek and potato soup-stew

postre: dessert

potaje: soup-stew, generally with vegetables

pote: cabbage, bean, and meat stew typical of Western Asturias

pringá: kind of pâté made from the finely chopped fatty meats leftover from the *puchero*

prueba: 'proof', 'trial', sample of sausage mixture fried up for testing at the *matanza*, now become dish in its own right

puchero: cooking pot, also andaluz one-pot stew, related to *cocido*

pulpeira (Gal.): octopus cooks (Galicia), also refers to a place serving octopus (*pulpería* in Castilian)

pulpo a feira: gallego speciality, boiled and sliced octopus with cooked potato, olive oil, pimentón and sea salt, served on a wooden plate

R

rabo de toro: bull's tail

ración: 'serving', larger versión of tapa

rape: monkfish

rehogado: technique of sautéing previously cooked vegetables in olive oil

revuelto: scrambled eggs

ribeiro: white Galician wine

romesco: sauce of pounded almonds, hazelnuts, garlic, tomato, olive oil, etc, also refers to a fish dish typical of Tarragona

ropa vieja: chopped mixed leftovers from the *cocido*, sautéed in olive oil and garlic

rosca/rosco/roscón: varieties of baked goods

S

sagardotegia (Basq.): cider house

salazón: applied to any food preserved in salt, *en salazón*

salchichón: Spanish salami

salmorejo: silky-smooth variant of gazpacho, usually made without cucumber or peppers. Typical of the province of Córdoba

salpicón: cold (seafood) salad

samfaina: Catalan base sauce of peppers, aubergine, onion, tomato

serrano adj: 'of the mountain', e.g. jamón serrano

setas: (wild) mushrooms

sidra: cider. Principally made (and consumed) in the communities of Asturias, Cantabria, and the Basque country.

sobrassada (Cat.): pork sausage from the Balearic islands, of a spreading consistency, cured with large amounts of pimentón

socarrat (Cat.): highly valued by connoisseurs of paella, the rice at the centre of the pan's base which becomes caramelised or lightly burned during cooking

sofrit pagès (Cat.): (Ibiza) dish of boiled and sautéed meats and vegetables
sofrito/sofregit: sauce base, a sauté of onions and other finely chopped vegetables
solomillo: andaluz*sopas frías*: 'cold soups', generic term for andaluz family of gazpacho, salmorejo, etc.

T

tinto de verano: 'summer red', red wine with lemonade or fizzy pop and lots of ice
tocinillo de cielo: 'heavenly bacon', sweetmeat made of eggs yolks and sugar
tocino: fatty bacon
torta: 1) flatbread, 2) type of rich unctuous sheep's cheese, e.g. *Torta del Casar*
tortilla de patatas: Spanish potato omelette
tortillita de camarón: shrimp fritters, made with a thin batter and sizzled *a la plancha.*
turrón: honey and almond nougat, eaten at Christmas. There are two basic types: *t. de Alicante* (hard) and *t. de Jijona* (soft)
txakoli (Basq): acidic white wine from Basque country
txistorra (Basq.): long thin sausage sold in coils, of Basque/Navarrese origin
txoko (Basq.): gastronomic society

U

urta: fish common on the coast of Cadiz, most often prepared *a la roteña* (in the style of Rota) with peppers, tomato and potato

V

venta: roadside locale combining elements of restaurant, shop, bar, and petrol station, common in the south of Spain
vi d'agulla/vino de aguja: white, acidic 'needle wine', slightly sparkling
vi ranci (Cat.): a maderised [partly oxidised] wine made from the Garnatxa grape, commonly used in cooking
vieiras (Gal.): scallops
vinagreta: Spanish sauce, similar to French vinaigrette, traditionally including finely chopped onion, parsley and boiled egg
vuelta y vuelta: 'turn and turn', of anything briefly cooked on both sides

Y

yema: egg yolk, also refers to the convent sweetmeat made of it

Z

zorongollo: murciano dish of courgettes (zucchini), onion and egg
zurrukutuna (Basq.): salt cod, pepper and egg soup

BIBLIOGRAPHY

SPANISH FOOD: GENERAL

Adrià, Ferran, *Los Secretos de El Bulli*, Altaya, Barcelona, 1997
Almodóvar, Miguel Angel, *Rutas con Sabor*, RBA, Barcelona, 2001
Anson, Rafael, *La Gastronomía Española*, Everest, León, 2000
Bienzobas, Águeda, *Recetas Tradicionales*, Zendrera, Barcelona, 1999
Camba, Julio, *La Casa de Lúpulo o el Arte de Comer*, Espasa Calpe, Madrid, 1968
Capel, José Carlos, *Homenaje a la Tortilla de Patata*, Planeta, Barcelona, 2003
Cocina Monacal: Secretos Culinarios de las Clarisas, Planeta, Barcelona, 1999
Davidson, Alan, *The Tio Pepe Guide to the Seafood of Spain and Portugal*, Anness Publishing, London, 1992
Doménech, Ignacio, *Guía del Gastrónomo (Vademécum Culinario)*, Quintilla y Cardona, Barcelona, 1968
Doménech, Ignacio, *Ayunos y Abstinencias: Cocina de Cuaresma*, Alta Fulla, Barcelona, 1982
Domingo, Xavier, *Cuando Solo nos Queda la Comida*, Tusquets, Barcelona, 1980
García Santos, Rafael, *Lo Mejor de la Gastronomía*, Destino, Barcelona, 2004
García, Abraham, *El Placer de Comer, Síntesis*, Madrid, 2004
García, Jacinto, *Un Convento de Aromas*, Junta de Comunidades de Castilla-La Mancha, 2002
Herrera, Ana Maria, *Manual Clásico de Cocina*, El Pais Aguilar, Madrid 2000
Luján, Nestor, and Juan Perucho, *El Libro de la Cocina Española*, Tusquets, Barcelona, 2005
Martínez, Francisco. *Arte de Cocina, Pastelería, Vizcochería y Conservería*, Imprenta de Maria Angela Martí, Barcelona, 1763
Menús Familiares, Ministerio de Comercio, Madrid, 1974
Muñoz Redón, Joseph, *La Cocina del Pensamiento*, RBA, Barcelona, 2005
Muro, Ángel, *El Practicón*, Poniente, Madrid, 1982
Ortega, Simona, *Mil Ochenta Recetas de Cocina*, Alianza, Madrid, 1972

Pérez, Dionisio, *La Cocina Clásica Española*, La Val de Onsera, Huesca, 1994
Pérez, Dionisio, *Guia del Buen Comer Español*, Rivadeneyra, Madrid, 1929
Puga y Parga, Manuel María, *La Cocina Práctica*, Galí, Santiago de Compostela, 1972
Vázquez Montalbán, Manuel, *Contra Los Gourmets*, Mondadori, Barcelona, 1997
Vázquez Montalbán, Manuel, *Saber o no Saber*, Ediciones B, Barcelona, 2002
Vázquez Montalbán, Manuel, *Segundo Libro de Cocina*, Muchnik, Barcelona, 1982
Vega, Luis Antonio de, *Viaje por la Cocina Española*, Salvat, Madrid, 1969

REGIONAL SPANISH CUISINES

Amate, Pablo, *Gastronomía Granadina*, Ayuntamiento de Granada, 1996
Bennison, Vicky, *The Taste of a Place: Andalucía*, Chakula Press, London, 2005
Carpinell (viuda de), Eladia, *Carmencito o la Buena Cocinera*, Librería Universitaria, Barcelona 2001
Castro, Xavier, *Ayunos y Yantares*, Nivola, Madrid, 2001
Chela, José H, et al., *Cincuenta Recetas Fundamentales de la Cocina Canaria*, Cabildo de Tenerife, Santa Cruz de Tenerife, 2004
Cofradía Extremeña de Gastronomía, *Nuevo Recetario de Cocina Extremeña*, Caja Rural de Extremadura, Mérida, 2001 (check author)
Delgado, Carlos, *Comer en Madrid*, Penthalon, Madrid, 1981
Doménech, Ignasi, *La Teca*, Març 80, Barcelona, 1994
Iglesias, Pepe, *Asturias Gastronómica*, AG Ediciones, Posada de Llanera (Asturias), 2004
Lladonosa i Giró, Josep, *La Cuina que Torna*, Empúries, Barcelona, 1997
Núñez, Elisa, *Cocina Charra*, Alianza, Madrid, 2002
Osona Terra de Cuina, Osona Cuina, 2001
Osorio, Carlos, *Tabernas y Tapas de Madrid*, Ediciones La Librería, Madrid, 2004
Palacin, Montse de, *Barcelona Served: Cuina Catalana Contemporània*, Ajuntament de Barcelona, 2005
Parellada, Ramón, *El Llibre de les Picades*, La Magrana, Barcelona, 2000
Pla, Joseph, *El Que Hem Menjat*, i-ii, Destino, Barcelona, 1992
Richardson, Paul, *Foods of the World: Barcelona*, Oxmoor House, San Francisco, 2005
Suárez Granda, Juan Luis, *La Fabada*, Trea, Gijón, 2001
Taibo, Paco Ignacio, *Breviario de la Fabada*, Mondadori, Barcelona, 1988
Thibaut i Comalada, Eliana, *La Cuina dels Països Catalans*, Pòrtic, Barcelona, 2001

Vergara, Antonio, *Anuario Gastronómico de la Comunidad Valenciana*, Gratacels, Valencia, 2004
Zarzalejos, Maria de, *Cocina del Camino de Santiago*, Alianza, Madrid, 1993

HISTORY

Almodóvar, Miguel Angel, *El Hambre en España*, Oberón, Madrid, 2003
Altimiras, Juan, *Nuevo Arte de Cocina*, De la Luna, 2001
Cunqueiro, Álvaro, *La Cocina Cristiana de Occidente*, Tusquets, Barcelona, 1991
Díaz, Lorenzo, *Cocina del Quijote*, Alianza, Madrid, 1979
Díaz, Lorenzo, *Cocina del Barroco: la Gastronomía del Siglo de Oro*, Alianza, Madrid, 2003
Domingo, Xavier, *De la Olla al Mole*, Cultura Hispánica, Madrid, 1984
Espinet, Miguel, *El Espacio Culinario: de la Taberna Tomana a la Cocina Profesional y Doméstica del Siglo XX*, Tusquets, Barcelona, 1984
Fausto Rodríguez de Sanabria, Luis, *Recetas Para Después de una Guerra*, Aguilar, Madrid, 2000
Fernández-Armesto, Felipe, *Historia de la Comida*, Tusquets, Barcelona, 2004
Gutiérrez Rueda, Carmen and Laura, *El Hambre en el Madrid de la Guerra Civil*, Ediciones La Librería, Madrid, 2003
Huici, Ambrosio, *Cocina Hispano-Magrebí durante la Época Almohade*, Trea, Gijón, 2005
Martínez Llopis, Manuel, *Historia de la Gastronomía Española*, Alianza, Madrid, 1989
Nola, Ruperto de, *Libro de Guisados, Manjares y Potajes, Intitulado Libro de Cozina* Logroño, 1529, facs edn Espasa Calpe, Barcelona, 1992
Núñez Florencio, Rafael, *Con la Salsa de su Hambre*, Alianza, Madrid, 2004
Redon, Odile, *Delicias de la Gastronomía Medieval*, Anaya y Mario Muchnik, Madrid, 1996
Revel, Jean-François, *Un Festín en Palabras: Historia de la Sensibilidad Gastronómica*, Tusquets, Barcelona, 1996
Rodinson, Maxine, et al., *Medieval Arab Cookery*, Prospect Books, Totnes, 2001
Sánchez Jiménez, José, *La Vida Rural en la España del Siglo XX*, Planeta, Barcelona, 1975

OTHER WORKS CONSULTED

Altman, Donald, *Del Cielo a la Mesa*, Integral, Barcelona, 2000
Berger, John, *Pig Earth*, Vintage, London, 1992
Ford, Richard, *Handbook for Travellers in Spain and Readers at Home*, Centaur Press, Arundel, 1966

Lee, Laurie, *As I Walked Out One Midsummer Morning*, Penguin, London, 1979

Lewis, Norman, *Voices of the Old Sea*, Picador, London, 1996

Martínez, Angel, *De Techo y Olla: Alojamiento y Cocina en los Libros de Viaje*, Miraguano, Madrid, 2002

Sen, Miguel, *Un Artículo de Encargo*, RBA, Barcelona, 2004

INDEX

A NOTE ON THE AUTHOR

Paul Richardson was born on the shores of the Mediterranean and grew up in rural Hampshire, where he first saw the connection between food and quality of life. He studied at Cambridge and worked as a journalist in London, before leaving England for Spain, where he has lived since 1990. Paul Richardson's books include *Cornucopia: A Gastronomic Tour of Britain*, *Our Lady of the Sewers and Other Adventures in Deep Spain* and *Indulgence: One Man's Selfless Search for the Best Chocolate in the World*. He is a contributing editor for *Condé Nast Traveller* magazine, and also writes for *Gourmet* in the US.

A NOTE ON THE TYPE

The text of this book is set in Linotype Sabon, named after the type founder, Jacques Sabon. It was designed by Jan Tschichold and jointly developed by Linotype, Monotype and Stempel, in response to a need for a typeface to be available in identical form for mechanical hot metal composition and hand composition using foundry type.

Tschichold based his design for Sabon roman on a font engraved by Garamond, and Sabon italic on a font by Granjon. It was first used in 1966 and has proved an enduring modern classic.